INTRODUCTION TO ACCOUNTING
for the Banking Certificate

INTRODUCTION TO ACCOUNTING

for the Banking Certificate

H. J. Mellett, MSc(Econ), FCA
J. R. Edwards, MSc(Econ), FCA, ATII

The Chartered Institute of Bankers

10 Lombard Street, London EC3V 9AS

First published 1990
Reprinted 1990, 1992

BANKERS BOOKS LIMITED
c/o The Chartered Institute of Bankers
10 Lombard Street
London EC3V 9AS

CIB Publications are published by The Chartered Institute of Bankers, a non-profit making, registered educational charity, and are distributed exclusively by Bankers Books Limited which is a wholly-owned subsidiary of The Chartered Institute of Bankers.

ISBN 0 85297 274 1

 British Library Cataloguing in Publication Data

Mellett, H. J. (Howard J.)
    Introduction to accounting.
    1. Accounting
    I. Title II. Edwards, J. R. (John Richard) 1946–
    657

Typeset in 8pt and 10pt Times by Style Photosetting Ltd, Mayfield, East Sussex
Text printed on 80gsm Intercity bond, Cover on 275gsm Sovereign matt art.
Produced by AJ Press, Hertford, Herts.
Printed and bound by Stephens & George Ltd, Merthyr Tydfil, Glamorgan

Contents

CHAPTER 3 The Preparation of Accounts from Cash Records

CHAPTER 4 The Double Entry System

CHAPTER 5   Periodic Accounting Reports

CHAPTER 6   Asset Valuation, Profit Measurement and the Underlying Accounting Concepts

CHAPTER 7 **Partnerships**

CHAPTER 8 **Limited Companies**

CHAPTER 9 Accounting for Limited Companies

CHAPTER 10 Decision-Making

CHAPTER 11 Performance Assessment: Ratio Analysis

CHAPTER 12   Performance Assessment: Funds Flow

Preface

This book is designed to meet the requirements of students studying for the Introduction to Accounting paper of The Chartered Institute of Bankers' Banking Certificate examination. A knowledge of the scope and potential of accounting is a useful tool for bankers, and students should view this subject as a means of obtaining financial and analytical skills which will be of long-term benefit. *Introduction to Accounting for the Banking Certificate* has been written to provide readers with a sound understanding of accounting, rather than simply to equip them with a series of unrelated techniques solely to enable the examination to be passed. The text is essentially practical but makes reference to accounting theory, where relevant, to provide an understanding of accounting practice.

The syllabus of the Introduction to Accounting paper assumes a knowledge of, and builds on, the material covered by the accountancy section of the syllabus for Business Calculations. Students who have sat the Business Calculations paper in the preliminary section of the Banking Certificate will therefore have already met some of the material covered in the early part of this book. For those students coming directly into the subject, this book contains all the material which they require.

Chapter 1 introduces the student to what is, for the banker, the principal accounting statement: the balance sheet. Information is provided about the various assets and sources of finance which appear in the balance sheet, and the relationship between assets and sources of finance, which must always remain in balance, is carefully explained. Chapter 2 builds on Chapter 1 by showing how profit results in an increase in net assets. Chapter 3 introduces the method of measuring profit by establishing the difference between revenue and expenditure, and shows how to prepare a trading and profit and loss account and balance sheet from cash records.

Chapters 4 and 5 explain the operation of a formal system for recording and reporting business transactions based on double entry book-keeping. Chapter 4 deals with how the system operates and establishes the link between economic events, their entry in the books of account, and their conversion into accounting reports. Chapter 5 shows how the summarised information taken from the account books, in the form of a trial balance, is converted into a set of final accounts (the profit and loss account and balance sheet) by making the necessary post-trial balance adjustments.

Chapter 6 goes into greater depth on a number of valuation and conceptual issues central to the text. For example, it discusses alternative approaches to depreciation and shows their impact on reported profit. Basic accounting concepts, such as prudence and accruals, are also explained and related to the preparation of accounting statements.

Chapters 7 to 9 deal with the specialised accounting requirements of partnerships and limited companies. Chapter 7 is concerned with partnerships and explains how they differ from sole traders, so that, for example, a profit and loss appropriation account is needed to divide the profit made between the partners. Chapter 8 contrasts limited companies with the sole trader, and concentrates on the legal and regulatory consequences of incorporation, such as the need to have their annual accounts audited. Chapter 9 covers the more practical aspects of accounting for limited companies.

The production of accounting information is not limited to the annual accounts, and management has many demands for, and uses of, special accounting reports. These are of particular interest to the banker as they are likely to form the basis of negotiations with clients when loan requests are made. Chapter 10 therefore deals with the response of costs to changes in levels of activity and the preparation of forecast results based on planned activity.

It is important that bankers should be able to interpret the accounting information with which they are presented, and a number of techniques, described in Chapters 11 and 12, have been developed to assist with this. Chapter 11 explains and illustrates how accounts can be analysed using accounting ratios so that a judgment can be reached on a firm's progress, position and, to some extent, its prospects. Chapter 12 deals with the assessment of performance using funds flow analysis and also extends this to a full financial appraisal which also makes use of ratios.

The text of each chapter is fully illustrated with worked examples, and at the end of each chapter there are questions, which are referenced in the text, designed to test the extent to which the subject matter is understood. A full solution is provided for every chapter-end question in an Appendix.

As an additional aid to testing comprehension, each chapter ends with a 'Review', listing the matters that the student should have learnt and understood. We recommend that the book is read, and the questions worked, in chapter order. Every attempt must be made to master both the theoretical and the practical aspects of the subject, as it is important for bankers to appreciate what lies behind the figures presented to them by their customers.

H J Mellet
J R Edwards
Cardiff Business School, April 1990

Acknowledgements

We should like to express our gratitude to the entire team at The Chartered Institute of Bankers, who have encouraged us in the preparation of this book, and to Sandie Edwards for typing much of the manuscript.

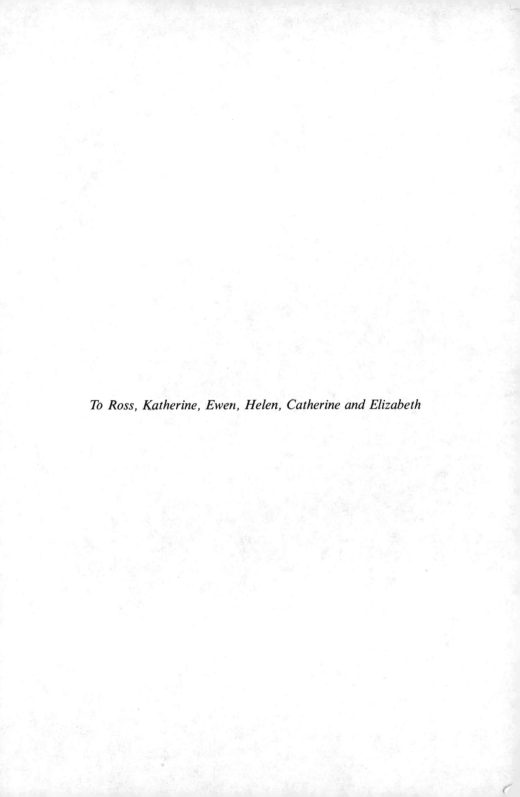

To Ross, Katherine, Ewen, Helen, Catherine and Elizabeth

CHAPTER 1

The Balance Sheet

1.1 INTRODUCTION

An introductory textbook should start with a definition of the topic under consideration. For this purpose, we may define accountancy as follows:

Accountancy is a system for recording and reporting business transactions, in financial terms, to interested parties who use this information as the basis for performance assessment and decision making.

The two main elements of the accounting process, 'recording' and 'reporting', are interrelated, since accounting records are kept as the basis for preparing accounting reports. For instance, when the bank makes a loan to a customer, a record is made of this transaction, and the terms of the agreement provide for the loan to be repaid after a specific time period. Periodically, the bank manager will examine a list of loans outstanding and, if it transpires that the loan has not been repaid by the due date, steps can be taken to demand immediate repayment.

We can therefore see both why the transaction is recorded and why the report is made:

- The loan is recorded so that it is not forgotten, i.e. it helps to protect money belonging to the bank.
- The report brings to the bank manager's attention the fact that the loan is overdue. He can then take the necessary steps to ensure repayment takes place.

The loan report is an example of a detailed accounting statement since it contains full information relating to each advance. At the other extreme, accounting statements are prepared in a highly summarised form. A good example is the annual report published by banks for their shareholders. This report includes a number of accounting statements, amongst which the best known — the profit and loss account and the balance sheet — are the main subjects of this book.

The profit and loss account is usually confined to a single sheet which summarises the financial effect of all the business transactions which produce either a profit or a loss for the bank during the year. The profit and loss account of the National Westminster Bank for 1988 showed a profit before tax of £1,407,000,000; the cumulative effect of many millions of individual transactions. The balance sheet, on the other hand, reports the assets belonging to the bank, at the end of the financial year, and the various ways in which those assets were financed at that date. The balance sheet of Barclays Bank, at 31 December 1988, reported total assets of £104,645,000,000 divided into just seven major categories. The theory is that shareholders need financial information to judge the overall performance of their investment, and as the basis for deciding whether to retain or sell shares; the inclusion of vast amounts of detail would not be helpful for either of these purposes, and might even be positively damaging by obscuring the major financial developments.

We can therefore see that accounting is a device for communicating relevant information as the basis for assessing performance and reaching decisions about how money should be invested. The accounting report is the means for communicating this information, while the accounting record forms the basis for the report. The nature of the information and degree of detail contained in the report depend on the kind of decision which the recipient wishes to take.

1.2   THE ENTITY CONCEPT

Within the private sector of the economy there are three basic forms of business organisation:

Sole trader.   This is a business which has a single owner who also takes all the major managerial decisions. Examples are a shopkeeper or a plumber in business on their own account.

Partnership.   This exists where two or more people share the ownership and managerial functions. Professional people such as accountants, solicitors and doctors, commonly organise their business activities in the form of partnerships.

Limited company.   A limited company may be private (Ltd) or public (plc). The main significance of the distinction is that only the latter can make an issue of shares to the general public. In the case of public companies, there is the further distinction between listed companies, whose shares are traded on the stock exchange, and unlisted companies. In general, public companies are larger than private companies and listed companies larger than unlisted.

There are two important differences between sole traders and partnerships, sometimes referred to as 'firms', on the one hand and limited companies on the other.

1. *The relationship between ownership and management.* In the case of firms, the owner(s) is (are) also the manager(s). By this we mean that the individual who provides the money to set up the firm also runs its day to day operations. In the case of the limited company, on the other hand, these functions may well be the responsibilities of quite separate individuals. This is particularly likely in the case of the public limited company where the bulk of the finance is raised from the general public, and perhaps the banks, as in the case of Eurotunnel plc, while the business is run by professional managers who have only a relatively small financial investment in the concern.

2. *The owner's liability for business debts.* Sole traders and partners normally have unlimited liability for the debts of their firm, whereas the shareholders of limited companies are not required to contribute beyond the amount of their original investment. This distinction is significant when a business runs into financial difficulties. In the case of firms, the creditors claim first again the business assets but, if these are insufficient to satisfy the amounts due, creditors can then claim against the owner's private assets. In an extreme situation, the owner of a bankrupt firm can be forced to sell his/her home and all other personal belongings to meet demands from the firm's creditors. This is in stark contrast with the respective positions of investors and creditors in a limited company, where any deficiency of business assets compared with liabilities at the date of liquidation is borne by the creditors.

   Company Law therefore regards a limited company as a separate legal entity. The creditor contracts with the company and can claim only against its assets. No such legal distinction is recognised where the business is carried on by a sole trader or by partners.

The position in accountancy is quite different It is always assumed, for accounting purposes, that the business entity has an existence separate and distinct from owners, managers, or any other individuals with whom it comes into contact during the course of its trading activities. The assumption of a separate existence, for accounting purposes, usually referred to as the *Entity Concept,* requires a careful distinction to be drawn between business affairs and personal transactions.

Why is the distinction important? There are three main reasons:

1. *To measure business performance.*   The main reason for starting a business is because the owner hopes that it will provide a comfortable, or even luxurious, standard of living. To measure performance requires profit to be calculated and, to measure profit accurately, a clear distinction must be drawn between personal and business affairs so that the calculation can be confined to the latter.
2. *To enable tax liabilities to be calculated.*   Firms pay income tax on their profits, while companies pay corporation tax. In either case *business* profits must be calculated as the basis for the Inland Revenue's assessments.
3. *To enable limited companies to prepare accounts in compliance with the requirements of the Companies Acts 1985 and 1989.*   These accounts must be sent to shareholders and debenture holders. Copies of the accounts must be filed with the registrar of companies where they are available for inspection by the general public.

The distinction between private and business transactions is considered in Example 1.1.

Example 1.1

Mr Little won a premium bond prize of £10,000 on 1 January 19X1. He spent the cash in the following manner:

(i)   Purchased a bracelet for his wife, £1,900
(ii)   Went on holiday to Italy, £2,000
(iii) Purchased a new cricket bat for £100
(iv)   Decided to form a business called Little Enterprises and, as a first step, opened a business bank account and paid in £6,000

Required:
Identify which of the above transactions you consider to be private and which business.

Solution
  Private transactions: (i), (ii), (iii)
  Business transaction: (iv)

The crucial point to grasp, at this stage, is that Little Enterprises is immediately regarded as an entirely separate entity from Mr Little. The accounting treatment of its business transactions is demonstrated in sections 1.3–1.6, below.

Assignment   Students should now work Question 1.1 at the end of the chapter. Throughout this book it is imperative that students should *first* work the question and *then* compare their solution with the model answer in the Appendix.

1.3   REPORTING CAPITAL IN THE BALANCE SHEET

Because the business is regarded as a separate accounting entity, business transactions must be recorded *twice*.

First, to show the effect of the transaction on the assets belonging to the business, and

Secondly, to show the effect of the transaction on the relationship between the business, on the one hand, and providers of finance on the other.

If we apply this rule to transaction (iv) in Example 1.1, the effect is as follows:

Effect On:

Business assets	Source of finance
Increase from zero to: £6,000	Business owes Mr Little*: £6,000

Tutorial note:
*Remember that Mr Little is deemed, for accounting purposes, to be quite separate from the business entity, Little Enterprises. Transactions with him are therefore treated as a 'Sources of Finance'.

The transaction may now be recorded in the balance sheet as follows:

Illustration 1.1

Balance Sheet of Little Enterprises at 1 January 19X1

Assets	£	Sources of Finance	£
Cash at bank	6,000	Capital: Mr Little	6,000

The right side of the balance sheet shows that Mr Little has made a capital investment of £6,000 in the business. Put another way, the business owes Mr Little £6,000. The left side of the balance sheet shows that the assets belonging to the business, at present, consist of cash amounting to £6,000. Readers should note that there is numerical equality between the two sides of the balance sheet. This must always be the case since assets belonging to the business cannot be 'conjured out of thin air' and have to be financed in one way or another. The corresponding finance is shown on the right side of the balance sheet and the fundamental equation *Assets* = *Sources of Finance* therefore continues throughout the life of the business. We can now define the balance sheet as follows:

The balance sheet is a financial statement which shows on the one hand the sources from which the business has raised finance and on the other the ways in which those resources are employed.

It should also be noted that the balance sheet sets out the business's financial position at a particular moment in time: on 1 January 19X1 in the above example. It is for this reason that the balance sheet is sometimes colourfully described as an *instantaneous financial photograph* of the business. This description highlights both the major strength and major weakness of the balance sheet. It sums up, in a single statement, a large number of important financial facts, but only at one point in time; a day earlier or a day later the financial facts might be quite different. This provides scope for management to engage in 'window dressing' in order to improve the apparent financial position of the business. An example is the raising of a short-term loan, just before the date of the balance sheet, to boost the business's cash balance. The banker must always be on guard against the use of such schemes which, although often perfectly legal, can give a misleading impression of business prosperity.

1.4 RAISING FURTHER FINANCE

It is essential for management to make, at the outset, a careful estimate of cash needed to support the planned level of activity. Steps must then be taken to raise the full amount required. Where insufficient cash is raised, the early years of the firm's life will be marked by recurring cash flow problems, occupying much of management's time which would be more productively directed towards identifying and exploiting business opportunities. Many businesses fail through lack of funds before they get off the ground.

A major portion of the initial financial requirement is, of course, provided by the owner, and this is described as the capital investment in the concern. It is, however, likely than an additional source of finance will have to be raised if the business is to be placed on a sound financial footing. Mr Little has made a personal investment of £6,000 in Little Enterprises and we will assume that he has estimated that a total initial investment of £10,000 is required. He is £4,000 short and is likely to explore a number of avenues in the endeavour to obtain this sum. One possibility is to borrow from family or friends, another is to seek government aid, and a third might involve acquiring some of the business assets on hire purchase. We will assume that

Mr Little convinces his bank manager that there are sound prospects for Little Enterprises and on 2 January the bank lends him £4,000 secured by the deeds of his house. The effect of the transaction is as follows:

Effect On:

Business assets	Source of finance
Cash increases by: £4,000	Amount owed to bank increases from zero to: £4,000

Illustration 1.2

Balance Sheet of Little Enterprises at 2 January 19X1

Assets	£	*Sources of Finance*	£
Cash at bank (6,000 + 4,000) . .	10,000	Capital: Mr Little	6,000
		Loan from bank	4,000
	10,000		10,000

The equality between assets and sources of finance is maintained with the increase in business assets financed by the bank loan. There are now, however, two different types of finance. The amount advanced by Mr Little, his capital, is a permanent investment which will not usually be withdrawn until the business is wound up, whereas the amount advanced by the bank is a liability which must be repaid in due course. The relationship *Assets = Sources of Finance* therefore needs to be extended, as follows, by dividing the sources of finance into the two component parts — capital and liabilities. The formula now becomes:

$$\text{ASSETS} = \text{CAPITAL} + \text{LIABILITIES}$$
which may be abbreviated to
$$A = C + L$$

Assignment Students should now work Question 1.2 at the end of the chapter.

1.5 THE INVESTMENT DECISION

It is the job of Mr Little, when performing his role as manager of Little Enterprises, to decide how the cash raised at the outset is to be employed, i.e. he must make an investment decision. Let us assume that Mr Little decides to go into business as a wholesaler specialising in the acquisition of stationery from manufacturers and its resale to retail shops. After careful enquiries, he purchases, for cash, premises for £7,000 and stock-in-trade for £2,500 on 10 January 19X1. The effect of the transaction is as follows:

Effect On:

Business assets		Source of finance
Premises increase by:	£7,000	No change
Stock-in-trade increase by: ...	£2,500	
Cash at bank reduces by:	(£9,500)	

Illustration 1.3

Balance Sheet of Little Enterprises at 10 January 19X1

Assets	£	Sources of Finance	£
Premises	7,000	Capital: Mr Little	6,000
Stock-in-trade	2,500	Loan from bank	4,000
Cash at bank (10,000 − 9,500) .	500		
	10,000		10,000

No additional sources of finance have been raised and the right hand side of the balance sheet remains unchanged. The effect of the investment decision is merely to cause a redistribution of available resources, and the above balance sheet shows the revised financial position at 10 January.

Little Enterprises is now in a position where it is almost ready to commence trading. However, Mr Little must first make sure that the firm is in possession of a stock of stationery sufficient to enable sales to be made and still leave available a full range of products to display to potential customers. He estimates that further stock-in-trade (usually abbreviated to stock) costing £2,000 is required. The above balance sheet shows that the company has insufficient cash available and an additional source of finance must be obtained. In practice, very few businesses operate entirely on the cash basis; instead a proportion, often a high proportion, of purchases and sales are made on credit, i.e. a period of time elapses between the date that goods are supplied and when they are paid for. Normally businesses take the maximum period of credit allowed because, during this time, stock is financed by suppliers rather than by the firm itself, i.e. the firm enjoys 'free' credit. The period of credit allowed by suppliers varies a great deal but 30 days is most common.

Little Enterprises acquires stationery costing £2,000 on 11 January 19X1. The supplier allows 30 days' credit. The effect of the transaction is as follows:

Effect On:

Business assets		Sources of finance	
Stock increases by:	£2,000	Trade creditors increase by: ...	£2,000

Illustration 1.4

Balance Sheet of Little Enterprises at 11 January 19X1

Assets	£	Sources of Finance	£
Premises	7,000	Capital: Mr Little	6,000
Stock (2,500 + 2,000)	4,500	Loan from bank	4,000
Cash at bank	500	Trade creditors	2,000
	12,000		12,000

The above balance sheet shows that the firm now owns assets totalling £12,000, made up of premises, stock and cash at bank. The finance has been obtained from three sources: ownership, the bank, and suppliers who are described as trade creditors for balance sheet purposes. The investment made by the owners is normally permanent, while the loan is likely to be the subject of a formal agreement which deals with such matters as the repayment date and the rate of interest payable. Trade creditors expect to be repaid in accordance with the normal practice of the particular trade, in this case 30 days. An important feature of trade credit is that it is a renewable source of finance in the sense that, provided the firm pays money currently owed, it will be able to acquire further supplies on credit, thereby maintaining a constant level of indebtedness.

Assignment   Students should now work Question 1.3 at the end of the chapter.

1.6   BUSINESS DEVELOPMENT

Little Enterprises is now ready to start trading. Mr Little established the business in the expectation that it would earn profits, and stock must therefore be sold for a sum sufficiently in excess of its cost to convince Mr Little that his capital is efficiently employed and would not yield a larger return if invested elsewhere.

On 12 January Little Enterprises sells stationery costing £2,000 to a local chain of newsagents for £3,500, payment to be made by the end of the month. Ignoring interest charges and other operating costs, a profit of £1,500 (sales price £3,500 minus cost £2,000) is earned which accrues to Mr Little and is added to his capital to show that the value of his investment in the business has increased. The effect of the transaction is as follows:

Effect On:

Business assets		Sources of finance	
Stock decreases by:	(£2,000)	Capital increases by:	£1,500
Trade debtors increase by	£3,500		

Illustration 1.5

Balance Sheet of Little Enterprises at 12 January 19X1

Assets	£	Sources of Finance	£
Premises	7,000	Capital: Mr Little	6,000
Stock (4,500 − 2,000).......	2,500	Add: Profit	1,500
Trade debtors	3,500		7,500
Cash at bank	500	Loan from bank	4,000
		Trade creditors	2,000
	13,500		13,500

The total assets of Little Enterprises, alternatively described as the 'gross assets', have increased from £12,000, to £13,500. This is because one asset (stock) costing £2,000 has been replaced by a new asset (trade debtors) worth £3,500. A similar increase occurs in the sources of finance as the result of adding the profit earned to Mr Little's initial capital investment. It should be noticed that profit is recognised despite the fact that the cash due for the goods has not yet been received. This brings us to a second assumption made by accountants when preparing accounting statements, namely the *Realisation Concept*. This concept assumes that profit is earned or realised when the sale takes place, and the justification for this treatment is that Little Enterprises now possesses a more valuable asset, since the £3,500 is a legally enforceable debt.

The trade cycle is completed by Little Enterprises collecting £3,500 on 31 January 19X1 and paying £2,000 to its supplier on 8 February 19X1, 30 days after the goods were supplied. The effect of these transactions is as follows:

Effect On:

Business assets		Sources of finance	
Trade debtors decrease by: . . .	(£3,500)	Trade creditors decrease by: . .	(£2,000)
Cash increases by	£3,500		
Cash decreases by:	(£2,000)		

Illustration 1.6

Balance Sheet of Little Enterprises at 8 February 19X1

Assets	£	Sources of Finance	£
Premises	7,000	Capital: Mr Little	6,000
Stock	2,500	Add: Profit	1,500
Cash at bank (500 + 1,500) ...	2,000		7,500
		Loan from bank	4,000
	11,500		11,500

Assignment   Students should now work Question 1.4 at the end of the chapter.

1.7 THE TRADING CYCLE

A trading cycle, based on credit transactions, can now be expressed in the following diagrammatic form:

Figure 1.1

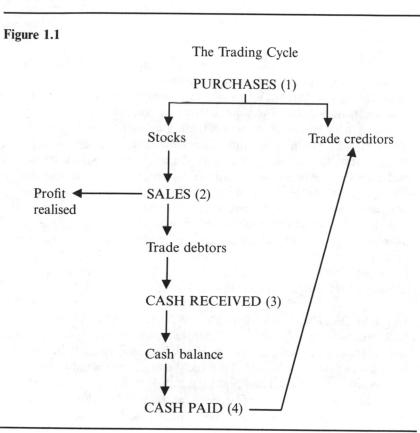

The Trading Cycle

PURCHASES (1)

Stocks   Trade creditors

Profit ◄──── SALES (2)
realised

Trade debtors

CASH RECEIVED (3)

Cash balance

CASH PAID (4)

The cycle consists of the following four stages:

Stage 1:   The purchase of goods on credit which gives rise to balance sheet entries for trade creditors and stock.

Stage 2:   The sale of stock results in a profit being realised or a loss incurred. At this stage some of the stock is replaced by trade debtors in the balance sheet.

Stage 3: The collection of trade debts. This produces a change in the composition of the firm's assets, from debts to cash.

Stage 4: The payment of the amounts due to suppliers. This causes a reduction in cash and the removal of trade creditors from the balance sheet.

A comparison of the position before (Illustration 1.3) and after (Illustration 1.6) the trading cycle is undertaken shows just two differences: cash rises by £1,500 and the owner's capital investment increases by a similar amount to reflect profit earned.

The trading cycle examined above is obviously a simplified version of what happens in practice. A company does not complete one cycle before commencing another, but is involved in a continuous series of overlapping business transactions. The purchases cycle consists of ordering goods, receiving them into stock as an asset, and paying for them by means of a cash outflow. At the same time there will occur the sales cycle which consists of making a sale, parting with the stocks sold as an asset outflow, and collecting the money due from the customer to produce a cash inflow. Therefore, even before one creditor is paid another is created, and debtors are turned over in a similar manner.

A simplified version of the trading cycle occurs when purchases and/or sales are made for cash. There are just two stages: Stage 1, the purchase of goods, involves the exchange of cash for stocks; Stage 2, the sale of goods, involves the exchange of stock for cash of a greater or lesser value, with the amount of the difference recorded as a profit or a loss.

1.8 REPORTING CHANGES IN OWNER'S CAPITAL

Each enterprise is regarded as a separate entity for accounting purposes, and the statement of capital in the balance sheet records the indebtedness of the business to its owners. This indebtedness is initially created by ownership introducing finance into the business, but the amount changes over time as the result of trading activity. A profit increases the indebtedness, whereas a loss reduces the value of the owner's capital investment.

Because it embraces the whole relationship between the business and its owner, the capital section of the balance sheet also reports all other transactions between these two entities. For instance, it reports any additional capital investments made by the owner during the life of the business, and also the regular withdrawals of cash and goods made for personal use. The owner does not normally wait until profit is calculated before making withdrawals; he/she is often dependent on the business for a living, and profits are withdrawn, for personal use, as they are earned during the year.

The manner in which these matters are reported is shown in Illustration 1.7. Because we are only interested in changes in capital, the remainder of the balance sheet is omitted.

Illustration 1.7

Newman started in business on 1 January 19X1 and paid £2,000 into the business bank account. On 30 June he transferred to the business his car valued at £1,400. Each week he withdrew £150 from the business in cash. The accounts prepared for 19X1 showed that his business had earned a profit of £8,000 during the year.

Extract from the Balance Sheet at 31 December 19X1

	£
Opening capital, 1 January 19X1	2,000
Add: Additional capital investment	1,400
Profit for 19X1	8,000
	11,400
Less: Drawings (£150 × 52)	7,800
Closing capital, 31 December 19X1	3,600*

*The closing capital for 19X1 is the opening capital for 19X2.

Tutorial notes:
- Where profits exceed drawings, as is the case in Illustration 1.7, the surplus of £200 (profit £8,000 minus drawings £7,800) is retained in the business and increases the owner's capital by an equivalent amount. These extra resources may be used to finance an expansion in the level of business operations.
- It can be seen that capital may be introduced in the form of assets other than cash. The motor vehicle, transferred to the business by Newman, appears as an asset in the balance sheet, and is matched by a corresponding increase in the value of his capital investment. Similarly, drawings may be made in a non-cash form (e.g. the family of a farmer is likely to consume some of the farm produce) though this has not happened in the above illustration.

Assignment Students should now work Question 1.5 at the end of the chapter.

1.9   ASSETS = CAPITAL + LIABILITIES

In the case of Little Enterprises we saw that the equality between sources of finance and assets was maintained throughout the trading cycle and, because all assets must be financed in some manner, we can be confident that this equality will continue throughout the firm's life. In this context there are four basic categories of business transaction:

1. Where an increase in a source of finance is matched by an increase in an asset. For example, extra capital invested by the owner which increases the cash balance by an equal amount.
2. Where an increase in a source of finance is matched by a decrease in another source of finance. For example, an increased overdraft to enable trade creditors to be paid the amount due to them.
3. Where a reduction in a source of finance is matched by a reduction in an asset. For example, trade creditors paid out of the balance of cash at bank.
4. Where an increase in an asset is matched by a reduction in another asset. For example, a new motor vehicle purchased for cash.

A complication occurs in the case of a transaction involving the sale of goods, since this gives rise to a profit or a loss which must also be recorded. For example, assume an item of stock which cost £80 is sold on credit for £100. In the balance sheet stock is replaced by debtors, i.e. a category 4 transaction takes place. In addition a category 1 transaction occurs, because the higher value of debtors, £20, gives rise to a profit which must be added to the owner's capital.

Assignment   Students should now work Questions 1.6 and 1.7 at the end of the chapter.

1.10   CLASSIFICATION OF ASSETS AND SOURCES OF FINANCE

1.10.1   Assets   The main characteristics of business assets are as follows:

- They are legally owned by the business entity.
- They have the potential to provide the entity with future economic benefits in the sense that such assets help to generate future cash inflows or reduce future cash outflows.

The fact that a business asset exists, however, does not necessarily mean that it will be reported in the balance sheet. For this to be done, the asset must satisfy the following further requirement:

A business asset is shown in the balance sheet only if the financial benefit it is expected to provide can be quantified, in money terms, with a reasonable degree of precision.

This rule is called the *Money Measurement Concept.* For example, stock-in-trade is reported as a business asset because it meets all the above requirements: it is owned by the firm; it is expected to provide a financial benefit for the firm when it is sold; and it has an identifiable monetary value (its cost). Expenditure incurred on training staff, on the other hand, presents a more difficult problem. While it is possible to identify the amount of the expenditure, it is not possible to forecast with a high degree of certainty whether the firm will benefit from the expenditure. Employees may be poorly motivated and fail to improve their competence as the result of attending training courses. In addition, they may leave the firm and take their new expertise elsewhere. Because of this uncertainty concerning the likely extent of any future benefit, such expenditure is not reported as a business asset but is instead written off against profit as it is incurred.

Assets reported in the balance sheet are divided into two categories:

1. *Current Assets.* These are defined as assets which are held for resale, conversion into cash, or are cash itself. There are three main types of current assets: stock-in-trade, trade debtors, and cash. A *temporary* investment of funds in the shares of a listed company or in government securities should also be classified as a current asset. A characteristic of current assets is that the balances are constantly changing as the result of business operations.

2. *Fixed Assets.* These are assets which a firm purchases and retains to help carry on the business. It is not intended to sell fixed assets in the ordinary course of business and it is expected that the bulk of their value will be used up as the result of contributing to trading activities. Examples of fixed assets are premises, plant, machinery, furniture and motor vehicles. A characteristic of fixed assets is that they usually remain in the business for long periods of time and will only be sold or scrapped when they are of no further use. A fixed asset which a firm uses but does not own, e.g. rented premises, must not be reported in the balance sheet, but any expenses incurred to obtain the use of the asset must be treated as a business expense.

It is important for students to realise that it is possible to classify an asset as current or fixed only by examining the reason why it was purchased, i.e. was it purchased for resale or retention? Assets purchased by one company for resale may be purchased by another for retention. For example, a car dealer purchases motor vehicles for resale, while a manufacturing concern acquires them as fixed assets to be used, for example, by sales representatives.

Assets are reported in the balance sheet in the order of increasing liquidity, i.e. the list starts with the items least likely to be turned into cash and ends with the items expected to be converted into cash in the near future. A typical balance sheet presentation, in what is technically described as the 'Horizontal Format', is given in Figure 1.2.

Figure 1.2

Balance Sheet of the Nut and Bolt Engineering Company

	£	£		£	£
Fixed Assets			Capital		179,000
Land and Buildings		75,000			
Plant and Machinery		49,000	*Non-Current Liabilities*		
Motor vehicles		21,500	Loan repayable 19X8		50,000
		145,500			
Current Assets			*Current Liabilities*		
Stock	145,700		Trade creditors	170,000	
Trade debtors	143,700		Expense creditors	1,900	
Investments	2,600		Bank overdraft	36,700	
Cash in hand	100				
		292,100			208,600
		437,600			437,600

Tutorial note:
The column headings *'Assets'* and *'Sources of Finance'* have been omitted from the above balance sheet. This is the normal practice.

1.10.2 Sources of Finance We have already seen that sources of finance include both the capital invested by the owners and the liabilities due to non-ownership groups. These liabilities may be further classified into current liabilities, defined as amounts repayable within 12 months of the balance sheet date, and non-current liabilities. Typical examples of current liabilities are:

- amounts owing to trade creditors for goods supplied,
- amounts owed to creditors for other business expenses,
- a bank overdraft, since this is normally repayable on call,
- loans repayable within the following year.

The only loan outstanding in the case of Nut and Bolt Engineering is repayable in seven years' time (in 19X8), and is therefore classified as a 'non-current liability' and positioned between the capital section and current liabilities in the balance sheet.

We can see from Figure 1.2 that sources of finance are listed in order of permanence, with the most permanent sources at the top and amounts repayable, or potentially repayable, in the near future at the bottom of the balance sheet.

Most sources of finance are easily classified into one or other of the three categories, but certain items cause a little more difficulty. For example, the terms of a bank loan may provide for an advance of £100,000, repayable by five equal annual instalments of £20,000. In these circumstances the liability must be divided into two parts, with the next instalment repayable, of £20,000, shown as a current liability and the balance reported as a non-current liability. Therefore, a balance sheet prepared soon after the loan is raised will show £20,000 as a current liability and £80,000 as a non-current liability.

1.10.3 Balance Sheet Presentation   Accountancy is a device for communicating relevant financial information to interested parties. It is therefore important that the information reported should not only be technically accurate but also be presented in an orderly fashion so that it can be readily understood by owners, managers and others who wish to assess progress. The balance sheet of the Nut and Bolt Engineering Company is drafted in a manner which helps to achieve this objective. It is divided into five sections and, for each of these, an appropriate description is given and a sub-total provided. Users of accounting statements are therefore able to see, at a glance, the amount of finance provided by the owners, the volume of long-term loans, and the quantity of short-term finance. The statement also shows how the total finance has been allocated between fixed and current assets. If a firm is to be financially stable, it is normally important for long-term investments in fixed assets to be substantially financed by the owners and for current assets to be sufficient to meet current liabilities falling due over the next 12 months. A well prepared balance sheet enables these and other forms of financial analysis, considered in chapters 11 and 12, to be carried out efficiently.

Assignment   Students should now work Questions 1.8–1.10 at the end of the chapter.

1.11   REVIEW

After reading the chapter and working the chapter end questions, students should be able to:

- Define 'Accountancy'.
- Understand the meaning and significance of the 'Entity Concept', the 'Realisation Concept' and the 'Money Measurement Concept'.
- Understand the relationship between 'Assets' and 'Sources of Finance' and incorporate the effect of individual transactions in the balance sheet.
- Prepare a simple balance sheet in horizontal format.
- Distinguish between 'Fixed Assets' and 'Current Assets'.
- Distinguish between different sources of finance: 'Capital', 'Current Liabilities', and 'Non-current Liabilities'.

1.12   QUESTIONS

Question 1.1

Indicate which of the following transactions relate to Clive's business as a newsagent and which are his personal transactions:

(i)   £50 win on premium bonds owned by Clive.
(ii)   £100 paid for the following advertisement on a hoarding at the local football ground: 'Clive's for all the up to date news'.
(iii) Payment to the newspaper wholesaler, £1,260.
(iv)   Sale of unsold newspapers to a local fish-and-chip shop.
(v)   Purchase of a new car for family use, although it will be used each morning to collect papers from suppliers.

Question 1.2

John decides to start up in business on 1 April 19X2, and pays £4,000 from his private bank account into a newly opened business bank account. On 2 April 19X2 John's father loans the firm £600 to help with the new venture, and this amount is paid immediately into the business bank account. On 4 April the firm borrows £150 from John's friend Peter. This amount is kept in the form of 'ready cash' to meet small business expenses.

Required:
Balance sheet for John's business after the transactions on:

(a)   1 April
(b)   2 April
(c)   4 April

Question 1.3

Roger starts up in business on 1 September with a capital of £1,200 which he pays into his business bank account on that day. The bank agrees to provide him with a business overdraft facility of £500 for the first three months. The following business transactions take place:

2 September:	A machine is bought, on three months' credit from Plant Suppliers Ltd, for £750.
	£1,000 is borrowed from the Endridge Local Authority which is keen to encourage this type of enterprise.
3 September:	£1,820 is paid for a second hand machine.
	Stock is purchased, for cash, £420.
4 September:	Stock is purchased, on credit, for £215.

Required:

Balance sheets for Roger's business following the transactions on:

   (a) 1 September
   (b) 2 September
   (c) 3 September
   (d) 4 September

Question 1.4

The following balance sheet was prepared for Jeff's business at 1 October 19X5. The firm has an overdraft facility of £700.

Balance Sheet

	£		£
Machinery	2,200	Capital	5,300
Stocks	2,870		
Debtors	800	Trade creditors	690
Cash at bank	120		
	5,990		5,990

Jeff enters into the following transactions:

2 October:	Sells goods which cost £120 for £200, cash.
	Sells goods which cost £240 for £315, on credit.
3 October:	Collects £150 from customers.
	Purchases stock for £190, on credit.
4 October:	Pays trade creditors £75.
	Purchases a machine for £600, cash.

Required:
Balance sheets for Jeff's business following the transactions on:

(a)   2 October
(b)   3 October
(c)   4 October

Question 1.5

(a)   Prepare the balance sheet of Daley from the following list of assets and liabilities at 31 December 19X1:

	£
Cash	1,750
Stock	5,250
Owed by customers	3,340
Owed to suppliers	2,890
Business premises	9,000
Loan from Weakly	3,000

(b)   Prepare the balance sheet of Daley's business at the end of each of the first seven days of January taking account of the following transactions:

19X2:   January 1.   Purchased, on credit, a typewriter for office use, £500.
2.   Received £190 from a customer.
3.   Paid a supplier £670.
4.   Purchased stock, on credit, £260.
5.   Sold goods which had cost £350 for £530 cash.
6.   Repaid Weakly £1,000 of the balance due to him (ignore interest).
7.   Withdrew stock costing £100 for private use.

Question 1.6

Examine separately the effect of each of the following transactions on the relationship A = C + L.

1.   The owner of a business received a legacy of £2,000 and paid it into his business bank account.
2.   Machinery costing £3,000 is purchased for cash.
3.   Stock-in-trade is purchased on credit for £800.
4.   A business computer is purchased for £5,000 and is financed by a loan from a friend.
5.   Trade debts amounting to £750 are collected from customers.
6.   Stock-in-trade costing £1,000 is sold for £1,400.
7.   A supplier is paid £220 due to him.

8. Stock-in-trade is purchased for cash £350.
9. A filing cabinet is purchased for £60 by increasing an existing bank overdraft.
10. The owner of a business drew a cheque for £100 on his business bank account to meet private expenses.

You should present your answer in the following form:

TRANSACTION	ASSETS =	CAPITAL +	LIABILITIES
	£	£	£
1	+ 2,000 =	+ 2,000	0
2	+ 3,000 =	0	0
	− 3,000		

Note: In transaction 2, the machinery acquired increases assets by £3,000 but the payment reduces assets by the same amount. The net effect is zero.

Question 1.7

Prepare balance sheets to determine the amount missing from each of the following lists of balances at 31 December 19X1:

	A	B	C	D	E	F
	£	£	£	£	£	£
Capital at 1 January 19X1	2,500	2,000	3,000	4,000	3,800	?
Profit for 19X1	1,000	3,200	?	5,700	2,300	7,000
Drawings during 19X1	800	3,000	1,000	4,900	?	4,500
Current liabilities	750	?	600	1,300	1,700	2,100
Fixed assets	1,800	1,750	2,800	?	3,700	8,500
Current assets	?	850	1,200	1,900	1,600	3,500

Question 1.8

Review your understanding of the following concepts and terms discussed in this chapter by writing a short explanation of each of them.

(i)	Accounting	(vii)	A = C + L
(ii)	Entity concept	(viii)	Owner's capital
(iii)	Balance sheet	(ix)	Money measurement concept
(iv)	Realisation concept	(x)	Fixed assets
(v)	Trade credit	(xi)	Current assets
(vi)	Trading cycle, credit transactions	(xii)	Current liabilities
		(xiii)	Gross assets.

Question 1.9

For a fish and chip shop, indicate which of the following items are current liabilities, which are current assets, and which are fixed assets.

(i)   Microwave oven.

(ii)   2,000 kilos of 'King Edward' potatoes.
(iii)   Cash register.
(iv)   Amount owing to the Fat Fishy Company Ltd.
(v)   Capital investment of Mr V. Greasy, owner.
(vi)   Mrs Greasy's pearl necklace and gold wristwatch.
(vii)   250 Mackerel.
viii)   Loan from V. Greasy's father, repayable in two years' time.
(ix)   Last instalment due, in one month's time, on the microwave oven acquired on hire purchase.
(x)   Shop rented from a property company.

For items not classified as current liabilities or current assets or fixed assets, describe how they would be reported in the balance sheet, if at all.

Question 1.10
The following list of balances relates to the business of C. Forest at 31 December 19X3:

Plant and machinery	26,500
Stock-in-trade	14,200
Loan repayable June 19X4	2,500
Capital of C. Forest at 1 January 19X3	52,380
Trade creditors	10,600
Trade debtors	14,100
Cash-in-hand	270
Bank overdraft	3,940
Profit for 19X3	12,600
Owner's drawings during 19X3	10,950
Loan repayble 19X9	9,000
Leasehold premises	25,000

Required:
The balance sheet of C. Forest's business at 31 December 19X3 presented in good style.

CHAPTER 2

Profit Calculated as the Increase in Capital

2.1 THE IMPORTANCE OF PROFIT

The maximisation of profit has been traditionally regarded as the principal factor motivating the individual to invest in a business venture. In recent years, however, businessmen have often appeared reluctant to justify business activity in quite so direct a manner. This is in many ways a healthy development which demonstrates an increasing awareness of the fact that business organisations, particularly the very large ones, have responsibilities other than to produce an adequate return for their investors. A list of the responsibilities acknowledged by businessmen today can be obtained by examining the corporate objectives declared by company chairmen in their annual reports to shareholders. These often include a wide range of items, amongst which earning a profit appears to be accorded no particular priority. Other identified corporate goals include such matters as:

- an increase in the market share
- the improvement of product quality
- a contented work force
- a pollution free production process
- the maximisation of exports
- corporate survival.

It is difficult to say whether these aims are each of equal importance, but probably they are not. One view is that profit maximisation is the main objective, and all the other stated aims have as their sole purpose to contribute, either directly or indirectly, to the long-run achievement of the principal objective. This view may attach rather too much significance to profit, but widespread agreement that the desire to maximise profit is an essential feature of business activity in Great Britain today can safely be assumed.

There are basically two competing claims on the profits generated by business activity.

1. *Withdrawals.* The owner requires a satisfactory return on the investment, in the form of drawings or dividends, and an inadequate return will result in the owner closing down the business and investing the money elsewhere.

2. *Reinvestment.* Retained profits have always been a major source of finance for business expansion. In earlier times, it was quite common for businesses to develop from small beginnings and become very large industrial undertakings, entirely on the basis of retained earnings. Today it is usual for companies to speed up their rate of expansion by calling on a wide range of additional sources of finance, including bank loans and overdrafts, but there remain many companies in which profits retained and reinvested over the entire life of the concern far exceed the capital subscribed by the shareholders. For example, the balance sheet of the Royal Bank of Scotland plc at 30 September 1988 included capital invested by shareholders of £188.5 million, whereas retained profits amount to £904.9 million, i.e. nearly five times more. The retention of profits increases the value of the owner's investment in the business, of course, and should produce higher profits and withdrawals in the future.

When trading conditions are difficult there may be insufficient profit available to finance expansion or even to pay a return to the owners on their investment. In these circumstances management must look elsewhere for the finance required to carry on business. This is not a situation which can persist indefinitely. Just as consistent profitability generates the resources necessary for a healthy business, equally a succession of losses gradually deprives a company of the finance needed to support a continuation of business operations and, if unchecked, eventually results in the business being forced to close down. The accounting function can help guard against this outcome by providing management with the financial information required to monitor progress and ensure that resources are effectively employed.

2.2 PROFIT AND CHANGES IN GROSS ASSETS

Chapter 1 demonstrated the equivalence between *Assets* and *Sources of Finance*. It also showed us that, when profit is earned, a similar increase occurs in the assets under the control of management. These facts were illustrated by means of a series of balance sheets setting out the formation and financial development of a firm called Little Enterprises. Students should now revise their understanding of the relationship between profit and the level of business assets by working the following example.

Example 2.1

The balance sheet of Birch at 31 December 19X1 is as follows:

Balance Sheet of Birch at 31 December 19X1

	£		£
Fixed Assets		Capital	6,810
Plant and Machinery	5,000		
Current Assets		*Current Liabilities*	
Stock	1,600	Trade creditors.	1,350
Trade debtors	1,500		
Cash-in-hand	60		
	8,160		8,160

On 1 January 19X2 Birch sold stock (cost price £140) on credit for £220.

Required:
The balance sheet of Birch following the transaction on 1 January 19X2.

Solution

Balance Sheet of Birch at 1 January 19X2

	£		£
Fixed Assets		Capital	6,810
Plant and Machinery	5,000	Add: Net profit (220 − 140) .	80
Current Assets			6,890
Stock (1,600 − 140)	1,460	*Current Liabilities*	
Trade debtors		Trade creditors	1,350
(1,500 + 220)	1,720		
Cash-in-hand	60		
	8,240		8,240

A comparison of the two balance sheets shows that the financial effects of the single trading transaction undertaken by Birch are as follows:

1. Total assets (alternatively called 'gross assets') have increased from £8,160 to £8,240 as the result of stock costing £140 being replaced by a debt due from a customer of £220.
2. Total sources of finance have increased by the same amount as the result of adding the profit realised, of £80, to Birch's opening capital.

2.3 BALANCE SHEET PRESENTATION: VERTICAL FORMAT

The balance sheets so far examined are presented in what is conventionally described as the horizontal format, i.e. assets appear on the left side and sources of finance on the right. Since the early 1960s industry has gradually discarded the horizontal format in favour of the vertical format, though some financial institutions continue to favour the former method of presentation. Lloyds was one of the first major banks to change to the vertical format, first using it for the 1983 published accounts. The vertical presentation is illustrated below, using the same information as appears in the balance sheets contained in Example 2.1.

Figure 2.1

Vertical presentation of the balance sheets of Birch.

Balance Sheet of Birch

	1 January 19X2		31 December 19X1	
	£	£	£	£
Fixed Assets				
Plant and Machinery		5,000		5,000
Current Assets				
Stock	1,460		1,600	
Trade debtors	1,720		1,500	
Cash-in-hand	60		60	
	3,240		3,160	
Less: Current Liabilities				
Trade creditors	1,350		1,350	
Working capital		1,890		1,810
		6,890		6,810
Financed by:				
Opening capital		6,810		**
Add: Net profit		80		**
		6,890		6,810

** figures not provided

The advantages of the vertical format, compared with the horizontal format, are as follows:

1. It is easier to compare the position of a business at a series of accounting dates. The above illustration gives the position at just two

dates, but a columnar presentation dealing with five or even ten accounting dates would pose no particular difficulty, and it is then a relatively easy matter to glance across the series of figures to discover relevant changes and overall trends. For example, the analysis might show that large amounts of money are being spent each year on fixed assets, suggesting a policy of rapid expansion, whereas a continuous decline in the balance of cash, perhaps converting into a substantial overdraft, might be taken as an indication of the fact that the company is suffering from increasing cash difficulties.

2. It contains an extra item of useful information which does not appear in the horizontal balance sheet; namely the total for working capital, which is the balancing figure obtained by deducting current liabilities from current assets. A financially stable business is one which is able to meets its debts as they fall due for payment, and an adequate balance of working capital is an essential requirement if this desirable state of affairs is to exist. It is not possible to specify a figure for working capital which all firms should try to maintain. Much will depend on individual circumstances, such as the size of the firm, the speed with which creditors are paid, stocks are sold and cash is collected from customers. Nevertheless managers, shareholders, creditors and other users of accounting statements normally hold firm views concerning what can be regarded as an acceptable balance for a particular business. Working capital is examined further in chapter 11.4.

2.4   PROFIT AND CHANGES IN NET ASSETS

The vertical balance sheet contains the same basic financial information as does the horizontal balance sheet, since the facts are in no way altered by adopting a different method of presenting them. Similarly, the overall financial relationship between sources of finance and assets, expressed in the formula *Assets = Capital + Liabilities* (now abbreviated to A = C + L) remains unchanged. The revised presentation does, however, focus attention on a different aspect of the relationship between the three magnitudes, since it emphasises the fact that capital is equal to total assets (fixed plus current) minus liabilities, i.e:

$$C = A - L$$

In practice, the term 'total assets minus liabilities' is normally shortened to 'net assets'. We can therefore see that capital equals net assets; indeed these are two different ways of describing the same financial total. The only difference is the way in which the figure is calculated.

- Capital is computed by taking the owner's opening capital investment, adding profit earned and deducting withdrawals for private use to give the closing investment at a particular date.
- Net assets, on the other hand, are computed by adding together the values of the various assets owned on the date under consideration, and then deducting liabilities. Since assets are, by definition, financed either from capital or from liabilities, the balance which remains must necessarily be equal, in value, to the owner's investment.

Example 2.1 demonstrates the fact that profit produces an equivalent increase in the gross assets of a firm; the profit of £80 resulted in gross assets increasing from £8,160 to £8,240. If you now examine the vertical balance sheets given in Figure 2.1 you will see that profit also produces an equivalent increase in net assets which are up from £6,810 to £6,890. This is to be expected. The firm has earned a profit and this must be added to Birch's capital. We know that capital is equal to net assets, though calculated differently, so an increase in capital of £80 necessarily involves an increase in net assets of the same amount.

Although the aim of a business is to earn a profit, sometimes losses are suffered instead. This may be due to management inefficiency or, alternatively, events beyond their control for which they should not be blamed, e.g. a dock strike which makes it impossible to obtain delivery of imported raw materials which are essential for production. Where a firm suffers a loss, net assets, and therefore the owner's capital, are reduced by the amount of the loss. These circumstances are illustrated in Example 2.2.

Example 2.2

The following balance sheet has been prepared for Oak at 31 December 19X1.

Balance Sheet of Oak at 31 December 19X1

	£	£		£
Fixed Assets			Capital	15,200
Plant and Machinery		8,000		
Current Assets			*Current Liabilities*	
Stock	3,800		Trade creditors	2,400
Trade debtors	4,400			
Cash-in-hand	1,400	9,600		
		17,600		17,600

On 1 January 19X2 Oak sold, on credit for £480, goods which had cost £720 some weeks ago.

Required:
  (a) Calculations of:
    (i)   Oak's net assets at 31 December 19X1.
    (ii)   The profit or loss arising on the 1 January 19X2 sale.
    (iii) Oak's capital investment on 1 January 19X2, after the above transactions.
    (iv) Oak's net assets on 1 January after the above transactions.
  (b) Oak's balance sheet at 1 January 19X2, presented in vertical format, to show the figure for net assets at that date.

Solution

(a) (i)

	£
Assets	17,600
Less: Liabilities	2,400
Net Assets	15,200

(ii)

	£
Cost of stock	1,200
Less: Sales proceeds	960
Loss	240

(iii)

	£
Capital at 31 December 19X1	15,200
Less: Loss	240
Capital at 1 January 19X2	14,960

(iv) *Assets*

	£
Plant and machinery	8,000
Stock (3,800 − 1,200)	2,600
Trade debtors (4,400 + 960)	5,360
Cash-in-hand	1,400
	17,360
Less: Liabilities	
Trade creditors	2,400
Net Assets	14,960

(b)

Balance Sheet of Oak at 1 January 19X1

	£	£
Fixed Assets		
Plant and Machinery		8,000
Current Assets		
Stock	2,600	
Trade debtors	5,360	
Cash-in-hand	1,400	
Balance c/d	9,360	

Balance b/d	9,360	8,000
Less: Current Liabilities		
Trade creditors	2,400	
Working capital		6,960
		14,960
Financed by:		
Opening capital		15,200
Less: Net loss		240
Closing capital		14,960

We can therefore conclude from the above examples that

Profit = Increase in net assets (or capital)
Loss = Decrease in net assets (or capital)

An awareness of the relationship between a profit or a loss and changes in net assets (or capital) is fundamental to a sound understanding of the financial effects of business activity. The relevant connections between the various financial magnitudes can be expressed diagrammatically as shown in Figure 2.2.

Figure 2.2

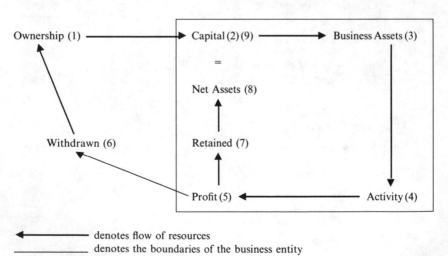

← ———— denotes flow of resources
———————— denotes the boundaries of the business entity

The ownership group (1) invests capital (2) which is used to acquire business assets (3). These assets form the basis for business activity (4) subsequently undertaken in order to generate profit (5). Some of the profit is likely to be paid out to the owners as a return on their investment (6). The remainder is retained (7), and this results in an increased volume of net assets (8) to be used for trading purposes during the following accounting period. There is, of course, an equivalent increase in the owner's capital investment (9), which is made in the expectation that the greater volume of net assets will enable a higher profit to be earned in the future.

Assignment   Students should now work Question 2.1 at the end of the chapter.

2.5   PROFIT MEASURED BY CAPITAL CHANGES

It sometimes happens that the accountant is faced with the task of measuring profit despite the fact that no record exists of business transactions undertaken during the period under review, e.g. because the records have been lost or destroyed by fire. In these circumstances it is not possible to calculate profit by comparing the cost of stock sold with its selling price, as in the previous examples worked. Instead the calculation must be based on the fact, established in section 4 of this chapter, that profit produces an equivalent increase in the owner's capital. Profit can therefore be found by comparing capital at the beginning of an accounting period with capital at the end of that period, i.e.

$$\text{Net profit} = \text{Closing capital} - \text{Opening capital}$$

If opening capital exceeds closing capital, the result of the calculation is a negative figure, and this means that a loss has been suffered.

The identification of proprietor's capital investment at the beginning and end of the period usually involves the need to exercise a significant element of estimation and judgment, particularly in relation to assets owned at the earlier of the two accounting dates. The main categories of assets and liabilities whose values need to be obtained are as follows:

1. *Fixed assets.*   The existence of fixed assets can usually be established by physical verification, but the valuation of these items may prove more difficult. Evidence of the price paid may well be available in view of the large sums often involved; otherwise it is necessary to use information which can be obtained from suppliers of the relevant items or, alternatively, to arrange for a professional valuation.
2. *Stock.*   Reliable figures for stock are difficult to obtain unless steps were taken to arrange for it to be physically counted and valued at each

of the balance sheet dates. If this task has not been undertaken, then an estimate of the likely values is required from the proprietor of the business.

3. *Trade debtors and creditors.*   The amounts involved can be constructed fairly easily, provided copies of the sales and purchase invoices have been retained. Where the company deals in products subject to value added tax, the likelihood of this information being readily available is much increased.

4. *Bank balance.*   The amount of money due to or from the bank can be established by an examination of the relevant bank statements.

The measurement of profit by capital changes is illustrated in Example 2.3.

Example 2.3

The following information is provided relating to the affairs of James who trades in fashionable garments from rented property.

Assets and Liabilities	31 Dec.19X1	31 Dec.19X2
Motor vehicles	1,800	1,350
Fixtures and fittings	450	820
Stocks	1,060	1,610
Trade creditors	730	810
Trade debtors	240	300
Bank overdraft	920	760
Cash-in-hand	40	50

Required:
(a)   Calculations of James's capital investment in the business at the end of 19X1 and 19X2, based on the relationship $C = A - L$.
(b)   A calculation of the profit earned by James during 19X2.
(c)   The balance sheet of James's business at 31 December 19X2, presented in horizontal format.

Solution

(a)   Capital is calculated at each date by deducting liabilities from assets:

Statement of Assets, Liabilities and Capital at 31 December

	19X1		19X2	
Assets	£	£	£	£
Motor vehicles		1,800		1,350
Fixtures and fittings		450		820
Stocks		1,060		1,610
Trade debtors		240		300
Cash-in-hand		40		50
		3,590		4,130
Less: Liabilities				
Trade creditors	730		810	
Bank overdraft	920	1,650	760	1,570
Capital (C = A − L)		1,940		2,560

(b)   Profit is calculated by deducting opening capital from closing capital:

	£
Closing capital	2,560
Less: Opening capital	1,940
Profit	620

(c)

Balance Sheet at 31 December 19X2

	£	£		£	£
Fixed assets			Opening capital		1,940
Motor vehicles .		1,350	Add: Net Profit		620
Fixtures and			Closing capital		2,560
fittings		820			
		2,170			
Current Assets			*Current Liabilities*		
Stocks	1,610		Trade creditors	810	
Trade debtors .	300		Bank overdraft	760	1,570
Cash-in-hand . .	50	1,960			
		4,130			4,130

Assignment   Students should now work Question 2.2 at the end of the chapter.

2.6   CAPITAL INJECTIONS AND WITHDRAWALS

There are two categories of business transaction which cause capital to increase or decrease during an accounting period:

1. Transactions which produce a profit or a loss.
2. Transactions involving the injection or withdrawal of capital by the owners.

Section 5 of this chapter demonstrated the measurement of profit by capital changes, based on the assumption that there are no capital injections or withdrawals during the year. This assumption is now dropped. Where capital injections or withdrawals occur, their financial effects must be isolated in order to obtain an accurate measure of profit. This is because, although an investment or withdrawal of funds, by the owner, causes capital to increase or decrease, these changes do not come about as the result of trading activity and therefore give rise to neither a profit nor a loss. The following adjustments must therefore be made.

1. *Capital injections.* These increase closing capital but they are not business profits and so their effect must be eliminated by deducting the amount of the additional investment from the increase in capital arrived at by deducting opening capital from closing capital.
2. *Drawings.* These reduce closing capital but, because they are not a business expense, they must be added back to the increase in capital arrived at by deducting opening capital from closing capital.

The calculation of profit therefore becomes:

$$\text{Profit} = \text{Closing capital} - \text{opening capital}$$
$$- \text{capital introduced} + \text{drawings}$$

Example 2.4

Assume the same assets and liabilities as are given in Example 2.3. In addition you discover that:

1. During 19X2 James withdrew cash totalling £1,000 to meet living expenses.
2. On 1 August James paid into his business bank account a first prize of £200 won in his golf club's raffle.

Required:
(a) A calculation of the corrected profit earned by James during 19X2.

(b)   The capital section of James's balance sheet at 31 December 19X2.

Solution

(a)   Profit is calculated, as follows, by applying the formula: Profit = Closing capital − opening capital + drawings − capital introduced.

	£
Closing capital	2,560
Less: Opening capital	1,940
Increase in capital	620
Less: Capital introduced	(200)
Add: Drawings	1,000
Profit	1,420

(b)   *Balance Sheet Extract 31 December 19X2*

Capital section	£
Opening capital	1,940
Add: Capital injection	200
Net profit	1,420
	3,560
Less: Drawings	1,000
Closing capital	2,560

Tutorial note:

The balance sheet now contains a full and accurate statement of transactions affecting the owner's capital during the year. It shows that James made an additional capital investment of £200, that he made personal withdrawals of £1,000 and that a profit figure of £1,420 (not £620) should be used as the basis for assessing the firm's performance and as a starting point for computing tax payable.

___

The accurate calculation of profit therefore requires the identification of any capital introduced and/or drawings made during the year. An injection of additional capital by the owner is an unusual event which is normally quite easy to identify. Possible sources of extra capital include the following: a legacy; gambling winnings; a premium bond prize; and the sale of a non-business asset belonging to the proprietor. Drawings are usually more difficult to calculate as they occur more often, may well vary from week to week, and may comprise both cash and stock-in-trade. The latter possibility is particularly likely in the case of a retail business. In the absence of a reliable record of withdrawals, a careful estimate is required from the proprietor.

The various matters discussed in this chapter are incorporated in Example 2.5.

Example 2.5

The following information is provided relating to the affairs of John who owns a tobacconist, confectionery and newspaper kiosk.

Assets and Liabilities	1 Jan.19X3	31 Dec.19X3
	£	£
Kiosk	2,000	2,000
Stocks of tobacco and confectionery ...	450	600
Trade creditors	250	320
Bank balance	160	940
Cash-in-hand	20	30

During 19X3 John received a legacy of £800 which was paid into his business bank account. Cash drawings are estimated at £200 per week and, in addition, John took from the business goods worth £150 for his own use during the year.

Required:
(a) A calculation of the profit earned by John during 19X3, based on the increase in capital.
(b) The balance sheet of John's business at 31 December 19X3, presented in vertical format.

Solution
(a) The capital at the beginning and end of the year must first be calculated using the relationship $C = A - L$

Statement of Assets, Liabilities and Capital at:

	1 Jan. 19X3	31 Dec. 19X3
Assets	£	£
Kiosk	2,000	2,000
Stocks	450	600
Bank balance	160	940
Cash-in-hand	20	30
	2,630	3,570
Less: Liabilities		
Trade creditors	250	320
Capital $(C = A - L)$	2,380	3,250

Profit can now be calculated on the basis of the increase in capital between the beginning and the end of the year, adjusted for capital injections and withdrawals.

	£
Closing capital	3,250
Less: Opening capital	2,380
Increase in capital	870
Less: Capital introduced	(800)
Add: Drawings	10,550W1
Profit	10,620

W1 Drawings: Cash, £200 x 52 =	10,400
Goods	150
	10,550

Tutorial note: John's capital has increased by only £870 during 19X3 (from £2,380 to £3,250). However, the legacy, which is a non-trading receipt, must be deducted from the increase in capital to calculate profits generated from trading activity. Similarly, during 19X3 John withdrew goods and cash totalling £10,550 which must be added. The combined effect of these two adjustments is to produce a 'true' profit figure of £10,620.

(b)   *Balance Sheet at 31 December 19X3*

	£	£
Fixed assets		
Kiosk		2,000
Current Assets		
Stocks	600	
Bank balance	940	
Cash-in-hand	30	
	1,570	
Less: Current Liabilities		
Trade creditors	320	
Working capital		1,250
		3,250
Financed by:		
Opening capital		2,380
Add: Capital introduced		800
Profit		10,620
		13,800
Less: Drawings		10,550
		3,250

Assignment Students should now work Questions 2.3 and 2.4 at the end of the chapter.

2.7 REVIEW

After reading the chapter and working the chapter end questions, students should be able to:

- Appreciate that profit maximisation is a major business objective.
- Distinguish between the two alternative applications of profit: withdrawal by the owner or reinvestment.
- Prepare a balance sheet in vertical format.
- Calculate capital as the difference between assets and liabilities (C = A − L).
- Appreciate the fact that profit increases both capital and net assets by an equivalent amount.
- Calculate profit as the increase in capital after making due allowance for any injections of capital or withdrawals of profit during the year.

2.8 QUESTIONS

Question 2.1

The following balance sheet relates to the affairs of Columbus, who works for the Government and also buys and sells second hand cars. The balance sheet of his second hand car business is as follows:

Balance Sheet at 31 December 19X1

	£	£		£
Fixed assets		2,000	Capital	6,500
Current Assets			*Current Liabilities:*	
Stock of cars	2,700		Trade creditors	200
Debtors	1,000			
Bank	1,000	4,700		
		6,700		6,700

Transactions undertaken in January 19X2:

1. Columbus collects the £1,000 owing in respect of the second hand car sold in December 19X1.
2. Columbus wins £500 on the football pools and pays the proceeds into his business bank account.
3. Columbus sells for £1,200 a car which was in stock on 31 December 19X1 at a value of £1,300.
4. Columbus withdraws £50 for private use.

5. Columbus purchases a friend's car for £150, and promises to pay him in February.
6. Columbus purchases a new machine for £700 and pays in cash.

Required:
   (a) Give the total for gross assets, net assets and working capital based on the figures in the above balance sheet.
   (b) Taking each of the transactions listed above separately, give their effect (increase or decrease) on:
       (i)   Profit.
       (ii) Net assets.
       (iii) Gross assets.
       (iv) Working capital.

Question 2.2
The balance sheet of Paul at 30 June 19X3 is as follows:

Balance Sheet as at 30 June 19X3

	£	£		£	£
Fixed assets		7,500	Capital		10,330
Current Assets			*Current Liabilities:*		
Stock	3,280		Trade creditors .	1,220	
Debtors	1,750	5,030	Bank overdraft .	980	2,200
		12,530			12,530

During the year to 30 June 19X4, Paul received a business loan of £3,000 from a friend. The loan is interest free and repayable at the end of 19X6. On 1 December 19X3 Paul purchased fixed assets costing £2,350. At 30 June 19X4, trade creditors amounted to £1,890, stock was valued at £4,270 and debtors amounted to £1,450. In addition Paul had £570 in the business bank account and cash-in-hand of £30.

Required:
   (a) A calculation of Paul's capital investment in the business at 30 June 19X4.
   (b) A calculation of the profit earned by Paul's business during the year to 30 June 19X4.
   (c) The balance sheet of Paul's business at 30 June 19X4, presented in vertical format.

Question 2.3

The balance sheet of Burnley's business as at 31 December 19X7 was as follows:

Balance Sheet as at 31 December 19X7

	£	£		£	£
Fixed assets		17,700	Capital		23,496
Current Assets			*Current Liabilities*		
Stock	5,062		Creditors		
Debtors	3,728		Goods	4,032	
Bank	1,242	10,032	Expenses	204	4,236
		27,732			27,732

The following information about Burnley's financial position at 31 December 19X8 was extracted from his books

	£
Stock	6,536
Debtors	4,864
Bank overdraft	2,492
Creditors:	
Goods	4,236
Expenses	168
Fixed assets	15,930

Burnley drew £10,800 from his business during 19X8 for private purposes.

Required:
  (a) A calculation of Burnley's capital at 31 December 19X8.
  (b) A calculation of the firm's profit for 19X8.
  (c) The firm's balance sheet at 31 December 19X8 presented in vertical format.

Question 2.4

The following information is obtained in connection with the business of G. Haze, a trader.

	31 December	
	19X3	19X4
	£	£
Fixed assets at book value	9,000	see below
Stocks	2,650	3,710
Trade debtors	5,200	5,600
Trade creditors	1,710	1,210
Bank balance (overdraft)	(360)	50

During 19X4 motor vehicles were purchased at a cost of £3,144, part of which was met by G. Haze trading in his private motor car at an agreed valuation of £600. Cash drawings made by G. Haze amounted to £150 per week and, in addition, stocks valued at £300 were taken during the year for personal use.

Required:

(a) A calculation of the profit earned by G. Haze's business during 19X4.

(b) The balance sheet of the firm at 31 December 19X4 presented in the horizontal format.

CHAPTER 3

The Preparation of Accounts from Cash Records

3.1 ACCOUNTING SYSTEMS AND INFORMATION REQUIREMENTS

The complexity of the accounting system for recording and reporting business transactions is principally a function of the size of the firm.* The large number of transactions undertaken each day and the separation of the management group from the ownership group, which is likely to occur in the case of a substantial business concern, requires the operation of a comprehensive accounting system for the dual purposes of control and performance assessment, *on a regular* (daily, weekly, or monthly) basis. These conditions do not apply in the small firm and, accordingly, the accounting system can be far more rudimentary for the following reasons:

- *Control* of valuable resources results from the owner's close personal contact with all aspects of the firm's business activities. Certain of its most vulnerable assets, e.g. the cash balance and the operation of the business bank account, are likely to remain under the direct control of the owner. Other resources, e.g. stocks, which may be placed in the custody of trusted personnel, also remain under the proprietor's close scrutiny.
- *Performance assessment* is also possible without the aid of accounting reports. The number of trade creditors and customers is relatively small, and any difficulties associated with the supply of, or demand for, the firm's products quickly come to the attention of a diligent proprietor. Similarly, in the absence of a significant level of capital expenditure, changes in the bank balance are likely to provide a fairly reliable indication of progress.

But although the small business does not require detailed accounting records to facilitate control and performance assessment, on a continuous

---

*The position is different in the case of a limited company which, irrespective of its size, is *legally* required to keep full accounting records.

basis, *annual* accounts must still be prepared as the basis for agreeing tax liabilities with the Inland Revenue. In the case of a partnership, annual accounts are also required as the basis for allocating profit between the partners. The annual accounts are, in principle, no different from those prepared for large companies. They consist of:

- a trading and profit and loss account. This document was referred to in chapter 1.1, and is considered in detail later in this chapter, and
- a balance sheet, with which you should by now be fully familiar.

The minimum information required to prepare each of these documents, where a rudimentary accounting system (or no system at all) is in operation, comprises details of:

1. Assets at the beginning and at the end of the year.
2. Liabilities at the beginning and at the end of the year.
3. Cash receipts and payments during the year.

The steps which must be taken to obtain details of assets and liabilities (items 1 and 2) were discussed in chapter 2.5. We also saw, in chapter 2, that the information obtained can then be used to prepare both an opening and a closing balance sheet.

Details of cash transactions during the year (item 3) are required as the starting point for preparing the trading and profit and loss. The business bank statements fulfil an essential role in this context, since they contain a wealth of reliable information concerning cash transactions during the year. There is, of course, usually a large number of bank statements and the analysis of these documents is a lengthy process, particularly because the statements provide few details. It is therefore important for cheque books and paying in books to be retained so that a full and accurate description of the various items appearing on the bank statements is available. Details must also be obtained of any cash transactions which have not gone through the bank. This information may be recorded in a 'petty' cash book; alternatively it may be possible to build up the relevant figures from files of cash receipts and payments.

In examination questions, it is usually assumed that the analysis work has been done, and figures for receipts and payments are given in a summary form similar to the following:

Figure 3.1

Cash Transactions During 19X1

Receipts	£	Payments	£
Opening balance of cash	510	Payments to suppliers	17,380
		Rent and rates	840
Sales of goods	23,750	Wages	2,560
		Lighting and heating	620
		General expenses	375
			21,775
		Closing balance of cash	2,485
	24,260		24,260

The 'Receipts' side of the summary shows cash receipts from customers of £23,750 which, when added to the sum available at the start, of £510, means that cash resources amounting to £24,260 became available to the business during 19X1. Cash payments totalling £21,775 must be deducted from the £24,260, leaving a cash balance at the year end of £2,485.

Provided the rudimentary financial facts referred to in this section can be assembled, it is possible to prepare a full set of final accounts. The process, described as the preparation of accounts from cash records, is examined in this chapter.

3.2 THE MATCHING CONCEPT:
PROFIT = REVENUE − EXPENDITURE

Chapter 2 demonstrated how profit can be measured in the absence of detailed information concerning trading transactions undertaken during a particular accounting period, i.e. it is computed by calculating the owner's capital at the beginning and the end of the accounting period and measuring the change which has occurred. Where there exists an adequate accounting record of transactions undertaken during the year, profit is instead computed in accordance with the *Matching Concept,* i.e. the accountant measures profit by comparing or 'matching' the total cost of the many trading transactions undertaken during an accounting period with the total revenues arising therefrom. A simple example is now considered.

Example 3.1

Mex Cars Ltd is a motor vehicle distributor which makes up its accounts on the calendar year basis. Ten cars are purchased during 19X1 for £4,500 each and sold for £6,000 each.

Required:
Calculate profit by matching revenues with expenditures.

Solution

	£
Revenue: Proceeds from sales of cars (£6,000 × 10)	60,000
Less: Expenditure: Cost of cars sold (£4,500 × 10)	45,000
Profit	15,000

3.3 GROSS PROFIT AND NET PROFIT

The balance of profit, which is arrived at by matching sales proceeds with the actual cost of goods sold, is called gross profit. In practice many other costs are also incurred. These include some or all of the following:

- wages and salaries paid to employees
- salesmen's commission
- rent and rates paid on the factory, showroom, or office accommodation
- telephone costs
- stationery.

Since these outlays are incurred to help generate sales revenue, they must also be deducted to leave a final balance called net profit. Revenues and expenditures are matched against one another in the trading account and the profit and loss account (usually abbreviated to trading and profit and loss account). The gross profit is calculated in the trading account, by deducting the cost of cars sold from sales revenue; the remaining expenses are deducted in the profit and loss account. The relationships may be expressed as follows:

TRADING ACCOUNT: Sales − Cost of goods sold = Gross profit

PROFIT AND LOSS ACCOUNT: Gross profit − Remaining expenses
= Net profit

A common method of presenting this accounting statement is illustrated in Figure 3.2.

Figure 3.2

The trading and profit and loss account of Mex Cars Ltd for 19X1 is as follows:

Trading and Profit and Loss Account for 19X1

Expenditure	£	Revenue	£
Cost of cars sold	45,000	Sales	60,000
Gross profit	15,000		
	60,000		60,000
Salaries	6,200	Gross profit	15,000
Commissions	600		
Rent and Rates	1,400		
Lighting and heating	250		
Telephone	150		
Postage and Stationery	220		
Advertising	370		
General expenses	500		
	9,690		
Net profit	5,310		
	15,000		15,000

It might occur to students that the calculation of profit on the basis of changes in capital is a rather more straightforward process than by comparing revenue with expenditure. The accumulation of figures for sales revenue and the various items of expenditure is a far more time consuming task than the identification of figures for capital on the basis of assets minus liabilities. The extra work involved is justified on the following grounds:

1. Trading transactions entered into during an accounting period are recorded, not only to enable profit to be measured, but also to facilitate effective control over inflows and outflows of cash and goods, e.g. records of sales and work done by employees are needed to ensure that cash is collected from customers and that employees are paid the amounts due to them.
2. The trading and profit and loss account provides a comprehensive statement of how the net profit balance has been achieved. This document includes, in addition to the net profit figure, both a calculation of gross profit and a detailed list of expenses. It therefore provides a valuable means for assessing performance, e.g. by

comparing this year's results with those achieved last year, and for reaching decisions concerning the future allocation of resources.

3.4   THE PROBLEM OF PERIODIC PROFIT CALCULATION

The frequency with which the trading and profit and loss account and balance sheet are prepared varies, depending on the circumstances of the particular business. As a minimum, however, accounts must be prepared once a year: limited companies are legally required to prepare annual accounts for publication, while sole traders and partnerships are under an effective legal obligation to prepare annual accounts for tax purposes. To provide the information needed to take day-to-day decisions designed to achieve the most effective use of available resources, management requires more frequent calculations of profit, and the preparation of quarterly or even monthly management accounts is a common feature within commerce and industry today.

The calculation of periodic profit causes difficulties because business activity is continuous. For example, a business may run for 10 years but, for financial reporting purposes, it must be split into at least 10 accounting periods, each lasting one year. The problem is how to deal with the transactions which cannot be completely identified with a particular accounting period. Many transactions cause no difficulties. For example, assuming accounts are prepared on the calendar year basis, an item of stock purchased and paid for in January 19X1 and sold for cash in February 19X1 is taken into account in computing the profit for the calendar year 19X1. Problems arise with transactions which overlap the end of one accounting period and the beginning of another. For example, consider the following cases, assuming a 31 December accounting date:

1.   Stocks are delivered to a customer in December 19X1 but are not paid for until January 19X2.
2.   Stocks are purchased and paid for in November 19X1 but not sold until March 19X2.
3.   Rates are paid on 1 October 19X1 for the six months to 31 March 19X2.
4.   Machinery is purchased and paid for in 19X1 which will last for eight years.

The problem of deciding whether these transactions give rise to revenues and expenditures in 19X1 or 19X2 or another accounting period is solved by the accountant making certain assumptions and applying a range of accounting conventions to the factual information generated by the accounting system. These procedures are examined in sections 5–7 of this chapter.

3.5 THE IDENTIFICATION OF REVENUE:
THE REALISATION CONCEPT

Revenue is obtained mainly from the sale of goods or services and, for accounting purposes, *it is assumed to arise at the point of sale.* For a cash sale this occurs when the goods are exchanged for cash; for a credit sale, it occurs when the goods and sales invoice are delivered to the customer and a debtor is created. We saw in chapter 1.6 that the assumption that revenue, and therefore profit, arises when the sale takes place is called the *Realisation Concept,* and it is a good illustration of how accounting procedures are based on generally agreed conventions rather than indisputable facts.

Illustration 3.1

Owen Ltd manufactures a specialised motor car for which demand exceeds supply. Immediately production is complete, a buyer can quickly be found. The company completes one motor car per week. The following information is provided.

1. Motor car, works no. Z23, is completed on Friday of the week ending 31 January 19X5. The total cost of production is £26,300.
2. The Getrich Finance Company Ltd orders the car for its managing director on Wednesday, 5 February.
3. The Getrich company takes delivery of the car on Friday, 14 February and is invoiced for the sales price of £37,000.
4. The Getrich company pays for the car on Monday, 17 March 19X5.

There are therefore four possible dates on which the profit arising, of £10,700 (£37,000-£26,300), could be recognised.

(a) *31 January 19X5 on completion of production.* A great deal of work goes into building the car and, by the time manufacture is complete, there is little more to do. Demand exceeds supply and so a sale is more or less guaranteed. No profit is recognised, however, because it is considered imprudent to anticipate sales which may not occur.

(b) *5 February 19X5 on receipt of the order.* The acceptance of an order produces a legally enforceable contract. However, it is unlikely that a motor vehicle manufacturer would attempt to enforce the contract, or sue for damages, if Getrich decides to withdraw. It is therefore again considered imprudent to anticipate profit at this stage.

(c)   *14 February 19X5 when the item is sold.*   Profit is recognised on the grounds that the sale gives rise to a legally enforceable debt which would be recognised by a court of law.

(d)   *17 March 19X5 on receipt of cash.*   It is sometimes argued that, in the case of a credit sale, it would be even safer to wait until the cash is actually collected before recognising a profit. But although accountants rightly have the reputation of being cautious, they are not that cautious. The collection of cash will in most cases be a mere formality, and any delay in the recognition of revenue, beyond the point of sale, is not considered justified.

3.5.1   Calculating Sales from Records of Cash Receipts   Where accounting records are incomplete, the sales figure is not usually available and must be built up from cash records and figures for the opening and closing balances of trade debtors.

Example 3.2

During 19X1, John received £17,500 from customers in respect of credit sales. At 1 January 19X1, his trade debtors amounted to £3,600 and at 31 December 19X1 they were £4,720.

Calculations of sales:	£
Cash received in respect of credit sales	17,500
Less: Opening trade debtors	3,600
	13,900
Add: Closing trade debtors	4,720
Sales	18,620

Tutorial note:
Of the £17,500 received during the year, £3,600 was collected from customers to whom goods were sold in 19X0 and which would have been reported as revenue in the trading account for that year. The difference, £13,900, represents the cash received in respect of sales during 19X1. To this must be added closing debtors for goods sold during 19X1, but not yet paid for, to produce the sales figure of £18,620.

The rule to remember for calculating the sales figure from cash records is therefore:

$$\text{Sales} = \text{Cash received from customers} - \text{Opening Debtors} + \text{Closing Debtors}$$

3.6   MATCHING EXPENDITURE WITH REVENUE: THE ACCRUALS CONCEPT

The first step in the calculation of profit for the year is to compute revenue; the second step involves identifying the expenditures which must be matched against revenue. The basic test is: 'Which accounting period benefits from expenditure?'

- If the answer is: 'The current accounting period', then the expenditure is charged against revenue for the current year.
- If the answer is: 'A future accounting period', then the expenditure must be carried forward as an asset in the balance sheet and charged against the revenue of the future accounting period.
- If the answer is: 'Both the current period and one or more future periods', an apportionment must be made between accounting periods.

This process, which relates the charge to benefits received during the year, rather than payment made during the year, is called the *Accruals Concept*. The application of this concept to specific business facts is now examined in sections 3.6.1 to 3.6.3.

3.6.1   Accounting for Stock   The calculation of the figure for cost of goods sold, to be compared with sales revenue for the purpose of computing gross profit, involves two steps:

1. *Calculate purchases.*   The procedure is analogous to that followed when computing sales, except that: payments to suppliers are substituted for receipts from customers; creditors are substituted for debtors. The following formula should be used:

   Purchases = Cash paid to suppliers − Opening creditors
   + Closing creditors

2. *Calculate cost of goods sold.*   It is unlikely that all the goods purchased during the year will have been sold by the end of the year. Some items will remain in stock and should be deducted from purchases and carried forward, in the balance sheet, to the following accounting period which will benefit from their sale. In a similar manner, stocks brought forward from the previous year, and sold during the current accounting period, must be added to purchases and matched with the current year's sales proceeds. The calculation which must be memorised in this case is:

   Cost of goods sold = Purchases + Opening stock − Closing stock

Example 3.3

James made payments by cheque to suppliers of goods on credit amounting to £27,300 during 19X2. In addition, he made cash purchases of £1,600. Trade creditors at 1 January 19X2 and 31 December 19X2 amounted respectively to £4,750 and £6,100. Opening stocks were £10,250, while closing stocks amounted to £9,640.

Required:
Calculate (a) purchases and (b) cost of goods sold for 19X2.

Solution

(a) *Calculation of purchases:* £

		£
Cash paid to suppliers: Credit purchases		27,300
Cash purchases		1,600
		28,900
Less: Opening creditors		4,750
		24,150
Add: Closing creditors		6,100
Purchases		30,250

(b) *Calculation of cost of goods sold:* £

	£
Opening stock	10,250
Add: Purchases	30,250
	40,500
Less: Closing stock	9,640
Cost of goods sold	30,860

The calculations discussed and illustrated in sections 3.5.1 and 3.6.1 of this chapter are central to the measurement of profit by matching revenue with expenditure.

Assignment Students should now work Question 3.1 at the end of the chapter.

3.6.2 Accounting for Services: Accruals and Prepayments When preparing accounts from cash records, it is also necessary to adjust cash payments for services rendered to the company, so that the amount charged in the profit and loss account reflects the cost of benefits actually consumed during the year.

For certain services, payments are made before the associated benefits are received, i.e. the payment is made in advance. In the case of rent and rates, advance payments are made for the right to occupy the property for a fixed future period of time. Where the period of occupation covers the end of one accounting year and the beginning of another, an arithmetic apportionment of the amount paid must be made between the two consecutive accounting periods. The value of the service consumed during the current period is written off in the profit and loss account; the value of the benefit carried forward to the following period is known as a 'prepayment', and is included in the balance sheet as a current asset.

Illustration 3.2
On 1 April 19X1 Griffin Ltd pays a rent of £600 for the occupation of premises over the forthcoming 12 months. The accounts are made up on the calendar year basis.

Nine months (or three-quarters) of the total benefit is received during 19X1 and three months (one-quarter) of the benefit is received during 19X2. Therefore:

Amount to be charged against revenue arising during 19X1 — £600 × ¾ = £450

Amount to be carried forward in the balance sheet, at 31 December 19X1 as a 'prepaid expense' — £600 × ¼ = £150. This amount is then charged against revenue in the profit and loss account for 19X2.

The majority of expenses are paid in arrears, rather than in advance. This is because the amount charged depends on the extent to which the service is utilised. Examples are electricity charges, telephone charges, and the wage bill. In these cases, it is necessary to raise an 'accrual' at the end of the accounting period, representing the value of the benefit received but not yet paid for. The amount of the accrual may be estimated on the basis of past experience. Alternatively, where the bill is received by the time the accounts are prepared, an arithmetic apportionment may be made. This is unlikely to produce strictly accurate results because the service will not have been utilised at an even rate throughout the period under consideration. However, the error is unlikely to be significant, and the extra work and cost involved in obtaining a more precise apportionment would not be justified. The amount of the accrual is carried forward in the balance sheet as a current liability under the heading 'accrued expense'.

Example 3.4

The following information is provided relating to Mark's business for 19X4:

		£
Payments during the year for:	rates	500
	telephone	375

Balances at	1 January	31 December
	£	£
Rates paid in advance	100	125
Telephone charges outstanding	50	62

Required:

Calculations of the amount to be charged against revenue for 19X4 in respect of (i) rates (ii) telephone.

Solution

			£
(i)	Rates:	Payments during 19X4	500
		Add: Amount prepaid at 1 January 19X4	100*
			600
		Less: Amount prepaid at 31 December 19X4	125
		Charge for the year	475
(ii)	Telephone:	Payments during 19X4	375
		Less: Amount accrued at 1 January 19X4	50**
			325
		Add: Amount accrued at 31 December 19X4	62
		Charge for the year	387

Tutorial notes:

*   This amount was paid in 19X3 but it relates to the occupation of the premises during 19X4 and must be charged against revenue arising during 19X4.

**   This amount was paid in 19X4, but it relates to services received during 19X3 and it will have been charged against revenue arising during 19X3.

3.6.3 Accounting for the Depreciation of Fixed Assets   Fixed assets are usually paid for at the date of acquisition, or soon afterwards, but they are

expected to benefit the firm for many years. For example, a motor vehicle used by a sales representative might last five years, a machine 10 years, and a building 50 years or more. It would therefore be unreasonable to burden revenue arising during the year that the asset is acquired with its entire cost. At the same time, most fixed assets have a limited useful life, and it would be equally wrong to keep these items indefinitely in the books at cost.

'Depreciation' is the term used to describe *the fall in the value of a fixed asset between the date it is acquired and the date it is sold or scrapped.*

The reduction in value is acknowledged, in the accounts, by making an annual depreciation charge designed to spread the loss over the periods which benefit from using the asset. The amount of the depreciation charge is written off, each year, in the profit and loss account, while the fixed asset is reported in the balance sheet, each year, at cost less the total amount written off to date, called 'accumulated' depreciation.

There are many different methods of charging depreciation, and we will concentrate on the one which is most common and easy to apply for the purpose of illustration, namely the straight line method (sometimes called the equal instalment method). This method assumes that each accounting period benefits to the same extent from using the asset, and the total decline in its value is therefore spread evenly over the period of ownership. The formula used to calculate the depreciation charge *for one year* is as follows:

$$\text{Straight line depreciation} = \frac{\text{Original Cost} - \text{Estimated value at end of useful life}}{\text{Estimated useful life, in years}}$$

Example 3.5

Paul purchased a machine for £130,000 on 1 January 19X1. It is estimated that the machine will have a useful life of 6 years and then be sold for £10,000. Calculate the annual straight line depreciation charge and show the relevant balance sheet entries for each of the years 19X1–X6.

Solution

$$\text{Straight line charge} = \frac{£130,000 - £10,000}{6} = £20,000 \text{ per annum}$$

Each year, for 6 years, a depreciation charge of £20,000 will be made against revenue, and the value of the machine will appear in the year end balance sheets as follows:

31 December	19X1	19X2	19X3	19X4	19X5	19X6
	£000	£000	£000	£000	£000	£000
Machine at cost	130	130	130	130	130	130
Less: Accumulated depreciation	20	40	60	80	100	120
	110	90	70	50	30	10

The effect of charging depreciation is that the balance sheet value of the machine is gradually reduced to its disposal value. If everything works out as planned, on 31 December 19X6 the machine will be removed from the balance sheet and replaced by cash of an equal value. Events may not progress quite so smoothly, and it may turn out that the estimates on which the calculation was based prove to be wrong, i.e. the machine might not last for six years or sell for £10,000 at the end of its useful life. These possible complications are considered later in this book.

3.7 THE PREPARATION OF ACCOUNTS FROM CASH RECORDS: A WORKED EXAMPLE

Example 3.6

William is a trader who has been in business for a number of years. In the past a friend has prepared accounts which were sufficient to enable William to agree his tax liabilities with the Inland Revenue. William's friend has now left the country and is therefore unable to help. William maintains separate files of invoices received from suppliers and issued to customers.

The following summary has been prepared from William's paying in books, cheque books and bank statements for 19X2.

Bank Summary

	£		£
Cash sales	39,640	Opening balance	3,520
Proceeds from credit sales ...	18,500	Payments to suppliers	31,910
		Rates	2,800
		Personal drawings	6,500
		Wages for part-time staff ...	5,930
		General expenses	3,180
		Vehicle	4,000
		Closing balance	300
	58,140		58,140

The following information has been obtained from the files of invoices and other books and records of William:

1. William has paid all sales proceeds into his bank account, except for £200 which was used to pay additional part-time staff over the busy Christmas period.
2. Assets and liabilities at 31 December, based on an analysis of the invoice files, and from discussions with William, were as follows:

	19X1	19X2
	£	£
Premises at cost	6,600	6,600
Furniture at book value (cost £6,000)	3,000	Note 3
Stocks	4,250	5,760
Trade creditors	4,630	4,920
Trade debtors	2,140	2,320
Rates paid in advance	180	200
General expenses accrued	320	290

3. William charges depreciation on furniture at the 5% on cost. The vehicle was purchased on 1 July 19X2 and is to be written off over five years assuming a resale value of £1,000 at the end of that period. Ignore depreciation of premises.

Required:
The trading and profit and loss account of William's business for the year ending 31 December 19X2 and the balance sheet at that date.

Solution

Tutorial note:
Questions involving the preparation of accounts from cash records should usually be answered by tackling each of the following steps in the order indicated:

Step 1: Establish the financial position at the beginning of the year by preparing an opening balance sheet. This shows the proprietor's opening capital which is needed when preparing the balance sheet at the year end.

Step 2: Calculate revenues and expenditures for inclusion in the trading and profit and loss account.

Step 3: Prepare the trading and profit and loss account.

Step 4: Prepare the closing balance sheet.

Step 1

Balance Sheet at 1 January 19X2

	£	£
Fixed Assets		
Premises.............................		6,600
Furniture		3,000
		9,600
Current Assets		
Stocks	4,250	
Trade debtors	2,140	
Prepaid expenses	180	
	6,570	
Less: Current Liabilities		
Trade creditors	4,630	
Accrued expenses	320	
Bank overdraft	3,520	
	8,470	
Working capital		(1,900)
Capital.............................		7,700

Step 2

Workings

W1 Sales

	£
Paid into bank	
cash sales	39,640
credit sales	18,500
Proceeds not paid in .	200
Total cash received ..	58,340
Less: Opening debtors	(2,140)
Add: Closing debtors	2,320
	58,520

W2 Purchases

Payments to suppliers	31,910
Less: Opening creditors	(4,630)
Add: Closing creditors	4,920
	32,200

W3 Rates

Paid during year	2,800
Add: Opening advance payment	180
Less: Closing advance payment	(200)
	2,780

W4 General expenses

	£
Paid during year	3,180
Less: Opening accrual	(320)
Add: Closing accrual .	290
	3,150

W5 Wages

Paid by cheque	5,930
Paid in cash	200
	6,130

W6 Depreciation of furniture
£6,000 × 5% = £300

W7 Depreciation of vehicle:
(£4,000 − £1,000)/5 × ½* = £300

*The vehicle has only been owned for 6 months.

Step 3

Trading and Profit and Loss Account for 19X2

	£			£	
Purchases	32,200	W2	Sales	58,520	W1
Add: Opening stock	4,250				
Less: Closing stock	(5,760)				
Cost of goods sold	30,690				
Gross profit	27,830				
	58,520			58,520	
Rates	2,780	W3	Gross profit	27,830	
General expenses	3,150	W4			
Wages	6,130	W5			
Depreciation: furniture . .	300	W6			
vehicle . . .	300	W7			
	12,660				
Net profit	15,170				
	27,830			27,830	

Step 4

Balance Sheet at 31 December 19X2

	£	£		£	£
Fixed Assets			Opening capital . . .		7,700
Premises at cost . .		6,600	Add: Net profit . . .		15,170
Furniture	3,000		Less: drawings . . .		(6,500)
Less: Depreciation .	300	2,700			16,370
Vehicle at cost	4,000		*Current Liabilities*		
Less: Depreciation .	300	3,700	Trade creditors	4,920	
		13,000	General expenses		
Current Assets			accrued	290	5,210
Stocks	5,760				
Trade debtors	2,320				
Prepaid rates	200				
Bank	300	8,580			
		21,580			21,580

3.7.1   Trading and Profit and Loss Account Presented in Vertical Format

Chapter 2.3 drew attention to the fact that today the balance sheet is often presented in the vertical format rather than the horizontal format, and the same is the case with the trading and profit and loss account. The reasons are similar; the layout is thought to be more easily comprehended by the non-accountant; it is possible to present a number of years' results on a single sheet; and comparison of results between years is made much easier. The trading and profit and loss account of William is now reproduced in vertical format for the purpose of illustration.

Figure 3.3

Trading and Profit and Loss Account of William for 19X2

	£	£
Sales		58,520
Less: Purchases	32,200	
Add: Opening stock	4,250	
Less: Closing stock	(5,760)	
Cost of goods sold		30,690
Gross profit		27,830
Less: Rates	2,780	
General expenses	3,150	
Wages	6,130	
Depreciation: furniture	300	
vehicle	300	12,660
Net profit		15,170

Tutorial note:

In exam questions, instructions to use either the horizontal format or vertical format must be complied with, but where no instruction is given, either presentation may be used.

Assignment   Students should now work Questions 3.2, 3.3 and 3.4 at the end of the chapter.

3.8 REVIEW

After reading the chapter and working the chapter end questions, students should be able to:

- Understand what is meant by the following: 'Matching Concept', 'Accruals Concept', 'Gross Profit' and 'Net Profit'.
- Understand why the need to calculate 'periodic' profit causes difficulties for the accountant.
- Apply the 'Matching Concept' and the 'Accruals Concept' to the calculation of gross profit and net profit.

- Prepare final accounts from cash records together with details of assets and liabilities at the beginning and the end of the year.
- Prepare a trading and profit and loss account using the vertical format.

✗ 3.9   QUESTIONS

Question 1

The following information is provided relating to Peter's business for 19X3:

	£
Cash collected from customers in respect of:	
credit sales	41,750
cash sales	12,350
Payments to suppliers	36,590

Balances at	1 January £	31 December £
Trade debtors	12,650	11,780
Trade creditors	6,540	8,270
Stock	9,150	9,730

Required:
  (a)   Calculations for 19X3 of:
    (i)   receipts from customers,
    (ii)   sales,
    (iii)   purchases,
    (iv)   cost of goods sold.
  (b)   The trading account of Peter's business for 19X3.

Question 3.2

David owns a fruiter's shop and his annual accounting date is 30 September. David's balance sheet at 30 September 1988 was as follows:

Balance Sheet at 30 September 1988

	£	£
Leasehold shop at cost	12,100	
Less: Depreciation	8,150	
		3,950
Shop equipment at cost	19,634	
Less: Depreciation	11,585	
		8,049
		11,999
Stock	931	
Trade debtors	358	
Deposit account	6,412	
	7,701	
Less:		
Trade creditors	2,150	
Bank overdraft	32	
	2,182	
		5,519
		17,518
Financed by:		
Capital account		17,518

David's bank account for the year to 30 September 1989 may be summarised as follows:

Bank Current Account

	£		£
Takings paid to bank	60,205	Balance 1 October 1988	32
Interest on deposit account	428	Payments to suppliers	37,014
		Wages	10,398
		Rent and rates	7,500
		Heating and lighting	1,201
		Bank charges	314
		Transfer to bank deposit account	500
		Sundry trade expenses	1,792
		Personal drawings	1,047
		Balance 30 September 1989	835
	60,633		60,633

Other information relating to the year ended 30 September 1989 is given below.

1. All cash takings had been paid into the bank with the exception of £5,500 which David withheld for personal expenditure.
2. At 30 September 1989 stock was valued at £1,240; debtors amounted to £241; David owed his suppliers £786.
3. Depreciation to be charged for the year is to be £1,210 in respect of the leasehold shop, and £1,422 in respect of the shop equipment.
4. At 30 September 1989 rent and rates were prepaid by £824, and electricity charges accrued were £210.

Required:
  (a) A trading and profit and loss account for the year ended 30 September 1989. [10]
  (b) A balance sheet at 30 September 1989. [10]
           [Total marks for question — 20]
(Taken from Banking Certificate. Introduction to Accounting, October 1989)

Question 3.3

Barry is a taxi-driver who owns his taxi. It cost £10,500 new at the beginning of his financial year and he is taking depreciation into account at 25% p.a. on the straight line basis.

At 30 April 1987, he had prepaid expenses of £453 in respect of the licence and insurance on his vehicle, he was owed £312 for fares incurred by regular customers (with whom he operates a monthly account) and in turn owed a garage £209 for servicing and petrol.

At 30 April 1988, his prepaid expenses on licence and insurance amount to £531, his regular customers owe him £587, and his debt to the garage is £317.

A summary of his bank account for the year 30 April 1988 is given below.

Summary Bank Account

	£		£
Balance b/fwd	34	Taxi operating expenses	10,317
Bankings	16,013	Hire of two-way radio	540
Advertising revenue from		Advertising in telephone	
roof sign	200	directory	192
		Trade subscription	75
		Supply and fitting of	
		illuminated roof sign to	
		carry advertisements	520
		Bank charges	48
		Foreign currency	
		(for Dutch holiday)	427
		Personal expenses	
		(including mortgage	
		payments on house,	
		income tax, rates)	3,147
		Balance c/fwd	981
	£16,247		£16,247

The bankings represented all monies received for fares (including tips) after £75 per week for each of 50 weeks had been deducted: the latter sum he has retained in cash for housekeeping and personal expenses.

Required:
  (a)   A balance sheet at 30 April 1987.   [6]
  (b)   A profit and loss account for the year ended 30 April 1988.   [8]
  (c)   A balance sheet at 30 April 1988.   [6]

(Taken from Banking Certificate. Introduction to Accounting, May 1988)

Question 3.4
The following is the balance sheet of Stondon, a trader, at 31 December 19X2:

Balance Sheet

	£		£
Furniture and fittings	800	Capital	7,940
Stock	5,384		
Trade debtors	4,162	Trade creditors	3,294
Balance at bank	888		
	11,234		11,234

In January 19X3 Stondon sold certain private investments for £4,200; he purchased a motor van for business use for £3,000 and paid the balance of the proceeds into his business bank account.

At 31 December 19X3, trade debtors amounted to £4,124, stock-in-trade was valued at £6,891 and trade creditors amounted to £3,586. Stondon's business bank account was overdrawn by £782. His drawings during 19X3 were £12,840.

The total of running expenses charged to the profit and loss account for the year 19X3 amounted to £14,420; this total included £500 for depreciation of the motor van.

Stondon's gross profit is at the rate of 25% of selling price for all goods sold during 19X3.

Required:
(a) Prepare Stondon's balance sheet at 31 December 19X3.
(b) Calculate Stondon's net profit for 19X3 on the basis of changes in capital.
(c) Reconstruct the trading and profit and loss account of Stondon's business for the year 19X3.

Note: Ignore depreciation of furniture and fittings.

CHAPTER 4

The Double Entry System

4.1 INTRODUCTION

The first three chapters of this book have dealt with situations where entities have not maintained a full set of double entry accounting records. In this chapter, and the one which follows, the operation of accounting systems using double entry ledgers to record information and produce accounting reports is examined.

The initial step in the process of recording and reporting activity is to ensure that all business transactions are accurately and promptly recorded immediately they take place. They may then be summarised and entered in the firm's books from which accounting reports are periodically prepared. This chapter explains the operation of double entry book-keeping to maintain a ledger, describes how the initial record of transactions is created in the 'Books of Prime Entry', and shows how the balances which form the basis of periodic accounting reports are extracted from the ledger. The preparation of accounting reports is examined in chapter 5.

4.2 DOUBLE ENTRY BOOK-KEEPING

This section explains the operation of double entry book-keeping and shows how data from the books of prime entry, described in section 4.3 of this chapter, are recorded using this technique.

4.2.1 The Interlocking Effect of Transactions
It was demonstrated in chapter 1 that, in the balance sheet, assets remain equal in value to sources of finance after any transaction, and the relationship

$$A \text{ (assets)} = C \text{ (capital)} + L \text{ (liabilities)}$$

remains true in all circumstances. The system of double entry book-keeping is based on this interlocking effect and, to maintain the relationship $A = C + L$, each transaction must be accounted for as having two equal, but opposite, effects. These are known as 'debits' and 'credits'. In the balance sheet, debit entries increase assets or decrease liabilities, while credit entries increase liabilities or decrease assets. The accounting system must enable the production of a profit and loss account as well as the balance sheet, so the double entry effect of a transaction on the former document must also be considered. The impact of an expense is to decrease capital (the liability owed to ownership), and so it is recorded as a debit in the profit and loss account, while revenue increases capital and so is a credit. Periodically the effects of revenues and expenses are compared to calculate the firm's net profit or loss. A net profit is then added to capital, while any net loss is deducted from it. A full chart of debit and credit entries is given in Figure 4.1.

Figure 4.1

THE IMPACT OF DEBIT AND CREDIT ENTRIES

DEBIT	CREDIT
Increase Asset	Decrease Asset
OR	OR
Decrease Liability	Increase Liability
OR	OR
Decrease Capital	Increase Capital
OR	OR
Increase Expense	Decrease Expense
OR	OR
Decrease Revenue	Increase Revenue

A single transaction can affect any of the items listed as 'Debits' and be paired with any item from the 'Credits' list. The interlocking effect means that the total value of either of the two impacts must be the same as that of the other.

The practical application of the interlocking effect is shown in Example 4.1.

Example 4.1

The following transactions were undertaken by Commencer, a sole trader, when starting his business:

Transaction Number	Description	Value £
1	Introduce cash as capital	4,000
2	Raise a loan for cash	1,000
3	Buy plant for cash	3,000
4	Purchase stock for cash	1,250
5	Purchase stock on credit	1,400
6	Sell stock (which cost £700) on credit	1,100
7	Collect cash from debtors	600
8	Pay cash to creditors	750
9	Pay cash for wages	180

Required:
State the dual impact of each transaction, and for each debit and credit
whether it affects an asset, liability, revenue or expense.

Solution

Transaction Number	Value £	DEBIT	CREDIT
1	4,000	+ Asset (cash)	+ Capital
2	1,000	+ Asset (cash)	+ Liability (loan)
3	3,000	+ Asset (plant)	− Asset (cash)
4	1,250	+ Expense (purchases)	− Asset (cash)
5	1,400	+ Expense (purchases)	+ Liability (trade creditors)
6	1,100	+ Asset (debtor)	+ Revenue (sales)
7	600	+ Asset (cash)	− Asset (debtor)
8	750	− Liability (creditor)	− Asset (cash)
9	180	+ Expense (wages)	− Asset (cash)

Tutorial note:
Trading transactions 4 and 5 are recorded as purchases, i.e. as expenses.
However, as the cost of goods sold is less than the total stock acquired,
some of the goods must remain in stock; this is adjusted when preparing the
trading account (see chapter 5.2.1).

The dual effect of each transaction has given rise to the system called *double
entry book-keeping,* under which each transaction is recorded twice: once as
a debit and once as a credit. The equality between debits and credits holds
true even if more than two elements are affected by a single deal. For
example, a shop's customer buys, and has delivered, goods for £800; the
price is settled by an immediate cash payment of £200, and an agreement to
pay the remaining £600 in one month's time. The facts to be recorded at the
time of sale, together with their impact, are:

	Value	Debit		Credit	
	£	£		£	
Sales	800			800	+ Revenue (sales)
Cash received	− 200	200	+ Asset (cash)		
Creation of debtor	600	600	+ Asset (debtor)		
		800		800	

There is a credit of £800 and total debits of £800; equality has been sustained.

4.2.2 Ledger Accounts

The practical operation of a set of double entry books to record transactions involves the use of a separate record for each type of revenue, expense, asset and liability. Each record is named according to the item to which it relates, and is known as an 'account' — for example, each company maintains a cash account in which all inflows and outflows of cash are recorded. Similarly, all transactions between a sole trader and the business which he or she has founded are entered in a capital account. The complete set of accounts kept by a firm is called its 'ledger', and the guiding principle when designing a system of accounts, and deciding which accounts to open, is that it must provide sufficient information to prepare the trading and profit and loss account and balance sheet.

4.2.3 'T' Accounts

The ledger accounts in which business transactions are recorded are known as 'T' accounts, a name derived from each account's appearance, since it represents an open ledger, or book, which has two sides; the left is used to record debits and the right credits. This is apparent from Figure 4.2, which contains no accounting entries.

Figure 4.2

A 'T' Account	
Debit	Credit
£	£

We can now return to the transactions of Commencer given in Example 4.1. The first was the introduction into his firm of £4,000 capital in the form of cash. The two accounts needed to record this transaction are 'cash' and 'capital'; cash, an asset, is increased by an inflow of £4,000 and so is debited with this sum, while capital, the liability to ownership, is increased by £4,000 and the account is credited. The accounts appear as follows when the transaction has been entered:

	Cash				Capital	
Debit		Credit		Debit		Credit
	£		£		£		£
Capital	4,000					Cash	4,000

A system of cross-reference is used whereby, in each account, the location of the corresponding entry is named. Thus, for this transaction, the credit entry corresponding to the debit entry in the cash account can easily be traced to the capital account. This referencing is necessary as the separate accounts would not necessarily be adjacent to each other in the ledger.

Example 4.2

The transactions undertaken by Commencer, given in Example 4.1, are reproduced for ease of reference:

Transaction Number	Description	Value
		£
1	Introduce cash as capital.	4,000
2	Raise a loan for cash	1,000
3	Buy plant for cash	3,000
4	Purchase stock for cash	1,250
5	Purchase stock on credit	1,400
6	Sell stock (which cost £700) on credit	1,100
7	Collect cash from debtors	600
8	Pay cash to creditors	750
9	Pay cash for wages	180

Required:
Record the transactions of Commencer in a set of 'T' accounts. Insert the transaction number before each item.

Solution

Cash

Debit		£	Credit		£
1	Capital	4,000	3	Plant	3,000
2	Loan	1,000	4	Purchases	1,250
7	Debtor	600	8	Creditor	750
			9	Wages	180

Capital

Debit		£	Credit		£
			1	Cash	4,000

Loan

Debit		£	Credit		£
			2	Cash	1,000

Plant

Debit		£	Credit		£
3	Cash	3,000			

Purchases

Debit		£	Credit		£
4	Cash	1,250			
5	Creditors	1,400			

Creditors

Debit		£	Credit		£
8	Cash	750	5	Purchases	1,400

Debtors

Debit		£	Credit		£
6	Sales	1,100	7	Cash	600

Sales

Debit		Credit	
	£		£
		6 Debtor	1,100

Wages

Debit		Credit	
	£		£
9 Cash	180		

At the end of the accounting period, the accountant prepares the trading and profit and loss account and balance sheet. It is necessary first to prepare a TRIAL BALANCE; this is done by finding the balance on each of the accounts and listing them in columns according to whether they are debit or credit balances. The entries in the Trial Balance which relate to items of revenue and expense are transferred to the trading and profit and loss accounts where the net result of trading is calculated; the balances remaining, together with the net result of trading, are then used to compile the balance sheet. This process is demonstrated in Example 4.3, in part (b) of which the purchases figure of £2,650 is split between the cost of the goods which have been sold (£700) and those which remain in stock (£1,950). The accounting entries to achieve this split are described in chapter 5.2.1.

Example 4.3

Required:
(a) Prepare the trial balance by listing the balances from the ledger accounts in Example 4.2 in two columns, one for debit balances and one for credit balances.
(b) Prepare Commencer's trading and profit and loss accounts and balance sheet from the balances listed in answer to part (a).

Solution

(a)

	Debit £	Credit £
Cash	420	
Capital		4,000
Loan		1,000
Plant	3,000	
Purchases	2,650	
Creditors		650
Debtors	500	
Sales		1,100
Wages	180	
	6,750	6,750

Tutorial note:
The debit balances are equal in value to the credit balances; this provides a check of accuracy, the importance of which is discussed in section 4.4 of this chapter.

(b)
   Trading and Profit and Loss Account

	£
Sales	1,100
Less: Cost of Goods Sold*	700
Gross Profit	400
Less: General Expenses	180
Net Profit	220

Balance Sheet of Commencer

	£	£		£
FIXED ASSETS			CAPITAL	
Plant		3,000	At start of period	0
			Introduced	4,000
			Profit for period	220
CURRENT ASSETS				
Stock*	1,950			4,220
Debtors	500		LOAN	1,000
Cash	420			
		2,870	CURRENT LIABILITIES	
			Trade creditors	650
		5,870		5,870

Tutorial note:
* The balance on the Purchases Account shown in the trial balance was £2,650. To prepare the above statements, this has been split between the Cost of Goods Sold (£700) and Stock held at the accounting date (£1,950).

The balances on all accounts cleared to the trading and profit and loss account revert to zero, and these accounts are used to accumulate information for the next period. The asset and liability balances shown in the balance sheet are carried forward to the next accounting period where they are adjusted for any changes which then occur.

Assignment Students should now work Question 4.1 at the end of the chapter.

4.3 BOOKS OF PRIME ENTRY

It is unwieldy to attempt to enter each individual flow of cash, goods or services in the accounts ledger. To overcome this problem each transaction is entered, in the first instance, in a 'Book of Prime Entry' of which there are three types, namely, day books, the cash book, and the journal. The manner in which the information is initially recorded in the books of prime entry and then entered in the double entry ledger is now considered, together with how discounts, both received and allowed, are dealt with.

4.3.1 Day Books The day-to-day record of sales and purchases is kept in day books, which in their simplest form comprise lists of sales or purchases which have taken place on credit with the name of the customer or supplier entered next to each item. The total of each list gives the value of purchases or sales which have taken place during a period of time.

To produce final accounts, and provide management with relevant information, the inflows and outflows of goods and services must be broken down, and this is achieved by adding analysis columns to the day books. The analysis headings are determined on the basis of which aspects of the organisation are to be monitored. Excessive detail impairs comprehension and so too many headings should not be used; on the other hand, significant matters may be masked if the headings are too broad. Management needs to identify areas of strength and weakness, and this is achieved if, for example, sales and purchases are analysed by type of product, and/or the department or branch in which they originate.

Example 4.4

Party Ltd owns a shop which consists of two distinct departments, one selling tables and the other carpets. All sales are made on credit and management requires reports which show the individual results of each department. The following sales took place at the start of July:

Sales: 1 July to Modern — carpets £200; tables £150 (supplied on one invoice)
        2 July to Oldash — tables £100
        3 July to Contemp — carpets £180

Required:
Prepare from the above details the sales day book in a manner which provides the information needed by management.

Solution

Sales Day Book

Date July	Customer	Total £	Carpets £	Tables £
1	Modern	350	200	150
2	Oldash	100		100
3	Contemp	180	180	
		630	380	250

Tutorial note:
This record provides the following information: (a) the value of sales made by each department; (b) the total debt created (£630); and (c) the debt related to each individual customer.

Although they are the most common ones, the use of day books is not restricted to purchases and sales; they can be used for any routine transactions, such as the return of goods from customers or to suppliers. In all cases appropriate controls must be established to ensure that only valid entries are made in the records.

For accounting purposes, the sales day book must produce: (a) the total value of debtors created from sales to be debited to the debtors account; and (b) the value of credit sales to be credited in the sales account, possibly analysed according to type of sale. The purchases day book creates: (a) the total to be credited to the creditors account; and (b) the values to be debited to the various expense and asset accounts. For example, the following are the possible totals from a purchases day book:

Purchases Day Book

Total £	Purchases £	Stationery £	Motor Van (Fixed Asset) £
16,000	4,500	500	11,000

The totals of the analysis columns add up to the total value, and are entered in the following ledger accounts:

	Debit	Credit
Purchases (increase expense)	4,500	
Stationery (increase expense)	500	
Motor Van (increase asset)	11,000	
Creditors (increase liability)		16,000
	16,000	16,000

There should be clear cross referencing between the books of prime entry and the accounts so that the trail can be retraced if necessary. A note should be made in the day book of the account, and its location, to which the figures are posted; the entry in the account should refer to the source of the figure, preferably also stating the page in the book of prime entry on which it can be found.

For the purposes of the Banking Certificate it is not necessary to have a full knowledge of how these records are operated in practice, but it is useful to be aware of their existence as they provide a vital part of the input to the book-keeping system.

4.3.2 The Cash Book The cash book, unlike the day books, is itself a ledger account; it is therefore necessary only to complete the corresponding double entry for the transactions it contains. At the end of the accounting period the cash book is balanced and the result entered in the balance sheet. Just like the day books, the cash flows can be analysed in columns and only the analysis totals, rather than each separate transaction, need to be posted. For example, the following are the totals from an analysed cash book:

Cash Book

Receipts			Payments			
Total	Debtors	Cash Sale	Total	Wages	Creditors	Rent
£	£	£	£	£	£	£
5,000	3,500	1,500	4,000	1,000	2,500	500

The total of cash received, £5,000, is already debited in the ledger as the result of including it in the total column of the cash book, and so the double entry is completed by making the following credit entries:

	£
Sales (revenue)	1,500 (credit)
Debtors (reduce asset)	3,500 (credit)

The entries to complete the record of the effect of cash payments are:

	£
Wages (expense)	1,000 (debit)
Creditors (reduce liability)	2,500 (debit)
Rent (expense)	500 (debit)

Discounts The full value of each sale made on credit is entered in the debtors account, and in some cases this may be cleared by the receipt of cash together with the grant of a discount for prompt payment, that is, the cash received is less than the value of the debt. To remove the full amount of indebtedness shown in the debtor's account it is necessary to credit the account with the value of the discount; the corresponding debit is to the 'Discounts Allowed Account' in which all such discounts are accumulated. The balance on this account is transferred to the profit and loss account when the periodic accounting reports are prepared. If, alternatively, the company takes a discount offered by a supplier, the creditor account is debited and the 'Discounts Received Account' is credited; the balance on the latter account is income and is credited to the profit and loss account at the end of the accounting period. Where, as is the case with discounts given for purchasing large quantities, the discount is received as a reduction in price, that is, a trade discount, no entry in the discount column is needed as the amount invoiced is reduced by the discount. The procedure for recording discounts for prompt payment is illustrated in Example 4.5.

Example 4.5

Giver sells goods on credit to Taker for £500. A discount of 4% may be taken if the debt is settled within 10 days.

Required:
On the assumption that the discount is taken, prepare:

    (a)   the debtor and discount accounts in Giver's books; and
    (b)   the creditor and discount accounts in Taker's books.

Solution
(a)   The books of Giver

Debtor Account

	£		£
Sales	500	Cash	480
		Discounts allowed	20
	500		500

Discounts Allowed Account

	£		£
Debtor	20		

(b) The books of Taker

Creditor Account

	£		£
Cash	480	Purchases	500
Discounts received	20		
	500		500

Discounts Received Account

	£		£
		Creditor	20

It is useful to keep the discounts received and discounts allowed in separate accounts, rather than to net them, so that the cost of granting discounts and the benefit of taking them can be easily identified and their impact assessed. If discounts allowed rise in value, the question should be asked whether the terms are too generous, and the benefit of taking discounts must be weighed against the alternative advantages of retaining the cash in the business for a longer period of time.

Assignment   Students should now work Question 4.2 at the end of the chapter.

4.3.3 The Journal   There are a few transactions which, as they do not relate directly to the initial flows of cash, goods or services, are not entered in the cash or day books; these are instead entered in the 'Journal'. The use of a journal ensures that every entry in the ledger first passes through a book of prime entry which fully explains the nature of the transaction. Each entry in the journal should be authorised to ensure that no unsanctioned changes are made in the ledger. Journal entries are likely to be relatively small in number, and include such items as:

(a) *Transfers*   These occur when it is necessary to transfer value from one account to another, for example, to correct a mistake made in the original posting which placed the entry in the wrong account.

(b) *Adjustments* The original entry may be made in the correct account in the light of prevailing knowledge, but circumstances may change and require a further entry. For example, a debtor is created when a credit sale is made, but if, at a later date, it becomes apparent that the money will not be collected, the debt must be written off by transfer to the Bad Debts Account, since it no longer represents an asset. (Bad debts are considered further in chapter 5.2.5.)

(c) *Closing entries* Adjusting entries must be made at the accounting date to enable the periodic accounts to be drawn up. (These are dealt with in chapter 5).

The debit and credit entry for each transaction is entered in the journal together with a brief narrative to explain its purpose. Example 4.6 shows some specimen entries.

Example 4.6

J. Williams, a trader, wishes to record the following in his firm's ledger:

(a) The correction of a wrong posting which entered the purchase of a fixed asset costing £10,000 in the purchase of goods for resale account.

(b) The accrual of rent due for three months of £500.

(c) The introduction by J. Williams of additional capital in the form of a fixed asset worth £25,000.

(d) The scrapping of a fixed asset which cost £3,000 many years ago and was fully depreciated (i.e. it had a zero written down value).

Required:
Prepare the journal entries to enter the above facts in the firm's ledger accounts.

Solution
The journal entries are:

J. Williams — Journal

	Debit (DR) £	Credit (CR) £
(a) Fixed assets	10,000	
Purchases		10,000
Narrative: Transfer to fixed assets of incorrect posting		
(b) Rent	500	
Landlord – Creditor.........................		500
Narrative: Rent due for three months		

(c) Fixed Assets   25,000
    J. Williams — Capital   25,000
    Narrative: Introduction of capital in the form of a fixed asset

(d) Accumulated depreciation   3,000
    Fixed asset at cost   3,000
    Narrative: Removal from records of cost and accumulated depreciation on scrapping
    of fixed asset

Tutorial note:
'DR' and 'CR', used above as column headings, are usual abbreviations for the words 'debit' and 'credit' respectively.

Although, for practical purposes, the use of the journal is restricted to those cases where there is no other appropriate book of prime entry, it is theoretically possible to record all entries in journal form, and an exercise on these lines provides a useful way for examiners to test students' understanding of double entry accounting without calling for the preparation of a full set of 'T' accounts.

Assignment Students should now work Question 4.3 at the end of the chapter.

4.4 THE TRIAL BALANCE
The process by which an economic event becomes included in the final accounting statements is:

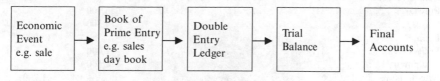

| Economic Event e.g. sale | → | Book of Prime Entry e.g. sales day book | → | Double Entry Ledger | → | Trial Balance | → | Final Accounts |

It can be seen that the stage prior to the production of the statements from the ledger (covered in chapter 5) is the preparation of a Trial Balance; the method by which this is obtained and its format were shown in Example 4.3.

Since each entry in the books consists of a debit and a credit of equal value, the two columns should possess the same total value. However, the fact that the trial balance shows equal totals for both debit and credit balances does not necessarily mean that it is correct, since there are some errors which are not revealed by an imbalance. These are:

- *Error of principle* An entry may be made in the wrong account, for example, wages may be debited to purchases.
- *Duplication* Both the debits and credits for a transaction could be entered in the accounts twice.
- *Omissions* A transaction may be omitted altogether.
- *Compensatory errors* There may be two or more errors, the effects of which cancel each other out.
- *Error in the original entry* An incorrect figure may be used as the basis for the double entry record.

Where the totals in the two columns of the trial balance are not the same, it is obvious that an error has been made. In these circumstances, investigations must be carried out to discover what is wrong, and the necessary adjusting entries made.

Example 4.7

Minter, who had no previous book-keeping experience, started trading on 1 January 19X1 and attempted to keep a full set of double entry books. At the end the first year of trading he extracted the following trial balance:

Trial Balance at 31 December 19X1

	£	£
Sales		78,600
Capital		27,000
Bank overdraft		11,700
Purchases	56,100	
Wages	14,300	
Loan		15,000
Delivery van	12,000	
Equipment	8,500	
Discounts received		1,200
Discounts allowed	400	
Light and heat	1,700	
Rent and rates	2,100	
Motor expenses	900	
Creditors		10,200
Drawings	10,000	
Difference	37,700	
	143,700	143,700

Investigation of the ledger accounts and other records of Minter revealed the following errors:

(a) Minter made cash sales of £2,200 which were not entered in the books. £1,200 of this money was spent on wages and £1,000 on sundries (to be recorded as part of General Expenses).

(b) The balance of debtors, £20,300, was omitted from the trial balance.

(c) Goods sold for £12,200 had been correctly recorded in the sales account, but no entry had been made in the debtors account.

(d) Goods costing £2,000 had been purchased on credit; the entry in the purchases account had been made correctly, but only £200 had been entered in the creditors account.

(e) Minter transferred his own car, valued at £8,600, to the business, but no entry had been made in the books to reflect this.

(f) The balance on the purchases account was wrongly extracted; it should be £58,100.

(g) Minter failed to extract the balance of £5,000 from the general expenses account and enter it in the trial balance.

Required
Prepare the trial balance of Minter after all the errors have been corrected.

Solution

Corrected Trial Balance at 31 December 19X1

	£	£
Sales (78,600 + 2,200)		80,800
Capital (27,000 + 8,600)		35,600
Bank overdraft		11,700
Purchases (56,100 + 2,000)	58,100	
Wages (14,300 + 1,200)	15,500	
Loan		15,000
Delivery van	12,000	
Equipment	8,500	
Discounts received		1,200
Discounts allowed	400	
Light and heat	1,700	
Rent and rates	2,100	
Motor expenses	900	
Creditors (10,200 + 1,800)		12,000
Motor vehicle	8,600	
Drawings	10,000	
General expenses (1,000 + 5,000)	6,000	
Debtors (20,300 + 12,200)	32,500	
	156,300	156,300

Tutorial notes:
1. Some corrections, such as that of the unrecorded sales, are corrected by a full double entry in the trial balance, while others, such as the omission of a balance, require only a single entry to be made.
2. The underlying records must also be corrected if they are found to be wrong, usually by means of a journal entry.

Assignment   Students should now work Question 4.4 at the end of the chapter.

4.5   ADVANTAGES OF DOUBLE ENTRY

The double entry system is very flexible. In this chapter, reference has been made to books of account and pages within these books. The records could, in practice, be kept on separate cards or be produced as computer print outs. Whichever method of operation is employed, however, the benefits derived from the use of double entry are:

● It enables all types of transactions undertaken by the business, which can be expressed in monetary terms, to be recorded; provided an economic event has a measurable financial impact it can be entered in the books using double entry.

● It enables large numbers of transactions to be recorded in an orderly manner; similar transactions are grouped together.

● Economic events are recorded both from the personal point of view, that is their impact on the relationship between the entity and outsiders, and also from their impersonal aspect, that is, their effect on the company itself in terms of assets owned, revenue and expenses.

● The debits entered to record a particular transaction must be of equal value to the credits. This equality enables a Trial Balance to be prepared which gives an initial check on the arithmetical accuracy of the records, although there are errors which are not revealed.

● The Trial Balance, an end product of the double entry system, is the basis for the preparation of the trading and profit and loss account and balance sheet. The former of these gives an indication of how well the business is performing, while the latter gives a picture of the financial position which has been reached as a result of all the transactions undertaken.

4.6 THE BANK RECONCILIATION

A company's cash account, kept in the cash book, should contain exactly the same receipts and payments as pass through its bank account. A valuable check on the accuracy of the cash account is provided by the routine preparation of the Bank Reconciliation Statement which agrees the cash account's balance with that shown on the bank statement. The reconciliation statement is prepared by comparing items in the cash account with those in the bank statement. Entries which appear in both during the period under examination are checked off, but usually these records, although covering the same period of time, do not correspond exactly. This is the result of some or all of the following:

(a) *Payments on the statement not in the cash account* Some payments, such as those for bank charges, are generated by the bank; the company may know that they have been paid only when a statement has been received, and they would not have been previously entered in the cash book. Other items which fall into this category are payments made by standing order and direct debits.

(b) *Receipts on the statement not in the cash book* It is common nowadays for sums to be paid directly into the recipient's bank account, and sometimes they are identifiable only when the statement is received.

(c) *Payments in the cash account not on the bank statement* These mainly result from the fact that there is a delay between the issue of a cheque, at which time it is entered in the cash account, and its clearance by the bank, when it appears on the bank statement.

(d) *Receipts in the cash account not on the bank statement* A company may enter the cash received each day in the cash account, but pay it into the bank the following day, or even allow it to accumulate for a short period of time. This causes a lapse of time between the cash account record and the bank statement entry. For security reasons, the delay should be kept to a minimum.

Items (a) and (b) represent new information which, if valid, should be entered in the cash account immediately the statement is received. Items (c) and (d) are merely timing differences and, although they must be included in the bank reconciliation, they require no further entry in the cash account.

The procedure for preparing a bank reconciliation statement is as follows:

1. Compare the entries in the cash account, for the period under investigation, with those shown on the bank statement. Mark off items

which appear in both sets of records. Items which are left unmarked must be examined and classified into types (a), (b), (c), and (d).

2. Items of types (a) and (b) are entered in the cash account from which the balance is then extracted.

3. The balance which results will still differ from that shown on the bank statement if there are any items of types (c) and (d), and so a memorandum statement is drawn up which adjusts the balance on the bank statement for these items, after which it should agree with that shown on the cash account.

Example 4.8

The following are the cash account and bank statement of Donor Ltd for the month of July:

Cash Account

Receipts (debit)			Payments (credit)		
		£			£
July			July		
1	Balance b/d	2,500		Cheques issued:	
9	Receipts paid into bank	875	4	No. 22	375
16	Receipts paid into bank	500	9	No. 23	563
23	Receipts paid into bank	1,187	15	No. 24	188
30	Receipts paid into bank	375	22	No. 25	1,112
			30	No. 26	400
			31	No. 27	825
			31	Balance c/d	1,974
		5,437			5,437

Bank Statement

		Debit	Credit	Balance
		£	£	£
July				
1	Balance brought forward			2,500Cr
6	Cheque No. 22	375		2,125
11	Lodgement		875	3,000
	Cheque No. 23	563		2,437
17	Cheque No. 24	188		2,249
18	Lodgement		500	2,749
24	Cheque No. 25	1,112		1,637
25	Lodgement		1,187	2,824
	Standing order	150		2,674
26	Direct credit		125	2,799
31	Bank charges	80		2,719
	Balance carried forward			2,719Cr

Tutorial note:
As the bank statement is prepared from the point of view of the bank, payments made by the company are shown as debits and deposits with the bank as credits, i.e., the terms are the opposite way round compared with the cash account in the company's books.

Required:
  (a) Compare the cash account with the bank statement and identify the differences between the two records.
  (b) Make the necessary adjustments to the cash account for the month of July.
  (c) Prepare the bank reconciliation statement at the end of July.

Solution
  (a) When the entries in the cash account are checked with those on the statement, the following differences are found:

  (i)   Payments on the bank statement not in the cash account:
        Standing order £150
        Bank charges £80
  (ii) Receipts on the bank statement not in the cash account:
        Direct credit £125
  (iii) Payments in the cash account not on the bank statement:
        Cheque No. 26 . . . .   £400
        Cheque No. 27 . . . .   £825
  (iv) Receipts in the cash account not on the bank statement:
        Lodgement £375

Items (i) and (ii) are used to complete the cash account, and items (iii) and (iv) appear in the bank reconciliation statement.

(b) Completion of the Cash Account for July

Receipts (debit)		£	Payments (credit)		£
July			July		
31	Balance b/d	1,974	31	Standing order	150
31	Direct Credit	125	31	Bank charges	80
			31	Balance c/d	1,869
		2,099			2,099

(c)   Bank Reconciliation Statement at 31 July

	£	£
Balance per bank statement		2,719
Less: Outstanding cheques:		
No. 26	400	
No. 27	825	
		1,225
		1,494
Plus: Outstanding lodgement		375
Balance as per cash account		1,869

Tutorial notes:

1. Subsequent bank statements should be checked to ensure that all outstanding items are cleared without undue delay.
2. It is possible for banks to make mistakes. Any unexplained entry on the bank statement should be queried as it may have been entered in the company's account in error. Until a satisfactory explanation is obtained, such items should be shown as part of the reconciliation statement and not entered in the cash book.
3. To provide additional control, the reconciliation should ideally be prepared or checked by an official of the company who is otherwise independent of the control and recording of the flows of cash.
4. When preparing answers to questions involving the completion of the cash account, it is not necessary to copy out the cash account given in the question and then add the new information; it is sufficient to start with the balance carried down.

Assignment   Students should now work Question 4.5 at the end of the chapter.

4.7   REVIEW

After reading the chapter and working the chapter end questions, students should be able to:

- Express individual transactions in terms of their related debit and credit effects and enter them in the appropriate accounts.
- Balance accounts and prepare and, if necessary, correct a Trial Balance.
- Make the link between the Trial Balance and the Trading and Profit and Loss Accounts and Balance Sheet.
- Understand how transactions are initially recorded in books of prime entry and subsequently entered in the double entry records.

● Appreciate the uses and limitations of the Trial Balance.
● Prepare a bank reconciliation statement.

4.8 QUESTIONS

Question 4.1
Dreamer, a trader, carries out all cash transactions through a bank account, and on 1 September 19X9 the balance on the business bank account was £550 debit. The following cash transactions were undertaken by Dreamer during September 19X9:

	£
Cash received from sales	10,000
Cash paid:	
Wages	2,000
Vehicle repairs	300
Petrol	250
Rent	1,400
Purchases	4,000
Salaries	1,000

Required:
Open 'T' accounts for: Cash, Sales, Wages and Salaries, Motor Expenses, Rent, and Purchases. Using double entry, record Dreamer's transactions for September, carrying down the balance on the cash account at the end of September.

Question 4.2
Getup, a trader, owns a shop with two separate departments and sells goods for cash and on credit. On 1 August 19X9 the firm is owed £15,000 by debtors.

During August 19X9 the following transactions took place:

(i)	Department A	Department B	Total
	£	£	£
Credit sales	10,000	22,000	32,000
Cash sales	12,500	11,000	23,500
	22,500	33,000	55,500

(ii)	Cash received from debtors	£35,000
(iii)	Discounts allowed	£1,500

Required:
Open 'T' accounts for Sales: Department A, Sales: Department B, Cash, Debtors and Discounts Allowed. Enter in these accounts the transactions

of Getup for August 19X9, carrying down the balance on the debtors account at the end of the month.

Question 4.3
The transactions undertaken by Commencer, given in Example 4.1, are reproduced for ease of reference:

Transaction Number	Description	Value £
1	Introduce cash as capital	4,000
2	Raise a loan for cash	1,000
3	Buy plant for cash	3,000
4	Buy stock for cash	1,250
5	Buy stock on credit	1,400
6	Sell stock (which cost £700) on credit	1,100
7	Collect cash from debtors	600
8	Pay cash to creditors	750
9	Pay cash for wages	180

Required:
Show, in the form of journal entries, how the above transactions are recorded using double entry techniques. Do not attach a narrative to each transaction.

Question 4.4
Badly established a business on 1 January 19X6, and at the end of its first year's trading produced the following draft balance sheet:

Balance Sheet at 31 December 19X6

	£	£
FIXED ASSETS		
At cost		200,000
Less: Depreciation		20,000
		180,000
CURRENT ASSETS		
Stock	38,700	
Debtors	42,800	
Cash	7,600	
	89,100	

CURRENT LIABILITIES
Trade creditors   47,400

WORKING CAPITAL   41,700
                                                                                                 221,700

Financed by:
Capital introduced   180,000
Profit for year   26,500
                                                                                                 206,500
Difference   15,200
                                                                                                 221,700

Subsequence investigation reveals the following:

1. The cash balance should be shown as an overdraft.
2. The purchase of a computer, at a cost of £6,000 on 1 January 19X6, was
    wrongly recorded in the wages account. The computer is expected to
    have a life of three years and no residual value.
3. Goods which cost £3,000 were included in the value of stock shown in
    the balance sheet, but were not included in purchases as the invoice was
    not received until January 19X7.
4. £1,600 was paid for rates in September 19X6. This amount was for the
    six months to 31 March 19X7.
5. A debt of £200 included in the balance sheet is considered to be bad and
    should be removed from debtors and written off against profit.
6. Bank charges of £300 were shown on the bank statement in December
    19X6, but no entry was made in the cash book to record them.

Required:
  (a) Calculate the value of profit to be included in the balance sheet at 31
       December 19X6 after making any amendments necessary as a result
       of notes 1 to 6 above.
  (b) Prepare the balance sheet of Badly at 31 December 19X6 after all
       necessary adjustments which result from notes 1 to 6 above have
       been made.

Question 4.5

(Adapted from the Autumn 1987 *Introduction to Accounting* paper.)
    Shown below is the cash book of General Traders Ltd for the month of
September 1987, together with the bank statement for that month.
    As the company's book-keeper you are required:

(a)   to complete the cash book for the month of September 1987;
(b)   to prepare the bank reconciliation statement between the revised balance from (a) above and the balance shown by the bank statement;
(c)   to state what action (if any) you would take in respect of the items you have entered in the cash book in part (a) above and the reconciliation statement in part (b).

CASH BOOK

Sept	1	Balance brought forward	281	Sept	1	Borough Treasurer ...	703
	1	Ajax	517		4	Export Agency	152
	1	Bertram	72		5	Publishers Association .	55
	2	Chorlton	314		9	Petty Cash	50
	3	Dennis	25		9	British Rail	172
	4	Ebury	152		9	Customs & Excise	795
	5	Franks	31		11	Smithers & Son	23
	8	Gordons	234		11	Blackburn Brothers ...	118
	9	Hastings	87		11	Johnson & Co.	257
	10	Ironside	125		17	Petty Cash	80
	11	Jolly	10		17	Office Services Ltd ...	37
	12	Fisherman	782		17	Higgins Supplies	179
	15	Leonard	87		26	Orb Construction	217
	16	Masters	131		26	Thames Water Authority	110
	17	Newton	252		26	Wages	752
	18	Oliver	304		30	Balance carried forward	293
	19	Parsons	57				
	22	Quinton	92				
	23	Rogers	12				
	24	Staveley	15				
	25	Thompson	108				
	26	Ullyses	92				
	29	Victor	178				
	30	Watson	35				
			3,993				3,993

Bank Statement

Date	Particulars	Debits	Credits	Balance
Sept 1	Balance forward			281
2	Paid in		903	1,184
5	081	703		
	Paid in		208	689
7	084	50		
	Paid in		321	
	Bank giro credit — Jones		825	1,785
10	083	55		
	Paid in		125	1,855
12	082	152		
	087	795		
	Paid in		792	1,700
17	085	117		
	086	172		
	091	80		
	Paid in		218	1,549
18	Returned cheque	782		767
19	089	118		
	Paid in		613	1,262
23	Direct debit — Moon Insurance Co . . .	375		
	088	23		
	Dividends — Excelsior Tdg plc		35	899
26	093	179		
	Paid in		319	1,039
30	Bank charges	97		
	092	37		
	094	217		
	096	752		64(OD)

CHAPTER 5

Periodic Accounting Reports

5.1 PERIODIC ACCOUNTS

The preparation of the profit and loss account and balance sheet should be a routine procedure as these documents are regularly needed by management, ownership, and other interested parties, such as bankers, to monitor the progress and position of the company. If decisions are delayed due to lack of financial information, then opportunities may be missed, possibly with disastrous consequences. For example, when losses are being made it is important to realise this fact at an early stage; this is helped by the frequent (perhaps monthly) and prompt production of a profit and loss account. The first evidence that losses are being incurred may otherwise be the collapse of the company, an eventuality which might have been avoided if the losses had been identified earlier and remedial action taken.

The procedures described in chapter 4 provide the foundations of the accounting process as they are used to record the flows of cash, goods and services and provide a summary of these flows in the form of the Trial Balance. This chapter deals with the adjustments necessary to the information contained in the Trial Balance to enable the production of the Trading and Profit and Loss Account and Balance Sheet, and, if appropriate, a Manufacturing Account as well.

5.2 ADJUSTMENTS TO THE TRIAL BALANCE

The transactions entered in the ledger accounts do not reflect precisely the economic events which have occurred during the period of time covered by the accounting statements. Adjustments to the trial balance are therefore needed to take account of:

1. *Timing differences.* These occur when an item recorded in the books during one accounting period has significance for the business not only in that accounting period, but also in previous or subsequent ones. In these circumstances an adjustment must be made to distribute the item accordingly. For example, the purchase of a fixed asset is initially recorded at cost in the year of purchase, but it is necessary to apportion this cost over the years which derive benefit from the expenditure. Timing differences also operate in the opposite direction. For example, there may be an interval between the receipt of a service or goods and

the arrival of the related invoice. (For a fuller explanation see section 5.2.3 of this chapter.)

2. *Incomplete information.* The entries in the books may not reflect all of the economic changes which must be reported, since some events are not supported by a documented flow of value on which a day book entry is based, for example, a debtor may be unable to pay the sum due to the company (see section 5.2.4 of this chapter). The routine documentation procedures for a sale or purchase do not apply in these cases, and care must be taken to ensure that allowance has been made for them when the accounts are prepared. The accountant must be satisfied that all the items relating to the period under review have been included, and also that items that are not relevant have been excluded.

The adjustments made to the trial balance must comply with the rules of double entry, and so each comprises a debit and a credit of equal value. The implementation of the adjustments which routinely arise when periodic accounts are prepared are examined in this chapter; the principles of valuation on which the adjustments are based are dealt with in chapter 6.

5.2.1 Stocks (Inventories) In a system of double entry accounting, it is usual to enter the opening stock in one account and to accumulate in another account, called purchases, the cost of all acquisitions made during the accounting period. The effect of this procedure is that the trial balance contains two separate balances: one for opening stock and another for purchases. These provide two elements of the formula used to calculate the value of the cost of goods sold, and the missing one, the figure for closing stock, is usually determined by means of a physical stock take to find the quantities of each type of stock held on the balance sheet date which are then valued.

A typical trading account, in vertical format, is shown in Figure 5.1.

Figure 5.1

Specimen Trading Account

	£	£
Sales.		X
Opening stock	X	
Add: Purchases	X	
Less: Closing stock.	(X)	
Cost of Goods Sold		(X)
Gross Profit		X

Tutorial notes:
1. In the above figure, the debits for opening stock and purchases and the credit for sales are transferred from the trial balance. The closing stock is recorded as a post trial balance adjustment by the accounting entry:

Debit	Credit	With
Stock Account	Trading Account	Value of Closing Stock

2. Since the closing stock is *deducted* from the total of the debit entries for opening stock and purchases, it is effectively treated as a credit item.

The closing balance on the stock account appears as an asset in the balance sheet and is subsequently included as opening stock in the trading account for the following accounting period.

Example 5.1 involves the preparation of final accounts from the trial balance where an adjustment has to be made for closing stock.

Example 5.1

The trial balance of Button, a sole trader, at 31 December 19X4 was:

	£	£
Capital		12,000
Drawings	10,000	
Sales		75,500
Purchases	45,250	
Stock 1 January 19X4	6,750	
Debtors	4,300	
Creditors		3,200
Cash	1,125	
Delivery Costs	2,875	
Wages	11,225	
Sundry Expenses	3,000	
Freehold Premises	6,175	
	90,700	90,700

The stock at 31 December 19X4 was £7,150

Required:
Prepare the Trading and Profit and Loss Account of Button for the year to 31 December 19X4 and a Balance Sheet at that date. The accounts should be presented in vertical format.

Solution

Trading and Profit and Loss Account

Year to 31 December 19X4

	£	£
Sales		75,500
Stock 1 January	6,750	
Purchases	45,250	
Stock 31 December	(7,150)	
Cost of Goods Sold		44,850
Gross Profit		30,650
Wages	11,225	
Delivery Costs	2,875	
Sundry Expenses	3,000	
		17,100
Net Profit		13,550

Balance Sheet at 31 December 19X4

	£	£
Fixed Assets		
Freehold Premises		6,175
Current Assets		
Stock	7,150	
Debtors	4,300	
Cash	1,125	
	12,575	
Current Liabilities		
Creditors	3,200	
		9,375
		15,550
Capital		
At 1 January		12,000
Profit for 19X4		13,550
		25,550
Drawings		10,000
		15,550

Assignment Students should now work Question 5.1 at the end of the chapter.

5.2.2 Depreciation   Fixed assets and their related accumulated depreciation are recorded in the double entry ledger by using an account for each type of fixed asset at cost and another for each type of fixed asset's accumulated depreciation. The number of accounts to be opened depends on the nature of the business, but usually separate accounts for land and buildings, plant and machinery, motor vehicles, and furniture and fittings suffice. Further accounts can be used if appropriate, for example computer equipment or assets out on hire may have a value significant enough to warrant separate identification. The totals of these accounts should be backed up by detailed analysis in a fixed asset register so that the individual assets can be identified.

When the trial balance is extracted at the end of the year it contains the following entries for each type of fixed asset:

1. *a debit balance* which is the accumulated historical cost of the assets at the end of the year; and
2. *a credit balance* which is the accumulated balance of depreciation brought forward at the *start* of the accounting period.

The value of the depreciation charge for the period for each class of asset has then to be calculated, and the amounts are debited to the profit and loss account and credited to the accounts containing the opening balances of accumulated depreciation; after this entry, the latter accounts hold the value of accumulated depreciation at the *end* of the year. The debit balance on each of the fixed assets (at cost) accounts is entered in the balance sheet, and the credit balance on the related accumulated depreciation account is deducted from it to give the written down value (also known as the 'book value' or 'net value'), that is, the portion of cost not yet written off and therefore carried forward to the next accounting period. It is helpful to the users of the accounts if both the total cost and the total related depreciation are shown in the balance sheet, rather than just the net figure; this procedure indicates how much of the value has been used up and therefore how long it is likely to be before replacement becomes necessary. In the case of a limited company, such disclosure is a legal requirement (see chapter 9).

Example 5.2

The following information relates to the machinery owned by Achilles Ltd:

	£
At cost, 1.1.19X9	65,000
Accumulated depreciation at 1.1.19X9	25,000
Acquired during 19X9	10,000
Depreciation charge for 19X9	8,000

Required:
  (a)   Prepare the ledger accounts for 19X9 to record the above information.
  (b)   Show the balance sheet extract for machinery at 31.12.19X9.

Solution

(a)   *Machinery at Cost Account*

		£			£
1.1.19X9	Balance b/d	65,000	31.12.19X9	Balance c/d	75,000
19X9	Purchases	10,000			
		75,000			75,000

Accumulated Depreciation Account — Machinery

		£			£
31.12.19X9	Balance c/d . . .	33,000	1.1.19X9	Balance b/d	25,000
			31.12.19X9	Profit and Loss Account	8,000
		33,000			33,000

(b)   *Balance Sheet Extract 31.12.19X9*

	£	£
Machinery at Cost	75,000	
Less: Depreciation	33,000	
		42,000

Assignment   Students should now work Question 5.2 at the end of the chapter.

5.2.3 Prepayments and Accruals   A business makes a number of payments which gives it the right to enjoy certain benefits over a period of time. Some of these payments, such as rates on the occupation of property, are paid in advance of the receipt of the benefit and give rise to a prepayment, while others, such as for the consumption of gas or electricity or the audit fee paid by limited companies, are made in arrears and create accruals. Unless the period of time covered by these payments coincides exactly with the firm's accounting period, an adjustment is needed when the final accounts are prepared to take account of the asset created where payments are made in advance and the liability which arises when benefits are paid for in arrears. The value of accruals and prepayments for items which relate to a period of time is found by apportioning the cost on a time basis, while, for goods or services received during the period to which the accounts relate but which are not billed until after the year end, the full individual invoices are accrued.

Prepayments The entries in the accounts to record a prepayment are:

Account Debited	Account Credited	With
Prepayment	Expense	Value of Prepayment

The credit of the prepayment to the expense account reduces the amount charged against profit, while the prepayment is shown in the balance sheet as a current asset. In practice, as a matter of convenience, the prepayment may be carried down in the expense account to which it relates. This is illustrated in Example 5.3.

Example 5.3

Fibia Ltd makes up its accounts to 31 December, and made the following cash payments in respect of rates:

Year	Month	Payment £
19X0	October	900
19X1	April	1,000
19X1	October	1,000

The payments for rates relate to the six-month period starting with the month in which they are paid.

Required:
Prepare the rates account for 19X1.

Solution

Rates Account

1.1.19X1	Balance b/d	450	31.12.19X1	Balance c/d ...	500
April	Cash	1,000		Profit and Loss	
October	Cash	1,000		Account	1,950
		2,450			2,450
1.1.19X2	Balance b/d	500			

Tutorial note:
The balance brought down at the start of the year is half of the payment of £900 made in October 19X0 and covers January, February and March 19X1. The balance of £500 carried down at the end of 19X1 is an asset since it pays in advance for the first three months of 19X2 and will appear as a current asset in the balance sheet at 31 December 19X1. The transfer to the profit and loss account is found as a balancing figure once all the other entries have been made. The balance brought down on 1 January 19X2 will be charged against profit as an expense in 19X2, even though payment was made in 19X1.

Accruals   The entries in the accounts to record an accrual are:

Account Debited	Account Credited	With
Expense	Accruals	Value of Accrual

The accrual increases the expense figure charged in the profit and loss account (debit) and is included as a current liability in the balance sheet (credit). In practice the accrual may be carried down in the expense account to which it relates. This is illustrated in Example 5.4.

Example 5.4

Fibia Ltd makes up its accounts to 31 December, and made the following payments in respect of electricity:

Year	Month	Payment £
19X0	October	400
19X1	January	600
19X1	April	630
19X1	July	400
19X1	October	500
19X2	January	750

The payments are for electricity consumed during the three months immediately prior to the months in which they are made.

Required:
Record the above transactions in the company's electricity account for
19X1 and 19X2.

Solution

Electricity Account

		£			£
19X1			1.1.19X1	Balance b/d. . .	600
January	Cash	600	31.12.19X1	Profit and Loss	
April	Cash	630		Account	2,280
July	Cash	400			
October	Cash	500			
31.12.19X1	Balance c/d	750			
		2,880			2,880
19X2			1.1.19X2	Balance b/d . . .	750
January	Cash	750			

Tutorial note:
The credit balance of £600 brought down would have appeared in the
balance sheet at 31 December 19X0 as a liability and relates to the
electricity consumed in the last three months of 19X0. It can be seen that it
is cancelled by the actual cash payment made in January 19X1, and at that
point the balance on the account is zero. The same reasoning relates to the
£750 carried down at the end of 19X1.

Assignment   Students should now work Question 5.3 at the end of the
chapter.

5.2.4   Aged Analysis of Debtors and Bad Debts   When a company makes
sales on credit there is a possibility that some of the customers will not be
able to pay their debts, with the result that bad debts are suffered. Although
known bad debts may be written off during the year, it is usual to review
carefully the list of debtors outstanding when the annual accounts are
prepared and write off any additional bad debts. The fact that a debt is
likely to prove bad becomes apparent when a great deal of time has elapsed
since the goods were supplied and no cash has been received despite
repeated efforts to collect the amount outstanding. This emphasises the
importance of monitoring debtors on a routine basis so that, when the
terms for payment are exceeded, further supplies can be stopped; such

action encourages the customer to pay the amount owed and also minimises the loss if the debt should prove to be bad. A useful aid to monitoring debtors is a report called an 'Aged Analysis of Debtors'. This lists individually all of the firm's debtors and shows for how long the money which comprises the debt has been owed. A much simplified version is shown in Figure 5.2

Figure 5.2

An Aged Analysis of Debtors Report

Debtor	Total	Outstanding for:			
		Less than 1 month	1 to 2 months	2 to 3 months	More than 3 months
	£	£	£	£	£
Alpha	5,000	5,000			
Beta	10,000	9,000	1,000		
Gamma	3,000				3,000
Delta	6,000	2,000	1,500	2,500	
Omega	8,000		8,000		
Total	32,000	16,000	10,500	2,500	3,000

The use of an aged analysis of debtors highlights those customers who are not complying with the normal terms of credit trade. In Figure 5.2, Gamma and Delta are causes for immediate concern. It is likely that no more goods should be supplied to either Gamma or Delta until their outstanding debts are settled. However, action should not be taken against debtors without first attempting to find out why the debt has not been paid. It may be that the debt is subject to some dispute, such as faulty goods being supplied, or the debt may have been recorded against the wrong customer's name.

When it becomes apparent that the full amount of the debt will not be received from the debtor, it is necessary to remove the value of the irrecoverable debt from the total debtors account and record the loss. The double entry to achieve this is:

Account Debited	Account Credited	With
Bad Debts	Debtors	Value of Bad Debt

The balance on the bad debts account appears as a debit balance in the Trial Balance, and is written off to the profit and loss account when the annual accounts are prepared since it represents the loss of an asset, and, therefore, is an expense.

In addition, a company may know, from experience, that a stable proportion of the debts outstanding at the balance sheet date will prove to be bad, although it is not possible to tell in advance which specific debts will remain unpaid. Prudence suggests that, in these circumstances, an allowance should be made for the likely bad debts contained in the value of debtors outstanding at the year end by the introduction of a provision for doubtful debts. When the amount to be provided has been determined, the provision is created by a debit to the Doubtful Debts Account with the corresponding credit to a Provision for Doubtful Debts Account; this credit balance is offset against the value of debtors in the balance sheet to show the net amount which is expected to be collected. The size of the provision required is usually determined by applying a set percentage to the value of debtors, after deducting any identified bad debts, at the balance sheet date. Where an aged analysis of debtors report is produced, different percentages may be applied to debts of different ages.

Once a provision has been created, it appears as a credit balance in the Trial Balance prepared at the end of the subsequent accounting period, and it is necessary only to adjust its value from year to year, rather than charge annually the full required value. This is because the provision created at the end of one year is carried forward to the next, and any debts which in fact prove bad are debited to the bad debts account and then written off to the profit and loss account. The double entry to record adjustments for doubtful debts is:

Account Debited	Account Credited	With
Doubtful Debts	Doubtful Debt Provision	Increase in Provision
Doubtful Debt Provision	Profit and Loss	Decrease in Provision

The operation of the doubtful debts account is now demonstrated in Example 5.5.

Example 5.5

The following balances appeared in the books of Fifth Ltd at the end of 19X1:

	Debit £	Credit £
Bad debts written off during 19X1	950	
Provision for doubtful debts brought forward		900
Debtors	125,000	

It is decided, after a review of the debtors' balances at the end of the year, to write off a further £1,000 of bad debts and create a provision of 1% of the value of the remainder for doubtful debts.

Required:
Write up the 'T' accounts to deal with these matters and show the appropriate extracts from the profit and loss account and balance sheet.

Solution

Bad Debts Account

		£			£
19X1	Debtors.	950	31.12.19X1	Profit and Loss	1,950
31.12.19X1	Debtors	1,000			
		1,950			1,950

Debtors Account

		£			£
31.12.19X1	Balance	125,000	31.12.19X1	Bad Debts	1,000
			31.12.19X1	Balance c/d	124,000
		125,000			125,000

Provision for Doubtful Debts Account

		£			£
31.12.19X1	Balance c/d	1,240*	31.12.19X1	Balance b/d	900
			31.12.19X1	Doubtful Debts	340
		1,240			1,240

* 1% of £124,000 = £1,240

Doubtful Debts Account

		£			£
31.12.19X1	Provision for Doubtful Debts	340	31.12.19X1	Profit and Loss	340

Profit and Loss Account (extract)

	£	£
Bad Debts	1,950	
Doubtful Debts	340	
		2,290

Balance Sheet (extract)

	£	£
Debtors	124,000	
Less: Provision for Doubtful Debts	1,240	
		122,760

Tutorial notes:

1. The bad debts of £950 have already been written off the value of debtors and so no further adjustment to the debtors account is required in respect of this loss.

2. All bad debts arising during 19X1 have been written off against profit. It is therefore necessary only to increase the provision to the revised value, that is, by £340 to £1,240. In some cases the review of debtor balances results in a reduction of the provision and hence a credit to the profit and loss account.

Assignment   Students should now work Question 5.4 at the end of the chapter.

5.3   THE ADJUSTED TRIAL BALANCE

The adjustments made to the trial balance when the trading and profit and loss accounts are prepared must be carried out in a systematic manner which complies with double entry procedures. Example 5.6 shows how this can be done.

Example 5.6

The following trial balance was extracted from the books of T. Jones on 31 December 19X5:

	£	£
Sales		100,000
Purchases	50,000	
Stock — 1 January	10,000	
Rent	5,000	
Wages	12,000	
Electricity	1,500	
Debtors	9,000	
Trade Creditors		8,000
Cash	1,000	
Fixed Assets at Cost	34,000	
Accumulated Depreciation — 1 January		13,000
Other expenses	6,000	
Capital — 1 January		17,000
Drawings	9,500	
	138,000	138,000

The following additional information is provided:

1. Goods which cost £1,000 were received during 19X5 and were included in closing stock. No invoice was included in purchases for them in 19X5.
2. Rent of £500 is prepaid.
3. Electricity of £350 is accrued.
4. The depreciation charge for the year is £6,000.
5. Jones took stock for his own use which cost £450. No entry was made in the books in respect of this.
6. The closing stock is £12,000.
7. Bad debts of £150 are to be written off.
8. A provision for doubtful debts of £100 is to be created.

Required:
   (a) Prepare the adjusted trial balance of T. Jones as at 31 December 19X5.
   (b) Prepare the Trading and Profit and Loss Account of T. Jones for the year to 31 December 19X5 and the Balance Sheet as at that date.

Solution

(a) Adjusted Trial Balance

| | Original Trial Balance at 31.12.X5 | | Adjustments | | Final Trial Balance | | | |
| | | | | | Trading and Profit and Loss Account | | Balance Sheet | |
	£ DR	£ CR	£ DR	£ CR	£ DR	£ CR	£ DR	£ CR
Sales		100,000				100,000		
Purchases	50,000		1,000(1)	450(5)	50,550			
Stock	10,000		12,000(6)	12,000(6)	10,000	12,000	12,000	
Rent	5,000			500(2)	4,500			
Wages	12,000				12,000			
Electricity	1,500		350(3)		1,850			
Debtors	9,000			150(7)			8,850	
Creditors		8,000		1,000(1)				9,000
Cash	1,000						1,000	
Fixed assets at cost	34,000						34,000	
Accumulated depreciation 1 January		13,000		6,000(4)				19,000
Other expenses	6,000				6,000			
Capital 1 January		17,000						17,000
Drawings	9,500		450(5)				9,950	
Accruals				350(3)				350
Prepayments			500(2)				500	
Depreciation charge			6,000(4)		6,000			
Bad and doubtful debts			100(8) 150(7)		250			
Provision for doubtful debts				100(8)				100
	138,000	138,000	20,550	20,550	91,150	112,000 −91,150 20,850	66,300	45,450 20,850 66,300

Tutorial notes:

1. The adjustment columns show the debit and credit entries needed to give effect to the additional information. The number in brackets by such figures refers to the note in the question on which it is based.
2. The opening balance of each line is taken, adjusted, and then entered in the Final Trial Balance.
3. The fact that the two adjustment columns have the same total shows that the double entry rules have been complied with.
4. The Final Trial Balance is separated into the Trading and Profit and Loss Account and the Balance Sheet. This is to aid the preparation of the final accounts. The proof of the trial balance in this format is that each section has an equal, but opposite, difference. This is the profit figure.
5. The accrual of £1,000 for the goods received but not invoiced at the year end represents a trade creditor and so is added to the existing balance of £8,000.

(b)   Trading and Profit and Loss Account

Year to 31 December 19X5

	£	£
Sales		100,000
Opening Stock	10,000	
Purchases	50,550	
Closing Stock	(12,000)	
Cost of Goods Sold		48,550
Gross Profit		51,450
Rent	4,500	
Wages	12,000	
Electricity	1,850	
Other Expenses	6,000	
Depreciation	6,000	
Bad and Doubtful Debts	250	
		30,600
Net Profit		20,850

Balance Sheet at 31 December 19X5

	£	£	£
FIXED ASSETS			
Fixed Assets at Cost			34,000
Less: Accumulated Depreciation			19,000
Balance c/d			15,000

	£	£	£
Balance b/d			15,000
CURRENT ASSETS			
Stock		12,000	
Debtors	8,850		
Less: Provision for Doubtful Debts	100		
		8,750	
Prepayment		500	
Cash		1,000	
		22,250	
CURRENT LIABILITIES			
Creditors	9,000		
Accruals	350		
		9,350	
WORKING CAPITAL			12,900
			27,900
CAPITAL			
Balance at 1 January			17,000
Profit for Year			20,850
			37,850
Less: Drawings			9,950
			27,900

An adjusted trial balance, as used in Example 5.6 above, should be prepared for inclusion in a set of permanent working papers when final accounts are prepared in practice. In examinations it is often too time consuming to prepare this, but, with practice, this process can be avoided. The important requirement is that students should adopt a systematic approach so as to ensure that all necessary adjustments are properly made. One useful technique is to note the double entry effects of all the adjustments to the trial balance on the question paper. The adjusted balances are then used to prepare the final accounts. This approach is now demonstrated in Illustration 5.1 which uses the data given in Example 5.6 for T. Jones. The notes on the trial balance which would in practice be made by hand are shown in italics, and the final accounts include workings to show how the figures have been calculated, so that the examiner understands how the figures are derived.

Illustration 5.1

Trial balance with workings in italics:

	£	£
Sales		100,000
Purchases	50,000 *+ 1,000 − 450*	
Stock — 1 January	10,000	
Rent	5,000 *− 500*	
Wages	12,000	
Electricity	1,500 *+ 350*	
Debtors	9,000 *− 150*	
Trade Creditors		8,000 *+ 1,000*
Cash	1,000	
Fixed Assets at Cost	34,000	
Accumulated Depreciation		
— 1 January		13,000 *+ 6,000*
Other expenses	6,000	
Capital — 1 January		17,000
Drawings	9,500 *+ 450*	
	138,000	138,000
Prepayments	*500*	
Accruals		*350*
Depreciation	*6,000*	
Bad debts	*150*	
Doubtful debt provision	*100*	*100*

Final accounts with workings in brackets:

Trading and Profit and Loss Account

Year to 31 December 19X5

	£	£
Sales		100,000
Opening Stock	10,000	
Purchases (50,000 + 1,000 − 450)	50,550	
Closing Stock	(12,000)	
Cost of Goods Sold		48,550
Gross Profit		51,450
Rent (5,000 − 500)	4,500	
Wages	12,000	
Electricity (1,500 + 350)	1,850	
Other Expenses	6,000	
Depreciation	6,000	
Bad and Doubtful Debts (100 + 150)	250	
		30,600
Net Profit		20,850

Balance Sheet at 31 December 19X5

	£	£	£
FIXED ASSETS			
Fixed Assets at Cost			34,000
Less: Accumulated Depreciation			
(13,000 + 6,000)			19,000
			15,000
CURRENT ASSETS			
Stock		12,000	
Debtors (9,000 − 150)	8,850		
Less: Provision for Doubtful Debts	100		
		8,750	
Prepayment		500	
Cash		1,000	
		22,250	
CURRENT LIABILITIES			
Creditors (8,000 + 1,000)	9,000		
Accruals	350		
		9,350	
WORKING CAPITAL			12,900
			27,900
CAPITAL			
Balance at 1 January			17,000
Profit for Year			20,850
			37,850
Less: Drawings (9,500 + 450)			9,950
			27,900

Assignment   Students should now work on the following questions at the end of the chapter.

Question 5.5 — As well as preparing an answer, students should concentrate on technique when doing this question so as to develop a systematic approach.

Question 5.6 — Errors may come to light during the examination of the books which takes place when the periodic accounts are prepared. The correction of errors dealt with in this question must be made in accordance with the double entry techniques described in this chapter.

Question 5.7, parts (a) and (c) — Revise bad debts and accruals and show in part (b) how, once the principles are grasped, double entry techniques can be used to record and analyse information relating to circumstances which may not have been previously encountered.

5.4 THE MANUFACTURING ACCOUNT

Where a company manufactures the product in which it trades, the cost of the goods produced is found by combining all the maufacturing costs in a 'Manufacturing Account'. The total cost of completed items is then transferred to the Trading Account, where it takes the place of purchases and is adjusted for the opening and closing stocks of finished goods to calculate the cost of goods sold.

Only factory costs must be included in the manufacturing account, and the analysis of costs carried out in the day books must be designed to produce the necessary figures. Separate accounts are opened in the ledger to record the individual costs on the basis of the day book analysis. In due course the various revenues and expenses of the concern are summarised in the trial balance which is then examined to determine which relate to manufacturing; these are transferred to the manufacturing account. Typical manufacturing costs are raw materials and depreciation of plant, and these can be identified directly with the production process. However, in some cases it is not possible to relate a cost entirely to one function, for example, a single rent payment may be made for premises which contain a factory, warehouse, transport depot and offices. When this occurs, the total cost recorded in the trial balance may be apportioned, that is, the proportion which relates to the factory is shown in the manufacturing account and the remainder in the profit and loss account. Such apportionments should be made on a rational basis, for example rent can be divided on the basis of the area occupied by each section.

The costs entered in the manufacturing account should be divided between prime costs and production overhead costs. Prime costs are the materials and labour used directly in the production process; they vary with the level of production and would not be incurred at all if output fell to zero. Overhead costs are those which do not usually vary with the rate of production, for example the rent must be paid whether the factory is producing very little or operating at full capacity. (The importance of the behaviour of costs in response to changes in output is discussed in chapter 10.) The sum of the prime costs and overhead costs is the total production cost, or factory cost, of the output.

To determine the cost of raw materials consumed, the value of purchases during a period must be adjusted by the opening and closing stocks by applying the formula:

Opening stock of + Purchases − Closing stock of = Cost of
raw materials raw materials materials
consumed

There may also be stocks of 'Work in Progress', that is, units of output which are partly completed at the accounting date; these are valued and used to adjust the total factory cost to give the cost of completed production. Work in progress is carried forward to the next period, when further costs are incurred to complete the items involved and make them ready for sale; work in progress appears in the balance sheet as part of the stock included in Current Assets. The adjustment is made by applying the formula:

Opening work + Total factory − Closing work = Cost of
in progress cost in progress completed
items

Example 5.7

The following balances were among those extracted from the books of Antler, a manufacturing business, on 31 December 19X4:

	Debit £	Credit £
Sales		270,000
Production Wages	50,000	
Purchase of Raw Materials	100,000	
Depreciation of Manufacturing Equipment in 19X4	10,000	
Production Overhead Expenses	7,500	
Rent	9,000	
Depreciation of Office Equipment in 19X4	2,000	
Salaries of Salesmen	16,000	
Delivery Costs	12,000	
Advertising Costs	6,000	
General Administration Expenses	22,000	
Stocks at 1 January: Raw Materials	15,000	
Work in Progress	1,500	
Finished Goods	20,000	

Notes:
1. Stocks at 31 December were:

	£
Raw Materials	12,500
Work in Progress	2,500
Finished Goods	27,000

2. Two-thirds of the rent charge relates to the factory.

Required:

Prepare the Manufacturing, Trading and Profit and Loss Accounts of Antler for 19X4.

Solution

*Manufacturing, Trading and Profit and Loss Account of Antler
for the year to 31 December 19X4*

	£	£
Stock of Raw Materials 1 January	15,000	
Purchases of Raw Materials	100,000	
Less: Stock of Raw Materials 31 December	(12,500)	
Raw Materials Consumed	102,500	
Production Wages	50,000	
PRIME COST	152,500	
Production Overhead Costs:		
Depreciation	10,000	
Expenses	7,500	
Rent	6,000	
TOTAL FACTORY COST	176,000	
Work in Progress 1 January	1,500	
Less: Work in Progress 31 December	(2,500)	
COST OF COMPLETED ITEMS TRANSFERRED TO TRADING ACCOUNT	175,000	
Sales		270,000
Stock of Finished Goods 1 January	20,000	
Transferred from production	175,000	
	195,000	
Less: Stock of Finished Goods 31 December	(27,000)	
Cost of Goods Sold		168,000
GROSS PROFIT		102,000
Rent	3,000	
Depreciation of Office Equipment	2,000	
Salesmens' Salaries	16,000	
Delivery Costs	12,000	
Advertising	6,000	
General Administration	22,000	
		61,000
NET PROFIT		41,000

The manufacturing account is used by management because it shows how much it has cost to produce the goods sold during a period. It enables management to compare individual elements of cost with the results of previous periods for control purposes. Also, the total cost of production can be compared with the cost of purchasing similar completed products to give an indication of the efficiency of the manufacturing section. If finished goods can be purchased elsewhere at a total cost lower than that of internal manufacture, then the cessation of manufacturing should be investigated and the possibility of simply buying the completed product for resale examined. Alternatively, such comparisons may give an incentive to achieve improved levels of productivity to match the costs of outside suppliers. On the other hand, a comparison with outside costs might reveal that additional profit is made by producing the goods internally.

Assignment Students should now work Question 5.8 at the end of the chapter.

5.5 REVIEW

After reading the chapter and working the chapter end questions, students should be able to:

- Appreciate why the trial balance has to be adjusted to prepare final accounts.
- Prepare a manufacturing account.
- Prepare final accounts from the trial balance, making adjustments for stocks, depreciation, prepayments, accruals, errors, and bad and doubtful debts.
- Develop a consistent technique for preparing final accounts from the trial balance.

5.6   QUESTIONS

Question 5.1

The trial balance of Tendon, a sole trader, at 31 December 19X9 was:

	£	£
Sales		130,000
Purchases	80,000	
Returns inwards	250	
Returns outwards		150
Stock 1 January 19X9	15,000	
Capital at 1 January 19X9		27,600
Cash at bank	3,100	
Debtors	15,400	
Creditors		5,000
Premises	8,000	
Wages	17,300	
Discounts received		300
Rent and rates	3,000	
Delivery costs	2,750	
Cash drawings	12,000	
Heat and light	3,500	
General expenses	2,750	
	163,050	163,050

The value of stock at 31 December 19X9 was £17,750.

Required:
- (a)   State the location in the final accounts of each item in the trial balance, i.e., whether it is entered in the trading account, the profit and loss account, or the balance sheet.
- (b)   Prepare the trading and profit and loss account of Tendon for the year to 31 December 19X9 and the balance sheet at that date.

Question 5.2

The following is the Trial Balance of Vert, a sole trader, at 30 April 19X8:

	£	£
Capital		30,350
Sales		108,920
Purchases	72,190	
Drawings	12,350	
Debtors	7,350	
Creditors		6,220
Cash at bank	1,710	
Stock at 1 May 19X7	9,470	
Plant and machinery at cost	35,000	
Accumulated depreciation at 1 May 19X7		12,500
Rent	1,000	
Wages	14,330	
Other costs	4,590	
	157,990	157,990

Notes:
1. The value of stock on 30 April 19X8 was £9,960.
2. The depreciation charge for the year to 30 April 19X8 was £3,000.

Required:
Prepare the trading and profit and loss account of Vert for the year to 30 April 19X8 and the balance sheet at that date.

Question 5.3

Frozer Ltd prepares its accounts to 31 December. The following facts relate to 19X8:

		£
1 January	Balance on insurance account (debit)	1,350
1 January	Balance on rates account (debit)	870
1 January	Balance on gas account (credit)	1,800
March	Pay for gas consumed during quarter to 28 February	2,550
	Pay rates for half year to 30 September	2,340
June	Pay for gas consumed during quarter to 31 May	2,520
	Pay insurance for the year to 30 June 19X9	3,060
September	Pay for gas consumed during quarter to 31 August	1,830
	Pay rates for half year to 31 March 19X9	2,340
December	Pay for gas consumed during quarter to 30 November	2,880
	Gas consumed during December 19X8	2,040

Required:

   (a)   Calculate the amounts to be charged in the profit and loss account of Frozer Ltd for the year to 31 December 19X9 in respect of insurance, rates and gas.

   (b)   Calculate the amounts to appear in Frozer Ltd's balance sheet at 31 December 19X8 in respect of insurance, rates and gas. State how they would be presented in the balance sheet.

All workings must be shown.

Question 5.4

At 31 December 19X0 the following balances were shown in the books of E. Rider Ltd:

	£
Debtors	156,937 (dr)
Provision for doubtful debts	2,600 (cr)
Bad debts	750 (dr)

The list of debtors contained balances which were considered to be bad or doubtful as indicated in the 'remarks' column of the schedule below:

Schedule of Bad and Doubtful Debts

Customer	Account Balance £	Remarks
B. Clyde	560	Irrecoverable
S. Wars	680	In liquidation. At least 50p in the £ is anticipated, but full recovery is a possibility.
M. Poppins	227	Irrecoverable.
M. Express	390	This debt is doubtful to the extent of 20%.
B. Mann	240	A provision of £80 is to be made against this debt.

The general provision for doubtful debts in respect of debts other than those dealt with individually above is to be raised to £3,750.

Required:

   (a)   Prepare the debtors account, bad debts account, and provision for doubtful debts account as they appear after recording the above information.

   (b)   Show the balance sheet extract for debtors at 31 December 19X0.

Question 5.5

The following trial balance was extracted from the books of Dellboy, a retail trader, at 31 December 19X6:

	£	£
Capital account		193,894
Freehold land and buildings at cost	114,000	
Motor vans at cost	37,500	
Provision for depreciation on motor vans at 1 January 19X6		15,450
Purchases	164,770	
Sales		234,481
Rent and rates	3,000	
General expenses	7,263	
Wages	26,649	
Bad debts	693	
Provision for doubtful debts at 1 January 19X6		876
Drawings	18,000	
Debtors and creditors	20,911	13,006
Stock in trade at 1 January 19X6	32,193	
Bank balance	32,728	
	457,707	457,707

You are given the following additional information:

(i)   Wages outstanding at 31 December, 19X6 amounted to £271.

(ii)   The provision for doubtful debts is to be increased by £104.

(iii)   Stock-in-trade at 31 December, 19X6 was £34,671.

(iv)   Rent and rates amounting to £300 were paid in advance at 31 December, 19X6.

(v)   During 19X6 Dellboy took stock costing £1,250 for his own use. No entry has been made in the books in respect of this.

(vi)   During 19X6 a motor van which had cost £2,500 and had a written down value of £1,000 was sold for £1,500. No entry had been made in the books to record this, other than to credit the cash received to the motor vehicles account.

(vii)   The depreciation charge for the year is £7,000.

Required:

A trading and profit and loss account for the year 19X6 and a balance sheet as at 31 December 19X6.

Question 5.6

During the preparation of the accounts from the books of S. Top, a sole trader, for the year to 30 June, 19X7, the following items were found:

1. Included in the Repairs to Machinery Account was £2,750 which was paid on 29 June 19X7 and was for the purchase of a new lathe.
2. Manufacturing Wages Account included £350 paid to an employee for time spent repairing a machine.
3. A debt of £1,290 due from J. Jones was included in debtors, but in fact was irrecoverable.
4. The electricity bill for S. Top's private house of £200 had been paid by the business and charged to the Rates Account.
5. Goods worth £1,500 had been received into stock on 30 June and included in the value of stock for accounts purposes. No entry had been made in the books to record this purchase.
6. An old machine which had cost £1,000 and was fully depreciated had been scrapped during the year. This fact had not been recorded in the books.
7. S. Top had taken stock to the value of £150 for his own use during the year. No entry appeared in the books in respect of this usage.
8. A payment of £125 for delivery of goods to customers had been entered in the Purchase Account.

Required:
(a) Prepare the journal entries to record the adjustments.
(b) Prepare a statement to show the effect of these adjustments on the profit for the year to 30 June 19X7.

Question 5.7

(Taken from the October 1989 *Introduction to Accounting* Paper.)

(a) A trader has total debtors of £35,208 at his balance sheet date of 30 June 1989. An analysis of the debtors at 30 June 1989 shows the following:

Invoiced within the last month	£24,906
Invoiced 1-2 months ago	£8,476
Invoiced over 2 months ago	£1,826

The company accountant knows from past experience that 5% of debts over two months old, 3% of debts between one and two months old, and 1% of debts less than one month old turn out to be bad. The balance on the Provision for Bad Debts Account at 30 June 1988 was £450 (credit).

Required:
(i)   Show the appropriate entry for debtors (net of provisions) in the balance sheet at 30 June 1989. *Show your workings.* [3]
(ii) Show the amount to be charged in the profit and loss account for the year to 30 June 1989 in respect of the provision for bad debts.

[3]

(b)   On 1 April 1989 Charles borrowed £5,000 for his business from a finance company. The terms of the loan were that he would make monthly capital repayments of £200 plus interest at the rate of 1.5% per month on the outstanding capital balance starting on 1 May 1989.

Required:
What charge for loan interest in connection with this transaction would you expect to find in his profit and loss account for the year ended 31 July 1989, and what entry would you expect to find in his balance sheet at 31 July 1989 in respect of the amount still outstanding? *Show your workings.*   [9]

(c)   A grocer's telephone bill has been fairly consistent in recent years. It rises during summer months as he has to make more calls to hotels and holiday camps to take orders.
     He always receives his quarterly accounts in the first week of January, April, July and October and pays them two weeks after receipt. Recent bills have been as follows:

April 1988	£87
July 1988	£214
October	£138
January 1989	£94
April 1989	£93
July 1989	£144
October 1989	£168

The accrued charge for telephones in his balance sheet dated 31 August 1988 was £92.

Required:
If you were preparing the grocer's annual accounts for the 12 months ended 31 August 1989, state the amounts you would show for telephone charges in:

    (i)   the profit and loss account;

    (ii) the balance sheet at 31 August 1989. *Show your workings.* [5]

[Total marks for question — 20]

Question 5.8

The following is the trial balance of Drinkle, a manufacturer, at 31 March 19X6:

	£	£
Capital		50,000
Sales		209,500
Long term loan		30,000
Raw materials:		
purchases	40,000	
stock at 1 April 19X5	12,000	
Production wages	30,000	
Production equipment:		
at cost	70,000	
accumulated depreciation at 1 April 19X4		14,000
Rent	6,400	
Light, heat and power	12,000	
Production overhead costs	17,500	
Administration expenses	12,500	
Administration salaries	15,000	
Work in progress 1 April 19X5	2,000	
Finished goods stock at 1 April 19X5	11,500	
Hire of office equipment	7,000	
Postage and telephone	5,350	
Loan interest	3,000	
Bank charges	1,250	
Overdraft		10,000
Hire of delivery vans	5,000	
Van driver's wages	17,000	
Petrol and other van expenses	3,000	
Debtors	20,000	
Creditors		5,000
Drawings	28,000	
	318,500	318,500

Notes:

1.   The production equipment has a life of 10 years and a zero scrap value.
2.   Stocks, all at cost, at 31 March 19X6 were:

	£
Raw materials	14,000
Work in progress	7,000
Finished goods	13,800

3. 75% of the rent and light, heat and power relates to the factory.

Required:
Prepare the manufacturing, trading and profit and loss accounts of Drinkle for the year to 31 March 19X6 and the balance sheet as at that date.

CHAPTER 6

Asset Valuation, Profit Measurement and the Underlying Accounting Concepts

The figure for profit appearing in the final accounts depends on the amounts at which assets, reported in the balance sheet, are valued. Any errors made when valuing assets have a corresponding effect on the level of reported profit and, therefore, reduce its usefulness as a basis for assessing performance. For example, if closing stock is over-valued by £1,000, the figure for cost of goods sold is understated and reported profit overstated by this amount. Great care should therefore be taken when calculating asset values for inclusion in the accounts. The procedures which are followed, in practice, are examined below.

6.1 STOCK VALUATION METHODS

The categories of stock owned by business organisations differ depending on the way it which their affairs are organised. For example:

1. Trading organisations, i.e. businesses which purchase and sell goods, but do not process them. Stock consists of goods purchased, in their completed state, and remaining unsold at the end of the accounting period.
2. Manufacturing concerns. The term 'stock' covers raw materials, work-in-progress and finished goods awaiting sale.
3. Service organisations, e.g. accountants and bankers. These hold very little, if any, stock in the conventional sense of the term, though accountants will have a significant balance of work-in-progress (representing services provided but not yet billed) while banks possess large investments which present their own valuation problems.

For many businesses stock is a large proportion of gross assets. For example, the accounts of Rolls-Royce plc, for 1988 included stock amounting to £559,000,000 and this represented 31.4% of its total assets.

The calculation of the figure for stock involves two steps: first, the physical quantities of stocks must be established; secondly, these physical quantities must be valued.

The quantity of stock on hand is usually established by a physical count after close of business at the end of the accounting period. Because of the importance of the 'stock count', stock-taking procedures should be worked out well in advance and the exercise undertaken in a systematic manner by reliable employees who are fully aware of their responsibilities. In these circumstances the likelihood of error, as the result of items being mis-described, counted twice, or completely omitted, is reduced to a minimum. It is also necessary for management to take steps to ensure that all goods sold and invoiced to customers on the last day of the accounting period have been despatched from the premises by the time the count takes place. Failure to ensure this happens may mean that profit will be substantially over-stated as the result of including certain items both in sales for the year and in the year-end stock figure. For similar reasons management operates controls designed to ensure that all goods on the premises, and included in stock, are recorded in the books as purchases made during the year.

We now examine the way in which quantities of stock, once identified, are valued.

6.1.1 The Basic Rule The fundamental rule is that stock should be valued at 'the lower of cost and net realisable value'. Students will be broadly familiar with what is meant by cost (examined further in section 6.1.2 of this chapter), but the term 'net realisable value' (NRV) is met here for the first time. Basically, NRV is the market selling price of stock less any further costs to be incurred by the firm in relation to the asset up to the time of disposal.

Example 6.1

The following information is provided relating to a vehicle held in stock by Thornhill Carsales Ltd.

	£
Cost	3,700
Market selling price	5,000

Salesmen are paid a commission of 2% on market selling price, and it is the company's policy to allow the customer a full tank of petrol at an estimated cost of £20.

Required:
Calculate the net realisable value of the vehicle.

Solution

Net realisable value:

		£
Market selling price		5,000
Less: Further costs — Commission	100	
— Petrol	20	120
NRV		4,880

NRV normally exceeds cost in a profitable concern, and this is the case in the above example; NRV (£4,880) exceeds costs (£3,700) by £1,180. Sometimes NRV is below cost. For example, where an existing model of car is to be replaced, the firm will be anxious to clear its 'old' stock before it becomes unsaleable, and is likely to accept a low price.

Example 6.2

The following information is provided for three vehicles held in stock by Reliable Cars Ltd.

Vehicle	Cost	NRV
	£	£
A	5,400	6,200
B	5,200	8,500
C	7,100	6,200

Required:

Calculate the value of Reliable Cars Ltd's stock for the purpose of its accounts.

Solution

Vehicle	Cost	NRV	Value for the Accounts: Lower of Cost & NRV
	£	£	£
A	5,400	6,200	5,400 (cost)
B	5,200	8,500	5,200 (cost)
C	7,100	6,200	6,200 (NRV)
	17,700	20,900	16,800

The total cost of the three vehicles is £17,700 compared with a total NRV of £20,900, i.e. total NRV exceeds total cost. It is to ensure that the fall in value of vehicle C is not ignored that the test is applied to each vehicle separately. Where the comparison between the cost and net realisable value of stock on an individual items basis would be excessively time consuming, e.g. because of the large number of items involved, groups of similar items of stock may be compared.

Most of a company's stock is usually valued at cost, with a small number of items reduced to net realisable value either because they are damaged or because they are no longer popular with customers.

Assignment   Students should now work Question 6.1 at the end of the chapter.

6.1.2 Calculating Cost   The calculation of the cost of stock is a straightforward matter in the case of a trading organisation, and normally consists of the price paid to the supplier plus delivery charges where these are not included in the purchase price. The calculation is more difficult for a manufacturing organisation because, in these businesses, cost consists of the price paid for raw materials plus the processing costs incurred to convert these materials into finished goods. This raises the question: 'Which processing costs should be included?' Clearly the wages paid to employees working with the materials should be included as part of the cost of the finished item, but what about the wages paid to supervisors and other essential manufacturing costs such as lighting and heating, rent and rates of the factory and depreciation of the machinery? In practice one of the following two procedures could be followed.

1. *The marginal cost basis.*   Only those costs which can be traced directly to the item manufactured are included in the valuation, e.g. materials costs and the wages paid to those employees directly involved in processing the materials.
2. *The total cost basis.*   All manufacturing costs are included, i.e. the marginal costs plus a fair proportion of incidental manufacturing expenses, called 'manufacturing overheads'.

The total cost figure for stock therefore exceeds the marginal cost figure by the amount of the fixed manufacturing overhead costs.

Example 6.3

The following data are provided relating to the manufacture of 'Nexo' for the month of January 19X1.

	£
Raw materials used (£5 per unit)	6,000
Wages paid to staff directly involved in manufacture	8,400
Salary paid to supervisor	850
Rent and rates	420
Light and heat	670
Depreciation of machinery	460

During January 1,200 items were manufactured, of which 1,000 were sold. There was no opening stock and no work-in-progress at the beginning or end of the month. Closing stock consists of 200 completed items.

Required:
  (a) Valuations of closing stock on the:
        (i) marginal cost basis
        (ii) total cost basis.
  (b) Comment on your results.

Solution

(a) (i)   Marginal cost basis:

		£
Direct material costs:	Raw materials	6,000
	Labour	8,400
		14,400

	£
Marginal cost per unit manufactured, £14,400 ÷ 1,200	12
Marginal cost of unsold stock, £12 × 200	2,400

(ii) Total cost basis: £   £
      Direct manufacturing costs   14,400
      Manufacturing overheads: Salary   850
                                Rent and rates   420
                                Light and heat   670
                                Depreciation   460   2,400
                                                                             ─────
                                                                            16,800

             Total cost per unit manufactured, £16,800 ÷ 1,200 .   14
             Total cost of stock, £14 × 200   2,800

(b)   The total cost basis produces a cost per unit which is £2 more (£14 − £12). This results
      from the inclusion of a proportion of manufacturing overheads which amount, in total,
      to £2,400, or £2,400 ÷ 1,200 = £2 per unit manufactured.

A company must be able to cover all its costs if it is to survive and flourish
in the long run, and for this reason companies are required to use the total
cost basis when valuing stock for inclusion in the accounts published for
external use. For internal reporting purposes, however, either total costs or
marginal costs can be used, and management may well regard the latter as
the more relevant basis for short-run business decisions. For example, a
business operating below its full productive capacity may find it worthwhile
to accept orders at prices below total costs, provided marginal costs are
covered, since overhead costs will be incurred anyway.

Assignment   Students should now work Question 6.2 at the end of the
                 chapter.

6.1.3   Identifying Purchases with Sales: First In First Out (FIFO)   Chap-

ter 3.2 showed us that profit is calculated by matching costs with related
revenues arising during an accounting period. The difficulty, in the case of
stocks, is to decide which costs to match with sales revenue in view of the
large number of items acquired at different times during the year, and
probably at different prices. It is theoretically possible to identify the actual
items sold and, where a firm deals in a relatively small number of high value
items which can be easily identified, e.g. cars, this procedure is followed in
practice. Where there are a large number of transactions, however, the
heavy additional cost involved in keeping such detailed records rules out
this option. Instead the matching process is facilitated by making one of a
number of arbitrary assumptions concerning the flow of goods into and out
of the business. The most common assumption which is used for published
accounts is:

First in first out (FIFO). This assumes that the first items purchased are the first items sold. The items in stock are therefore the most recent acquisitions.

Example 6.4

The following information is provided for Heath Ltd for 19X4.

		£
Opening stock:	200 units at £5 each	1,000
Purchases:	May, 1,200 units at £6 each	7,200
	October, 800 units at £6.50 each	5,200
Sales:	June, 900 units at £10 each	9,000
	November, 900 units at £10 each	9,000

Required:
   (a)   A calculation of the number of units in stock on 31 December 19X4.
   (b)   A calculation of the value of stock held on 31 December 19X4.
   (c)   The trading account for 19X4.

Solution

(a)

	units
Stock on 1 January	200
Add: Purchases, 1,200 + 800	2,000
	2,200
Less: Sales, 900 + 900	1,800
Stock on 31 December	400

(b)   Value of closing stock: 400 units at £6.50 2,600

Tutorial note:
The 1,800 items sold are assumed to be made up of the opening stock of 200 units, plus the next 1,600 units purchased, i.e. the 1,200 units purchased in May and 400 of the units purchased in October. Closing stock therefore consists of the remaining 400 units purchased during October and are therefore valued at £6.50 each.

(c)   *Trading Account for 19X4*

	£	£
Sales		18,000
Less: Opening stock	1,000	
Purchases	12,400	
Closing stock	(2,600)	10,800
Gross profit		7,200

Assignment   Students should now work Question 6.3 at the end of the chapter.

6.2 THE DISTINCTION BETWEEN CAPITAL EXPENDITURE AND REVENUE EXPENDITURE

All expenditure incurred by a business must be accounted for as either:

1. capital expenditure, or
2. revenue expenditure.

The basic test used to distinguish between the two types of expenditure is the effect that the outlay has on the company's long run ability to earn profits. If it is enhanced, the expenditure is capital, whereas if the expenditure merely maintains the business's ability to operate, it is revenue.

The distinction between capital and revenue expenditure is of crucial importance because it determines which items must be carried forward as assets in the balance sheet and which items must be written off immediately in the profit and loss account. Capital expenditure is recorded in the balance sheet at cost, and is subsequently charged against revenue over the period of years which benefit from using the asset. Revenue expenditure is normally charged against revenue arising during the period when the cost is incurred. An example of capital expenditure is money spent on the purchase of fixed assets, whereas examples of revenue expenditure are the cost of acquiring or manufacturing stock for resale and the day-to-day costs of running the business. It is important to achieve an accurate classification; otherwise the reported balances for profit and net assets are incorrectly stated (see Figure 6.1), and wrong conclusions may be reached regarding the performance and position of the firm.

Figure 6.1

Effect of wrongly allocating expenditure to capital or revenue

	Effect on	
	Profit	*Net assets*
Capital expenditure wrongly allocated to revenue	understated	understated
Revenue expenditure wrongly allocated to capital	overstated	overstated

---

Most items of expenditure can be identified fairly easily with the balance sheet or the profit and loss account, but there are some 'grey areas' where judgment is needed to help make a proper allocation in the light of all the available facts. The main grey areas are:

1. *Stock.* The cost incurred in acquiring or manufacturing stock is a revenue expense. The gap between the purchase and sale of stock is relatively short, and most stock acquired will be re-sold by the end of the accounting year. These items are correctly debited to the trading account for that year. There will, however, usually be a balance of stock, unsold at the year-end, and this is carried forward in the balance sheet, as a current asset, and written off against revenue in the following accounting period.

2. *Expenditure on fixed assets.* The cost of fixed assets acquired or built by the firm itself, to form the basis for business activity, is clearly a capital expenditure. Difficulties arise in connection with expenditure incidental to the acquisition of the fixed asset and expenditure on fixed assets currently in use. The following rules should be followed to achieve a proper allocation:

   (a) Expenditure incurred in getting a new fixed asset ready for business use is a capital expense. This includes, for example, any transport costs, import duties and solicitors' fees. In addition, costs incurred in modifying existing premises to accommodate a new fixed asset should be capitalised.

   (b) Expenditure on an existing fixed asset which enhances its value to the business, e.g. by increasing its capacity, effectiveness or useful life, should be capitalised.

   (c) Expenditure on an existing fixed asset intended to make good wear and tear and keep it in satisfactory working order is a revenue expense.

It is possible for an expenditure to contain elements of both improvement (item (b)) and repair (item (c)), in which case an apportionment between capital expenditure and revenue expenditure must be made.

Example 6.5

The following events occurred at Lawrence Ltd during 19X7.

1. Legal expenses incurred when acquiring a new building, £5,000.

2. Factory given a fresh coat of paint, £4,500.
3. 200 tiles on a roof damaged by a gale were replaced at a cost of £1,200.
4. Expenditure incurred demolishing part of a wall to make room for a recently purchased machine, £750.
5. Wooden office windows replaced by double-glazed metal windows at a cost of £12,000.
6. A system of ventilation installed in the factory at a cost of £4,500.

Required:
Classify each of the above items as capital expenditure or revenue expenditure. Give reasons for your classifications.

Solution

1. Capital. This is part of the cost of acquiring the new asset.
2. Revenue. This makes good wear and tear.
3. Revenue. This merely restores the roof to its pre-gale condition.
4. Capital. This is part of the cost of bringing the fixed asset into use.
5. Part capital/part revenue. The new windows should be more effective in eliminating draughts and making the office sound proof.
6. Capital. Working conditions and employee performance should improve.

---

3. *Advertising.* It is necessary to distinguish between expenditure designed to launch a new product (capital) and expenditure designed to maintain the level of sales by keeping the product in 'the public eye' (revenue). The former type of expenditure is likely to involve a heavy initial outlay which, if successful, will benefit the firm for a number of years. Such expenditure may be 'capitalised' and written off over the accounting periods which benefit from the sale of the new product. In the balance sheet, the amount not yet written off is reported under the heading 'deferred revenue expenditure' to emphasise the fact that special circumstances justify carrying forward a type of expenditure which is normally charged immediately against revenue.

Assignment Students should now work Questions 6.4 and 6.5 at the end of the chapter.

6.3 DEPRECIATION METHODS
Chapter 3.6.3 draws attention to the fact that depreciation must be charged in the accounts in order to recognise the fact that the business has benefited

from using fixed assets which, as a result, have declined in value. The pattern of benefit which arises differs from one type of fixed asset to another. For example, some fixed assets produce a greater benefit in the early years of ownership, when the asset is more efficient, whereas other fixed assets make a fairly steady contribution over their entire useful life. There are a number of different methods of charging depreciation, and management should choose the one which most closely reflects the pattern of benefits received. The two methods most commonly used are examined below.

6.3.1 Straight Line (Equal Instalment) Method Under this method the difference between original cost and ultimate disposal value is spread evenly over the asset's estimated useful life. The method assumes that each accounting period benefits to an equal extent from using the fixed asset. The annual charge is calculated on the basis of the following formula:

$$\frac{\text{Original cost} \; - \; \text{Estimated disposal value}}{\text{Estimated life}}$$

An attraction of this method is that it is easy to apply once the initial estimates have been made and, probably for this reason, it is the method most widely used in Great Britain.

Example 6.6

On 1 January 19X1 a manufacturing company acquired a new lathe for £23,000. It is estimated to have a useful life of 4 years and a disposal value of £3,000 at the end of that time.

Required:
A calculation of the annual depreciation charge using the straight line method.

Solution

$$\text{Straight line depreciation charge} = \frac{£23,000 \; - \; £3,000}{4}$$

$$= \quad 5,000$$

6.3.2 Reducing (Declining) Balance Method This is the second most popular method. A fixed depreciation rate is applied to the net book value (i.e. original cost less accumulated depreciation) of the asset brought forward at the beginning of each accounting period. The depreciation rate is pitched at a level which reduces cost to disposal value over the fixed asset's estimated useful life. The appropriate rate may be identified using the following formula:

$$r = \left(1 - n\sqrt{\frac{s}{c}}\right) \times 100$$

Where: r is the depreciation rate
n is the expected useful life
s is the expected scrap value, and
c the original cost.

Applying this formula to the facts provided in Example 6.6 gives the following results:

$$r = \left(1 - 4\sqrt{\frac{3{,}000}{23{,}000}}\right) \times 100 = 39.9\%$$

Depreciation charges, 19X1–19X4:

	£
Original cost	23,000
Less: 19X1 depreciation charge, £23,000 × 39.9%	9,177
Net book value at 31 December 19X1	13,823
Less: 19X2 depreciation charge, £13,823 × 39.9%	5,515
Net book value at 31 December 19X2	8,308
Less: 19X3 depreciation charge, £8,308 × 39.9%	3,315
Net book value at 31 December 19X3	4,993
Less: 19X4 depreciation charge, £4,993 x 39.9%	1,993
Net book value at 31 December 19X4	3,000

It will be noticed that the charge is highest in 19X1 and then falls, each year, because the fixed depreciation rate is applied to a declining balance. Indeed the charge for 19X1 (£9,177) is over *four times* higher than the charge for 19X4 (£1,993). Clearly the method is appropriate only when the bulk of the benefit arises early on. An argument sometimes put forward for using this method is that repair and maintenance costs normally increase as a fixed asset gets older, and the reducing balance basis therefore helps to ensure that the total annual charge (depreciation + maintenance) remains steady over the asset's useful life.

Tutorial note:
Where the reducing balance method is to be used, the appropriate depreciation rate will be given in examination questions.

6.3.3 Comparing the Methods

The charge made under each method, discussed above, may be compared as follows:

	19X1	19X2	19X3	19X4	Total
	£	£	£	£	£
Straight line	5,000	5,000	5,000	5,000	20,000
Reducing balance	9,177	5,515	3,315	1,993	20,000

It can be seen that the pattern of charges differs a great deal depending on the method used. The straight line method produces lower charges in the first two years and higher charges in year 3 and 4. This shows that great care should be taken when choosing between depreciation methods, as the option selected is likely to have a material effect on the level of reported profit in any one year, although, over the life of the asset, the total charge is the same in either case. The choice is rarely easy, however, as the depreciation policy must be decided upon immediately the asset is acquired, and management does not know, at that stage, the precise benefit that will arise in each future accounting period. The decision is therefore to some extent arbitrary and, if an error is made, profit will be either under- or over-stated.

6.3.4 Estimation Errors

In addition to the difficulty of selecting the most appropriate method, there is the problem of making accurate estimates of the useful life of the fixed asset and of its disposal value at the end of that period. Care should be exercised when making these estimates as errors produce an incorrect charge for depreciation and a consequent understatement or overstatement of profit.

Example 6.7

A machine is purchased for £60,000 on 1 January 19X1. It is estimated that the machine will last for five years and then have a zero disposal value. Management believes that each accounting period will benefit equally from the use of the machine, and the straight line method of depreciation is therefore considered appropriate.

Required:
(a) Calculate the depreciation charge to be made each year, 19X1–19X5.
(b) Assume it turns out that all management's estimates are correct, except that it totally misjudges the second hand demand for the machine which eventually sells for £20,000. Calculate the depreciation charge which would have been made each year if the disposal value had been accurately estimated.

Solution

(a) Depreciation charge $= \dfrac{£60,000}{5} = £12,000$

(b) Depreciation charge $= \dfrac{£60,000 - £20,000}{5} = £8,000$

Because the disposal value was wrongly estimated, the annual charge is overstated and profit is understated by £4,000 during each of the five years of ownership. This is balanced by crediting £20,000 to the profit and loss account when the fixed asset, by this time completely written off, is sold for that figure.

Assignment   Students should now work Question 6.6 at the end of the chapter.

6.4   GOODWILL

Business assets may be classified as either tangible or intangible. Tangible assets possess a physical existence; the most common examples are stocks and fixed assets, considered earlier in this chapter. Intangible assets possess no physical existence but they are valuable because they help the firm to earn a profit. The most common example of an intangible asset is goodwill, which was defined as follows by Lord MacNaughton in *CIR* v *Muller* (1901):

It is the benefit and advantage of the good name, reputation and connection of a business. It is the attractive force which brings in custom. It is the one thing which distinguishes an old established business from a new business at its first start.

Goodwill is therefore built up gradually over the years and, when a businessman 'sells up', he expects the buyer to pay a price which covers not only the tangible assets but also intangible assets such as goodwill. In these circumstances it is useful to value goodwill as a basis for negotiations. The following are two examples of the methods which may be used.

Weighted average profits basis. Goodwill may be valued as a multiple of past profits. For this purpose a number of years' profits may be averaged and 'weights' attached to the profits arising each year.

Example 6.8

The profits of a partnership for the last three years are as follows: 19X1, £20,000; 19X2, £26,000; and 19X3, £31,000.

Required:
Calculate goodwill on the basis of 1.5 times the weighted average profits of the last three years, using weights of 3 for the most recent year, 2 for the previous year, and 1 for the earliest year.

Solution

Weighted average profits are calculated as follows:

Year	Weight	Profits £	Total £
19X1	1	20,000	20,000
19X2	2	26,000	52,000
19X3	3	31,000	93,000
	6		165,000

$$\text{Weighted average} = \frac{£165,000}{6} = £27,500$$

Goodwill = £27,500 × 1.5 = £41,250.

Super profit basis. This method seeks to identify the extra profit, usually called 'super' profit, earned by a firm because of the existence of good connections. It then values goodwill as the capitalised value of this surplus, i.e. at the amount that would have to be invested, assuming a given rate of return, to produce the extra profit for an indefinite period of time. The rate of return considered appropriate naturally differs from one type of business to another.

Example 6.9

Leake Ltd has earned profits averaging £20,000 per annum in recent years. It is estimated that £17,000 represents a reasonable return on the existing tangible assets.

Required:
  (a) A calculation of the super profit.
  (b) A valuation of goodwill based on the capitalisation of super profit, assuming that 20% is considered a reasonable rate of return on intangible assets in this type of business.

Solution

		£
(a)	Actual profit	20,000
	Normal profit	17,000
	Super profit	3,000

(b) Goodwill $= £3,000 \times \dfrac{100}{20} = £15,000$

  i.e., at a 20% rate of interest, £15,000 must be invested to give an annual return of £3,000.

Each of the above approaches enables goodwill to be valued, but it does not necessarily follow that a buyer will be willing to pay the amount of the valuation or that the seller will accept it. The price actually paid for goodwill depends on negotiation between these two parties, and the main use of the above calculations is that they produce measures of value which can be referred to during discussions.

In examinations the total price paid for the business is often given, and the students are able to calculate goodwill simply by subtracting the value of tangible assets from this figure.

Example 6.10

Ted Anthony, who has been in business for many years, decides to retire and sells his business assets, other than cash and debtors, to William Jones for £30,000. At the date of sale Anthony's tangible assets consist of premises worth £20,000, machinery worth £3,500, and stocks valued at £2,500.

Required:
Calculate goodwill arising on the sale of the business and comment on the result.

Solution

	£	£
Purchase price		30,000
Less: Tangible assets:		
Premises	20,000	
Machinery	3,500	
Stock	2,500	26,000
Goodwill		4,000

The total value of the tangible assets is £26,000, and we can therefore conclude that William Jones was willing to pay an extra £4,000 to cover the goodwill built up by Ted Anthony over the years.

In the above example, goodwill is the 'balancing' figure which results from comparing the agreed purchase price with the total value of the tangible assets acquired. The price paid for goodwill is initially recorded in the books of the acquiring company at cost, but goodwill does not last forever, e.g. the range of customers supplied gradually changes and those 'taken over' with the business eventually leave. Goodwill must therefore be written off either immediately against retained profit, or gradually against profits over the estimated useful life of the asset. The latter approach is theoretically more sound as it complies with the accruals concept by attempting to match costs with revenues. Immediate write off is the option usually selected, however, because:

1. it is the method favoured by the accounting profession,
2. the great difficulty of estimating the asset's likely future life,
3. the write-off is not made in the profit and loss account, and so higher profits are reported under this method.

Assignment   Students should now work Question 6.7 at the end of the chapter.

6.5   ACCOUNTING CONCEPTS

Accounting records and statements are based on a number of assumptions, called accounting concepts. The 10 considered most important are examined below. The treatment is brief in those cases where the concept has already been discussed in an earlier chapter.

6.5.1   Entity Concept   This fixes the boundary for the financial affairs contained in an accounting statement and was considered in chapter 1.2. The boundary is often the business, but it may be a smaller or even a larger unit. For instance, a business may be split into a number of departments, each of which is treated as a separate entity for the purpose of preparing accounting statements for management (see chapter 10.2.2). At the other extreme, a number of companies may be regarded as a single entity for accounting purposes. This occurs where a company owns more than 50% of the shares of one or more other companies. The connected companies together form a 'group', and their separate accounts are 'consolidated' for the purpose of reporting to shareholders. This topic is examined in the Associateship examinations core subject 'Accountancy'.

6.5.2   Money Measurement Concept   A business asset is reported in the balance sheet only if its value can be measured, in money terms, with a reasonable degree of precision. This concept was discussed in chapter 1.10.1. A good example of the application of this concept concerns the accounting treatment of goodwill. We saw, in section 6.4 of this chapter, that goodwill consists of the reputation and business connections built up over a period of time. Most firms enjoy an element of goodwill, but its value continuously fluctuates, and is therefore difficult to quantify with any degree of precision. For this reason the existence of goodwill is usually acknowledged by an entry in the accounts only when its value is proved by a market transaction involving its purchase or sale.

6.5.3   Matching Concept   The accountant measures profit for a period of time, such as a year, by comparing or 'matching' revenue and expenditure identified with that period. The first step is to identify revenues and the second step is to deduct the expenditures incurred in producing the revenues. This concept was examined in chapter 3.2. It should be noted that many of the concepts are closely interrelated. For example, the matching concept is put into effect by applying the realisation concept and the accruals concept. These are considered next.

6.5.4 Realisation Concept   Revenue is assumed to be earned when a sale takes place and a legally enforceable claim arises against the customer. The effect of this rule is that stock usually remains in the books at cost until the sale takes place, at which stage a profit arises or a loss is incurred. This concept was discussed in chapter 3.5.

6.5.5 Accruals Concept   Costs are matched against revenues when the benefit of the expenditure is received rather than when the cash payment is made. Where the benefit is received before the payment is made, the amount owed is treated as a liability in the balance sheet. Where the benefit is received after the payment is made, the amount paid is treated as an asset in the balance sheet, and charged against revenues arising during whichever future accounting period benefits from the payments. This concept was examined in chapter 3.6.

Assignment   Students should now work Question 6.8 at the end of the chapter.

6.5.6 Historical Cost Concept   Assets are initially recorded at the price paid to the supplier. In certain circumstances further costs may be added. For example, in the case of a manufacturing concern, a proportion of the production costs should be added to the cost of raw materials to arrive at the cost of finished goods (see section 6.1.2 of this chapter). In the case of fixed assets their recorded cost includes not only the price paid to the supplier but also all incidental costs incurred to make the item ready for use (see section 6.2 of this chapter). A major advantage of this concept is that the accounting records are based on objective facts. A disadvantage of using historical cost is that, during a period of rising prices, the reported figures may significantly understate the asset's true value to the business. It is for this reason that some companies periodically revalue some or all of their fixed assets (see further discussion in chapter 9.6).

6.5.7 Going Concern Concept   This assumes that the business is a permanent venture and will not be wound up in the foreseeable future. Many fixed assets have low resale values, e.g. machinery might cost many thousands of pounds but, because it is specially designed for a particular business, there may be no possibility of selling it other than as scrap metal.

The going concern concept allows accountants to ignore this low resale value and instead spread the cost of an asset over the accounting periods which benefit from its use. The assumption that the business will continue indefinitely as a going concern is, however, in certain circumstances false and must be dropped. For example, if a company is about to be liquidated, forecasts of the amounts likely to be received by various providers of finance should be based on estimates of what the business assets are expected to realise in the market rather than their historical book value.

6.5.8 Consistency Concept The same valuation methods should be used each year when preparing accounting statements. We have seen that there exist a number of methods for valuing fixed assets and stocks. There are arguments in favour and against most of them and, to some extent, an arbitrary choice must be made. The effect on reported profit is unlikely to be significant, however, provided similar procedures are adopted each year. For example, the total cost method of valuing stock produces a higher figure for stock than the marginal cost method, but it does not necessarily produce a higher profit figure. Businesses have both opening and closing stock, and the consistent use of total cost produces a higher figure for stock at both dates.

Example 6.11

The following information is provided for one of the products manufactured by Mill Ltd during 19X8.

Opening stock
 100 units valued as follows: £
  Marginal cost basis, £5 per unit × 100 500
  Total cost basis, £8 per unit × 100 800
Production cost of 500 units
  Marginal costs, £5 per unit 2,500
  Fixed costs 1,500
  Sales, 500 units at £12 6,000

Required:
 (a) Valuations of closing stock using:
  (i) the marginal cost basis, and
  (ii) the total cost basis.
 (b) Profit statements for 19X8 using each of the above bases.

Solution

(a) Opening stock is 100 units and, as the same number of items are produced as are sold, closing stock is also 100 units.

(i) Marginal cost basis:

	£	£
Marginal costs, £5 × 100		500

(ii) Total cost basis:

	£	£
Marginal costs	500	
Fixed costs	300 W1	800

W1 £1,500 (total fixed costs) ÷ 500 (number of items produced) × 100 (number of items in stock at year end).

(b)

Profit Statement, 19X8

	(i) Marginal cost basis		(ii) Total cost basis	
	£	£	£	£
Sales		6,000		6,000
Less: Opening stock	500		800	
Production costs	4,000		4,000	
Closing stock	(500)		(800)	
Cost of goods sold		4,000		4,000
Gross Profit		2,000		2,000

The higher opening and closing valuations, on the total cost basis, cancel out, and gross profit is unaffected by the valuation method adopted. It should be noted, however, that the balance sheet figure for stocks, and therefore gross assets and net assets, are higher if total cost is used. It should also be noted that reported profit does vary when there are changes in the level of stock because, in these circumstances, the opening and closing balances no longer cancel out. However, the difference is unlikely to be large unless the change in the level of stock is substantial, such as occurs when new business operations commence.

The level of reported profit can be significantly inflated or deflated if a company changes from one method to another.

Example 6.12

Assume the same facts as for Example 6.11, except that marginal cost is used at the beginning of the year and total cost at the end.

Required:

The revised profit statement for 19X8.

Solution

Profit Statement, 19X8

	£	£
Sales		6,000
Less: Opening stock (marginal cost)	500	
Production costs	4,000	
Closing stock (total cost)	(800)	
Cost of goods sold		3,700
Gross profit		2,300

Gross profit is £2,300 in Example 6.12 as compared with £2,000 in Example 6.11. Profit is therefore inflated by £300 as the result of switching from one valuation method to another and using the total cost closing stock figure, £800, instead of the marginal cost closing stock figure, £500. As the result of the change, reported profits are greater than actual profits and wrong conclusions may be reached concerning the performance of Mill Ltd. It is therefore important for valuation procedures to be consistently applied so that reported results fairly reflect performance during the year, and valid comparisons can be made with results achieved in a previous accounting period.

While consistency is a fundamental accounting concept (see section 6.5.11 of this chapter), it does not mean that methods, once adopted, should never be changed, but sound and convincing arguments must be put forward to justify departures from existing practice. The essential test is whether management can show that the new procedures result in a fairer view of the financial performance and position of the concern. If it is decided that a change should be made to a previously accepted method of valuation, the impact on comparability between two sets of figures must be noted and, wherever possible, also quantified, so that it can be taken into account when measuring performance. For example, when a firm switches from marginal cost to the far more popular total cost method of stock valuation, relevant balances for the previous year, which are also reported, must be re-computed, using total cost, so that a proper assessment of comparative performance can be made.

It must be emphasised that inconsistent accounting methods can have a marked effect on the information contained in accounting statements. The changes are not always explained as clearly as they should be, and the banker must scrutinise the accounts vigilantly to ensure that distorted financial information does not cause him to make a wrong investment decision.

Assignment   Students should now work Question 6.9 at the end of the chapter.

6.5.9   Prudence Concept   The prudence concept (sometimes called the concept of conservatism) requires the accountant to make full provision for all expected losses and not to anticipate revenues until they are realised. A good example of how this concept affects accounting practice is the basic rule that stock should be valued at the lower of cost and net realisable value (NRV). Where NRV is above cost, the profit likely to arise in the near future is ignored and stock remains in the accounts at the lower figure until the sale occurs, i.e. revenue is not anticipated. On the other hand, where NRV is below cost, stock must be immediately re-stated at the lower figure so that full provision is made for the likely future loss.

Approval of a prudent approach to profit measurement is based on the potential dangers of an over-optimistic calculation which may be used as the basis for an excessive withdrawal of funds, by ownership, which deprives the concern of much needed resources. Another possible pitfall is that an attractive presentation of the current position, not justified by the underlying facts, may cause management wrongly to expand the level of operations and, when this happens, heavy losses can result. New projects often involve a substantial commitment of resources, the bulk of which is tied up in fixed assets. The only way the firm is likely to get its money back is by using these assets to produce and sell goods at a profit. Caution is therefore highly desirable when management is considering whether to make an investment, and any accounting statement used to help reach this decision should be prepared on a prudent basis. This may mean that, occasionally, good opportunities are missed, but this will not happen often, and the likely loss from an ill-conceived investment will be many times greater than the profit possibly forgone.

It is important, however, not to take the prudence concept too far. Where there are a number of likely outcomes, it is usually wise to choose the lower figure, but profit should not be deliberately under-stated. Accounting statements are used as the basis for decision-making, and they should contain realistic, not excessively pessimistic, financial information. Under-statement can be just as misleading as overstatement, and although the potential loss from the mis-allocation of resources which may result is less, it can be avoided by preparers of accounting reports exercising a reasonable level of caution.

6.5.10 Materiality Accounting statements should contain only those financial facts which are material, or relevant, to the decision being taken by the recipient of the report. It is therefore important for the accountant to be familiar with the user's requirement so that he can decide which information should be included and excluded. For example, if an accounting statement is prepared to help management assess which departments are most successful, it is clearly important for the report to show the profits earned by each of them. This means identifying the revenues and expenditures which relate to each department, but unnecessary detail is omitted. For example, a manager is interested in knowing the individual amounts expended on materials, wages, power, depreciation, etc., but not on Christmas gratuities, the ingredients for morning coffee, and paper towels. Trivial items are therefore grouped together under the heading 'sundry expenses'. For similar reasons balance sheets contain values for the various main categories of assets and liabilities but do not give figures for each item of plant, stock, etc.

Accounting statements prepared for shareholders of limited companies contain even less detail. This is partly because such information is of little interest to them. It is management's job to decide how to allocate resources between various investment opportunities, while the shareholder is primarily interested in assessing whether the overall performance is satisfactory. It is therefore considered desirable to keep to a minimum detailed facts which may be difficult to assimilate, and instead concentrate on the broad overall pattern of developments. It must be admitted that the sophisticated institutional investor would welcome far more detail than is provided in the published accounts, but there is a natural reluctance to publish sensitive material which could be of use to competitors. The banker is in a different position. Although he is an external user of accounting statements, confidential information can be made available to him, on an individual basis, and is normally insisted upon as one of the pre-conditions for a loan decision.

There is another aspect of materiality, and this concerns the amount of detail which the accountant goes into when measuring profit. A good example is the failure of the accountant to distinguish between capital and revenue expenditure where the amount spent on a fixed asset is small. For example, minor items of office equipment such as staplers and punches last for a number of years, but it is not usually considered worthwhile to capitalise and depreciate them systematically over their expected useful life. Instead they are written off immediately against revenue. A detailed treatment is justified only if the extra cost involved produces a significant improvement in the quality of the information contained in accounting statements. When applying this test, it must be remembered that, because of the need for estimates to be made and judgment to be exercised, the reported profit figure is at best an approximation, and is unlikely to be improved by making precise adjustments for trivial items.

6.5.11 SSAP2: Disclosure of Accounting Policies

This chapter has given some examples of the numerous different ways of valuing individual business assets. The number of possible combinations of values are endless and, for a firm of any size, it is possible to come up with literally thousands of different profit figures, depending upon which valuation methods are used to measure performance during a particular accounting period.

Up until the 1960s, the calculation of reported profit was normallly left to company directors, and the accounting profession did no more than indicate the kind of valuation procedures it considered most appropriate. A number of well-publicised scandals in the late 1960s, however, drew the public's attention to the fact that reported profit was not the precise calculation that they had previously believed it to be, and that two accountants could come up with totally different profit figures, depending upon the valuation procedures chosen. This caused a crisis of confidence within the accounting profession and led to the establishment of the Accounting Standards Committee (ASC) in 1970 (to be replaced by the Accounting Standards Board in late 1990).

The ASC's job is to reduce the range of accounting methods used by publishing instructions, called Statements of Standard Accounting Practice (SSAPs), setting out appropriate accounting procedures for companies to follow. SSAP2 (issued 1971) makes a major contribution to the achievement of this objective by striving to ensure that:

1. companies prepare their accounts in accordance with certain 'fundamental accounting concepts' specified in the statement. Any departure from these concepts must be disclosed.
2. companies report which 'accounting policies' they have chosen from the 'accounting bases' available for the purpose of valuing the assets and liabilities appearing in the accounts.

SSAP2 does not specifiy the procedures to be adopted in individual cases; this job is done in other statements issued by the ASC, e.g. SSAP9 which deals with the valuation of stock and long-term contracts.

The terms 'fundamental accounting concepts', 'accounting bases' and 'accounting policies' are given the following meanings by SSAP2.

1. *Fundamental Accounting Concepts*   Company accounts are based on the following four concepts, which are considered to be of fundamental importance if the accounts are to give a true and fair view:

    - the going concern concept
    - the accruals concept
    - the consistency concept
    - the prudence concept.

    The above list covers four of the 10 concepts discussed in the previous section of this chapter. Obviously it was the ASC's view that these four concepts were more important than the others, though no explanation for giving them special priority was provided.

2. *Accounting Bases*   The description 'accounting bases' means the same as accounting methods, and we have seen in this chapter that accountants have developed a wide range of different methods for valuing individual assets and liabilities. For example, the alternative methods available to account for the decline in the value of tangible assets includes the straight line and reducing balance methods; also there is the sum of the digits method, the units of service method, and the annuity method. Each of these methods is acceptable for the purpose of valuing fixed assets for inclusion in company accounts, and they all broadly comply with the four fundamental accounting concepts.

3. *Accounting Policies*   This is the term used to describe the particular accounting bases (methods) used by a company for the purpose of valuing assets and liabilities. The following extract from the 1988 accounts of TSB Group plc is a typical example of how companies disclose the accounting policies used for the purpose of calculating depreciation.

    Depreciation

    Depreciation on freehold buildings and leaseholds with more than 50 years unexpired is provided on a straight line basis at 2% per annum. Other leasehold interests are written off by equal installments over the unexpired term of the lease. No depreciation is provided on the freehold land.

Computers and other equipment are depreciated on a straight line basis over their estimated lives of generally between three and ten years.

The main provisions of SSAP2 were given statutory backing by the Companies Act 1985.

Example 6.13

Larchmont Ltd was established on 1 January 19X3 to manufacture a single product using a machine which cost £400,000. The machine is expected to last for four years and than have a scrap value of £52,000. The machine will produce a similar number of items each year and annual profits before depreciation are expected to be in the region of £200,000. The financial controller has suggested that the machine should be depreciated using either the straight line method or the reducing balance method. If the latter method is used, it has been estimated that an annual depreciation rate of 40% would be appropriate.

Required:
(a) Calculations of the annual depreciation charges and the net book values of the fixed asset at the end of 19X3, 19X4, 19X5, and 19X6 using:
(i) the straight line method,
(ii) the reducing balance method.
(b) A discussion of the differing implications of these two methods for the financial information published by Larchmont Ltd for the years 19X3-19X6 inclusive. You should also advise management which method you consider more appropriate bearing in mind expected profit levels.

Solution

(a)

Year	Straight line method Depreciation charge £	Net book value £	Reducing balance method Depreciation charge £	Net book value £
19X3	87,000	313,000	160,000	240,000
19X4	87,000	226,000	96,000	144,000
19X5	87,000	139,000	57,600	86,400
19X6	87,000	52,000	34,560	51,840
	348,000		348,160	

(b) Either method succeeds in reducing the book value of the machine to its expected scrap value at the end of four years. Also the aggregate depreciation charge amounts to approximately the same figure.

The allocation of the total depreciation charge between the four years varies significantly depending on which accounting policy is used. In 19X3 the reducing balance method produces a charge which is £73,000 *higher* than under the straight line method; the situation is substantially reversed in 19X6 when the reducing balance charge is £52,440 *lower*.

The effect of the different rates of asset write-off has significant implications for the level of reported profits and the balance sheet figures for capital employed. If the straight line basis is used, reported profit is expected to be fairly stable at £113,000 (£200,000–£87,000). The reducing balance basis will result in a reported profit of £40,000 in 19X3, increasing to £165,440 in 19X6. In the balance sheet, the book value of fixed assets will decline much more quickly under the reducing balance method.

The level of activity is expected to remain unchanged over the four years and so the straight line basis, which produces an equal annual charge, is to be preferred.

Assignment Students should now work Question 6.10 at the end of the chapter.

6.6 REVIEW

After reading the chapter and working the chapter end questions, students should be able to:

- Apply the 'lower of cost and net realisable value' rule to the valuation of stock.
- Account for stock on the FIFO, marginal cost and total cost bases.
- Distinguish between capital expenditure and revenue expenditure.
- Account for depreciation on the straight line and reducing balance bases.
- Account for goodwill.
- Be familiar with the nature and purpose of the 10 accounting concepts.
- Understand the main features and objectives of SSAP2.

6.7 QUESTIONS

Question 6.1

Give the basic rule for valuing stock. Apply this rule to the facts provided below and calculate the total value of stock to be included in the accounts.

Product	Cost	Net Realisable Value
	£	£
A	2,400	2,760
B	1,290	740
C	3,680	750
D	2,950	4,760
E	6,280	9,730

Question 6.2

The Wigan Manufacturing Company Ltd commenced business on 1 January 19X8. One product of a standard type is produced. The following information has been obtained from the company's books.

	19X8	19X9
	£	£
Material consumed	108,000	186,000
Manufacturing wages (all direct)	132,000	234,000
Fixed overhead expenses:		
Manufacturing	72,000	94,500
Administration, selling and distribution	34,000	25,800
	Units	Units
Output	12,000	21,000
Sales (at a selling price of £34 per unit throughout the two years) ..	11,700	12,900

There was no stock of partly finished units at the end of either year. The output of 19X8 was produced at an even rate throughout that year and, similarly, production was at an even rate during 19X9. Costs in both years were also evenly spread.

The company's accountant plans to prepare accounts, for internal use, valuing stock on the basis of marginal cost. The company's auditors, however, intend to value stock on the basis of total cost.

Required:
  (a) Calculations of the quantity of stock on hand at the end of 19X8 and 19X9.
  (b) Calculations of the value of stock on the basis of the following accounting policies at the end of each of the two years:
    (i)   the marginal cost basis, and

    (ii) the total cost basis.

(c) Comments of the effect of these valuations on reported profit.

Question 6.3

Seconds Ltd started trading on 1 January and during that month undertook the following transactions in respect of product Alpha:

Date-Jan	Purchases Units	Cost per Unit £	Sales Units	Price per Unit £
8	100	20	—	—
13	60	25	—	—
14	—	—	125	40
17	75	30	—	—
22	—	—	30	42

Required:

Using the FIFO basis for matching purchases with sales, calculations of the figures for (a) closing stock, (b) cost of goods sold, and (c) gross profit.

Question 6.4

(a) How would you distinguish between capital and revenue expenditure, and why is it important to make a correct allocation?

(b) State, with reasons, in which of the two categories you would place each of the following items:

    (i)   Replacement of the blade on a cutting machine which was damaged as the result of using poor quality raw material inputs.

    (ii)   A feeding device costing £1,000 which is fixed to a machine so as to enable a 20% increase in throughput each hour.

    (iii) The cost of transporting, to the factory, a new machine supplied by a Japanese company.

    (iv) Second hand plant purchased at a cost of £1,500.

    (v)   Repairs to the plant mentioned in (iv) above before it is ready for use £300.

Question 6.5

Simon is a surveyor who purchases old properties in poor condition. He incurs expenditure on improving these properties which he then resells. His balance sheet at 31 December 19X2 was as follows:

	£			£
Properties on hand (including		Capital		79,000
expenses on purchase):				
1	30,250			
2	29,350			
Bank Balance	19,400			
	79,000			79,000

During 19X3 he bought three more properties:

	Cost	Legal expenses borne by Simon	Cost of improvement
	£	£	£
3	36,250	1,000	260
4	24,000	750	1,000
5	25,000	800	520

and sold the following three properties:

	Sale price	Legal expenses borne by Simon
	£	£
1	34,000	400
3	42,500	500
4	31,250	350

General expenses incurred and paid during 19X3 amounted to £2,500.

Required:
   (a) Simon's bank account for 19X3.
   (b) A profit and loss account for the year 19X3 covering Simon's property deals and a balance sheet at 31 December 19X3.

Notes:
1.   Cash due from the sale of property 4 was not received until 5 January 19X4.
2.   There were no other transactions during the year and all receipts and payments were by cheque.

Question 6.6
A machine was purchased on 1 January 19X1 for £20,000. It is estimated to possess a five-year working life, at the end of which it will possess a residual value of £1,000.

Required:
   (a) Calculate the depreciation charge for each year and the net book value of the fixed asset at the end of each year using:

    (i)   the straight line method,

    (ii)   the reducing balance method, applying a depreciation rate of 45%.

(b)   Indicate which depreciation method would produce the higher reported profit for each of the years 19X1–X5, and for the entire five-year period.

Question 6.7

Buy Ltd paid Mr Sale £120,000, cash, to acquire his business, Sale & Co., as a going concern on 1 January 19X1. The assets taken over were considered to be worth the following amounts:

	£
Fixed assets	71,500
Stock	20,000
Debtors	10,000

In addition, Buy Ltd assumed responsibility for paying Sale & Co.'s outstanding creditors which amounted to £5,000. The policy of Buy Ltd is to write off goodwill over a five-year period.

Required:

(a)   Calculate the goodwill arising on the acquisition of Sale & Co.

(b)   Show how goodwill will appear in the balance sheet of Buy Ltd as at 31 December 19X1.

Question 6.8

Where accounts are prepared in accordance with the *accruals concept,* cash receipts and payments may precede, coincide with, or follow the period in which revenues and expenses are recognised. Give two examples of each of the following:

(a)   A cash receipt that precedes the period in which revenue is recognised.

(b)   A cash receipt that coincides with the period in which revenue is recognised.

(c)   A cash receipt that follows the period in which revenue is recognised.

(d)   A cash payment that precedes the period in which expense is recognised.

(e)   A cash payment that coincides with the period in which expense is recognised.

(f)   A cash payment that follows the period in which expense is recognised.

Question 6.9

The summarised trading account of Change Ltd for 19X1 contained the following information:

Trading Account for 19X1

	£	£
Sales		100,000
Less: Opening stock	7,000	
Purchases	80,000	
Closing stock	(11,000)	
Cost of goods sold		76,000
Gross profit		24,000

Opening stock is valued at marginal cost, but the directors have now decided that total cost is more suitable, and this basis was used for the purpose of valuing closing stock. The value of opening stock, on the total cost basis, is found to be £10,000.

Required:

(a) Prepare a revised trading account for Change Ltd complying with the consistency concept.

(b) Indicate the effect of the revision on the *net* profit figure reported by Change Ltd for 19X1.

Question 6.10

At the beginning of 19X1 Deer Ltd was incorporated and manufactures a single product. At the end of the first year's operations the company's accountant prepared a draft profit and loss account which contained the following financial information:

Profit and Loss Account of Deer Ltd for 19X1

	£	£
Sales (200,000 units)		600,000
Less: Prime cost of units manufactured during 19X1 (500,000 units)	800,000	
Deduct closing stock	480,000	
Prime cost of goods sold	320,000	
Fixed Costs:		
Factory expenses	200,000	
General expenses	100,000	620,000
Net loss		£20,000

Additional finance is required, and the directors are worried that the company's bank manager is unlikely to regard the financial facts shown above as a satisfactory basis for a further advance. The company's accountant made the following observation and suggestion:

'The cause of the poor result for 19X1 was the decision to value closing stock on the prime cost basis. An acceptable alternative practice would involve charging factory expenses to the total number of units produced and carrying forward an appropriate proportion of those expenses as part of the closing stock value.'

Required:
(a) A revised profit and loss account, for presentation to the company's bank, valuing closing stock on the total (absorption) cost basis suggested by the company's accountant.
(b) Assuming that, in 19X2, the company again produces 500,000 units but sells 700,000 units, calculate the expected profit using each of the two stock valuation bases. Assume also that, in 19X2, sales price per unit and costs incurred will be the same as for 19X1.
(c) Comment briefly on the accountant's suggestion and its likely effect on the bank manager's response to the request for additional finance.

CHAPTER 7

Partnerships

7.1 INTRODUCTION

A partnership is a firm (other than a limited company) with more than one owner. The most common reasons for forming a partnership are:

- to raise the necessary finance to fund planned operations,
- to pool together complementary skills, for example an engineer who is very capable at developing new products may need the services of a salesman to market them.

The legal background is provided by the Partnership Act 1890 which defines a partnership as

. . . the relation which subsists between persons carrying on a business in common with a view of profit.

There is no formal legal procedure necessary to create a partnership; it can be deemed to exist because people are trading in a way which brings them within the definition. It is very important to determine whether a person is a partner as the liability of each partner for all of the firm's debts is unlimited; if the firm cannot pay, then each partner becomes personally liable to the extent of the entire debt. This is obviously of great importance to the lending banker when considering whether to grant a loan.

The number of partners allowed to combine in a partnership is limited to 20, although some specific exemptions are granted, for example firms of Chartered Accountants can have any number of partners. If a firm which is limited to 20 partners wishes to seek funds from a larger group, then incorporation as a limited company is first necessary.

Partnerships use the same basic accountancy techniques as those described so far in this book in the context of the sole trader, although some modifications are required in their application to suit the different constitution of the partnership. There is no legal requirement for partnerships to prepare annual accounts, but the need to share profits between the partners and for partners to submit tax returns makes their routine production essential if the conduct of the partnership is to proceed smoothly. As with sole traders, there is no necessity for the contents of partnership accounts to be made public even though they may relate to significant economic entities; this contrasts with the disclosure requirements imposed on limited companies described in chapters 8 and 9.

7.2 THE PARTNERSHIP AGREEMENT

The owners of a partnership, the partners, also manage it, and each partner can enter into contracts on behalf of the firm which are binding on the partnership as a whole. In these circumstances, the partners must have a great deal of mutual trust, and it is best for the manner in which the partnership is to be run to be formally set out in a legally binding Partnership Agreement signed by all of the partners. Examples of the matters to be covered by such an agreement are:

- The purpose for which the partnership is formed.
- The amount of capital each partner is to contribute.
- How profits and losses are to be divided between the partners.
- Whether separate capital and current accounts are to be maintained.
- The extent to which partners can make drawings.
- The frequency with which accounts are to be prepared and whether they are to be subjected to an independent audit.
- Regulations to be observed when: a partner retires; a new partner is admitted; or the profit sharing ratio changes.

Where no formal agreement exists, the terms of the partnership may be concluded from past behaviour, for example if profits have always been divided between two partners in the ratio 2:1, without dissent from either partner, then this is presumed to be the agreed ratio. The Partnership Act 1890 provides a 'safety net' of regulations which apply when there is no agreement, either formal or informal, to the contrary. Among the major of these provisions are:

- All profits and losses are to be shared equally among the partners.
- No interest on capital or remuneration for conducting the partnership business is payable to any partner.
- Every partner is authorised to take part in the firm's management.
- All existing partners must agree to the admission of a new partner.

7.3 PARTNERSHIP ACCOUNTS

On a routine basis, usually yearly, the profit or loss made by a partnership must be divided between the partners; the basis on which this is done and the related accounting entries are dealt with in sections 7.3.1 and 7.3.2 of this chapter. On other occasions, not of a routine nature, further adjustments must be made because the value of profit calculated in the conventional profit and loss account of a going concern contains only realised profits. For example, the increase in value of a piece of land held as a fixed asset is only recognised when it is sold and the profit realised, even though at any particular date its actual value may be greatly in excess of its book value at historical cost. The procedures applied when it is necessary to bring into account changes in asset values which have not previously been recorded in the books are dealt with in section 7.3.3 of this chapter.

7.3.1 The Division of Profit The net profit of a partnership is calculated in the usual way, and is then transferred to the Appropriation Account where it is divided between the partners in the agreed manner. The agreement may provide for a straightforward allocation in accordance with a specific ratio, such as 3:2; alternatively, precise adjustments may be made to take account of the following factors:

- *Capital* The partners may provide different amounts of capital; this involves sacrificing different amounts of interest which could have been earned by, for example, putting the money in a bank deposit account. Compensation for this can be achieved by allowing a deduction to be made in the appropriation account for interest on partner's capital. The rate of interest may be fixed in the agreement or, because rates of interest fluctuate, it could be tied to some external indicator, such as the rate paid on long-term deposit accounts by banks. In whichever way the rate is determined, the greater the amount of capital a partner has invested in the firm, the greater is the interest received.
- *Salary* By deciding to join a partnership, each partner foregoes potential earnings as an employee of another firm. The sacrifice of alternative income may not be the same for each partner, for example one may contribute more valuable skills. This can be recognised by giving each partner a salary related to potential 'outside earnings'. Such salaries are also deducted from profit in the appropriation account.
- *Drawings* Partners make drawings from the firm which reduce the amount of their investment, and it may be decided to recognise this by charging partners interest on their drawings. This interest is then added to the profit to be shared between the partners. Students are not expected to be able to calculate the interest charged on

drawings; where such information is needed, it will be provided in
the question.

● *Residue* After any interest and salaries have been deducted, there
must be agreement on how to divide the residual profit or loss. The
ratio in which it is shared may be designed to reflect the partner's
seniority, or some other basis, such as equality, may be adopted.

Tutorial note:
Where there is no agreement on how profits are to be shared, the
Partnership Act 1890 applies, and the profit (or loss) is divided equally
between the partners.

The steps which are followed to carry out the division of partnership
profit are:

1. Determine the manner in which profit is to be divided.
2. Determine the value of profit or loss to be shared. The value found
   takes no account of any payments to the partners, for example in the
   form of interest or salaries, and is transferred to the appropriation
   account.
3. Add to profit any interest charged on drawings made by the partners.
4. Deduct from profit any interest allowed on capital account balances
   and any salaries payable to partners.
5. Split the residual profit or loss in the agreed ratio.

Steps 3 to 5 are recorded in the firm's books with the following entries:

Debit	Credit	With
Capital Account#	Profit and Loss Appropriation Account	Interest charged on Drawings
Profit and Loss Appropriation Account	Capital Account#	Interest allowed on Capital, Salaries and Share of Profit
Capital Account#	Profit and Loss Appropriation Account	Share of Losses

Tutorial note:
The entries marked '#' are instead made in the current accounts of partners
where such accounts are maintained (see section 7.3.2 of this chapter).

The division of profit in the appropriation account is illustrated in
Example 7.1.

Example 7.1

Oak and Tree are in partnership and prepare their accounts on a calendar year basis. They have agreed that profits are to be shared as follows:

1. Oak is to receive an annual salary of £5,000 and Tree one of £10,000.
2. 10% per annum interest is to be paid on each partner's capital account balance as on 1 January.
3. Residual profits and losses are to be shared equally.

On 1 January 19X6 the balance on Oak's capital account was £64,000 and on Tree's it was £30,000.

Required:
Prepare the partnership's appropriation account on the alternative assumptions that the profit for 19X6 was:

(a) £30,000
(b) £20,000

Solution

(a)   *Appropriation Account*

		£			£
Salary:	Oak	5,000	Profit		30,000
	Tree	10,000			
Interest:	Oak	6,400			
	Tree	3,000			
Residue:	Oak	2,800			
	Tree	2,800			
		30,000			30,000

(b)   *Appropriation Account*

		£			£
Salary:	Oak	5,000	Profit		20,000
	Tree	10,000	Share of loss: Oak		2,200
Interest:	Oak	6,400	Tree		2,200
	Tree	3,000			
		24,400			24,400

Tutorial note:
If there is no agreement to the contrary, the profits in the above example would have been divided between the partners in accordance with the terms

of the Partnership Act 1890. Each would have received an equal share, namely, £15,000 in (a), and £10,000 in (b).

Assignment Students should now work Question 7.1, which extends the above example to three partners and includes interest charged on drawings, and Question 7.2, both of which are at the end of this chapter.

7.3.2 Capital and Current Accounts The capital which each partner invests in the business can be divided into two elements:

1. The part which is permanently required to finance the ability of the firm to trade. It is invested in fixed assets and working capital and cannot be withdrawn without reducing the capacity of the business.
2. The part which can be withdrawn by the partners as drawings.

The permanent capital of each partner is entered in a 'Capital Account'. The partnership agreement usually stipulates the amount of permanent capital invested by each partner, and the balances remain constant until the partners agree to a change. Routine transactions between partners and the firm are entered in a 'Current Account'. The current account balance fluctuates as it is credited with each partner's share of profits, in the form of interest, salary and share of residue, and is debited with drawings and interest on drawings. To prevent partners withdrawing more than their entitlement, the partnership agreement should state that no current account is allowed to have a debit balance without the consent of the other partners.

Example 7.2

Disk and Drive trade in partnership. The following information relates to 19X7:

	Disk £	Drive £
Current Account Balance 1 January 19X7	9,130	8,790
Interest allowed on Capital	1,000	1,500
Interest charged on Drawings	150	390
Salary	5,000	3,000
Share of Residual Profit	6,250	6,250
Cash Drawings	7,160	8,240
Stock Drawings	120	80

Required:

Prepare the current accounts of Disk and Drive for 19X7. For each entry indicate clearly the location of its corresponding double entry.

Solution

Current Accounts

	Disk £	Drive £		Disk £	Drive £
Appropriation Account:			Balance b/d	9,130	8,790
Interest	150	390	Appropriation Account:		
Drawings:			Interest	1,000	1,500
Cash Account ..	7,160	8,240	Salary	5,000	3,000
Purchases A/c ..	120	80	Residue	6,250	6,250
Balance c/d	13,950	10,830			
	21,380	19,540		21,380	19,540

It is possible for substantial balances to accumulate in the current accounts where partners consistently withdraw less then their share of the profits. The funds represented by these balances may have been invested in trading assets, and so have taken on the aspect of permanent capital, that is, they are not available for quick withdrawal. This position is shown in Illustration 7.1.

Illustration 7.1

The following is the summarised balance sheet of Paper and Clip at 31 December 19X9:

			£000
Fixed Assets			75
Working Capital			25
			100

	Paper £000	Clip £000	Total £000
Capital Accounts	20	20	40
Current Accounts	30	30	60
	50	50	100

It is clear that the current account balances could not be withdrawn without reducing the size of the business, since a large proportion of these balances has been invested in fixed assets which would have to be sold to release cash. This is unlikely to happen, and so to bring the balance sheet into line with economic reality, the partners may agree that each of them should transfer, say, £25,000 from current to capital account. The transfer is entered in the books by a debit in each current account and a corresponding credit in each capital account. This increase in capital account balances does not provide the firm with any additional funds, but simply recognises that the partners have invested funds previously available as drawings in the permanent structure of the undertaking. When *additional* capital funds are required by a partnership, they must be introduced by the partners and credited to their capital accounts.

Assignment   Students should now work Question 7.3 at the end of this chapter.

7.3.3 Change in Profit Sharing Ratio   It is necessary to revalue the assets when there is an alteration in the ratio in which profits are split so that changes in value up to that time are shared in the ratio which prevailed while they accrued; subsequent changes are shared in the new ratio. Failure to adopt this approach means that all value changes would be shared in the new ratio, even though this did not apply while some of the changes took place. Some assets may have increased in value while others have lost value, and a value should be assigned to goodwill, that is, the excess of the value of the firm as a whole over that of its separate tangible assets. The necessary adjustments to values are made at the time of the change in the ratio through a revaluation account, in which the following entries are made:

Debit	Credit	With
Revaluation Account	Asset Account	Reduction in asset value
Asset Account	Revaluation Account	Increase in asset value

The revaluation account contains all the increases and decreases in value, and its balance, the net surplus or deficit, is shared between the partners in the agreed ratio. Each partner's share of the net adjustment is entered in his capital account as it is permanent in nature. If the original values of any assets are to be reinstated, the adjustments are also made through the revaluation account, the balance on which is transferred to the partners' capital accounts in accordance with the new ratio.

Example 7.3

Cut and Hack are in partnership sharing profits and losses equally. The firm's summarised balance sheet at 30 June 19X7 was:

	£
Fixed Assets	70,000
Working Capital	30,000
	100,000

financed by:
Capital Accounts

	£
Cut	50,000
Hack	50,000
	100,000

Hack decides to reduce the amount of time he spends working for the business, and it is agreed that from 1 July 19X7 profits should be shared between Cut and Hack in the ratio 2:1 respectively.

The partners consider that fair current values for the assets on 30 June 19X7 are:

	£
Fixed Assets	100,000
Working Capital	35,000
Goodwill	55,000

The assets are to be recorded in the books at their original values, after the necessary adjustments consequent upon the change in the profit sharing ratio have been effected.

Required:
- (a) Prepare the revaluation accounts of the partnership to record all the adjustments made to asset values.
- (b) Prepare the partners' capital accounts showing clearly the balances after all adjustments have been made.
- (c) Prepare the revised balance sheet of Cut and Hack.

Solution

(a)   *Revaluation Account (old profit sharing ratio)*

	£		£
Surplus: Cut	45,000	Fixed Assets	30,000
Hack	45,000	Working Capital	5,000
		Goodwill	55,000
	90,000		90,000

Revaluation Account (new profit sharing ratio)

	£		£
Fixed Assets	30,000	Cut	60,000
Working Capital	5,000	Hack	30,000
Goodwill	55,000		
	90,000·		90,000

(b)   *Capital Accounts*

	Cut £	Hack £		Cut £	Hack £
Revaluation			Opening		
Account	60,000	30,000	Balance	50,000	50,000
Balance c/d	35,000	65,000	Revaluation		
			Account	45,000	45,000
	95,000	95,000		95,000	95,000

(c)   *Revised Balance Sheet*

	£
Fixed Assets	70,000
Working Capital	30,000
	100,000

	£
financed by:	
Capital accounts	
Cut	35,000
Hack	65,000
	100,000

Assignments   Students should now work Questions 7.4 and 7.5 at the end of the chapter. Question 7.4 involves the preparation of full partnership final accounts from cash records, and Question 7.5 is based on the trial balance.

7.4 REVIEW

After reading the chapter and working the chapter end questions, students should:

- Be able to define a partnership.
- Understand the need for a partnership agreement and its usual coverage.
- Know the regulations for sharing profits laid down by the Partnership Act 1890 and when they are to be applied.
- Understand the difference between capital and current accounts and why they are maintained.
- Be able to share profits and losses between partners and enter the results in their accounts.
- Be able to use a revaluation account to record the adjustments necessary when there is a change in the profit sharing ratio or membership and understand why these adjustments are needed.
- Be able to prepare the annual accounts of a partnership from incomplete records and the trial balance.

7.5 QUESTIONS

Questions 7.1 to 7.3 test individual aspects of partnership accounts specifically dealt with in this chapter; Questions 7.4 and 7.5 deal with the preparation of a full set of partnership accounts.

Question 7.1

Jack, Jill and Jane trade together in partnership, and they have agreed to share profits and losses on the following basis:

1. Annual salaries of £10,000, £7,500, and £5,000 are to be paid to Jack, Jill and Jane respectively.
2. Interest of 12% is to be allowed on the average balance of each partner's capital account for the year.
3. Interest of 12% is to be charged on drawings.
4. Residual profits and losses are to be shared: Jack 40%; Jill 40%; and Jane 20%.

You are given the following additional information:

1. On 1 January 19X2, the balances on the partners' capital accounts were:

	£
Jack	30,000
Jill	20,000
Jane	40,000

On 30 June 19X2, Jill introduced further capital of £5,000.

2. The charges for interest on drawings for 19X2 are:

	£
Jack	600
Jill	450
Jane	400

3. The firm made a profit of £42,000 in 19X2.

Required:
Prepare the partnership appropriation account for 19X2.

Question 7.2
Required:
   (a) Prepare the partnership appropriation account of the Jack, Jill and
        Jane partnership using the information given in Question 7.1 and
        assuming that no partnership agreement exists.
   (b) Explain the basis on which you have divided the profit in part (a).

Question 7.3
Ice and Cube are in partnership, sharing profits and losses equally. The
balances on their capital and current accounts at 1 January 19X4 are:

	Capital £	Current £
Ice	50,000	30,000
Cube	60,000	20,000

The trading profit for 19X4 was £45,000, and during the year the cash
drawings of Ice were £12,500 and of Cube £14,000. In addition, Ice took
over one of the firm's cars at its book value of £1,500 to give to his daughter
as an eighteenth birthday present.

The partners review the accounts for 19X4 and decide that, as some of
their current account balances have been invested in the expansion of the
firm, Ice should transfer £20,000 and Cube £10,000 from current to capital
account.

Required:
Prepare the partners' current and capital accounts for 19X4.

Question 7.4

Second and Minute started trading as retail grocers in partnership on 1
January 19X4, but did not keep a set of double entry books. The firm's
bank account, for 19X4, prepared from the record of cheques issued and
cash paid into the bank, was:

	£		£
Capital introduced:		Purchases	160,000
Second	20,000	Wages	17,000
Minute	20,000	Rent and rates	3,500
Sales receipts banked	200,000	Light and heat	1,260
		Delivery van	19,000
		Drawings: Second	18,000
		Minute	16,000
		Balance c/d	5,240
	240,000		240,000

Notes:
1. The following payments were made directly from cash sales receipts:

	£
Petrol for van	2,000
Maintenance	1,000
Advertising	900
Purchases	2,500
	6,400

2. The van, purchased on 1 January 19X4, is expected to have a life of five
   years, at the end of which its scrap value will be £3,000.
3. The partners agree that separate capital and current accounts are to be
   kept and all profits and losses are to be shared equally.
4. At 31 December 19X4:

	£
Debtors	5,460
Trade creditors	3,800
Prepaid rent	100
Light and heat accrued	140
Stock	9,200

5. During 19X4 both Second and Minute took groceries for personal use
   at cost price as follows:

	£
Second	1,000
Minute	1,260
	2,260

Required:

Prepare the trading and profit and loss account for the year to 31 December 19X4 and the balance sheet at that date.

Question 7.5

The following is the trial balance of Bean and Stalk, who trade in partnership, at 31 March 19X3:

	£	£
Capital Account Balances 1 April 19X2:		
Bean		30,000
Stalk		10,000
Current Account Balances 1 April 19X2:		
Bean		3,000
Stalk		5,000
Sales		150,000
Stock 1 April 19X2	30,000	
Wages	14,500	
Rent	5,000	
Expenses	3,000	
Heat and light	1,200	
Debtors/creditors	14,000	11,500
Delivery costs	5,300	
Drawings		
Bean	7,000	
Stalk	9,000	
Cash	4,500	
Fixed assets	6,000	
Purchases	110,000	
	209,500	209,500

Notes:

1. Stock at 31 March 19X3 was valued at £40,000.
2. Depreciation of £1,500 is to be written off the fixed assets for the year to 31 March 19X3.
3. At 31 March 19X3 wages accrued amounted to £500 and rent of £1,000 was prepaid.
4. On 1 February 19X3 the firm ordered and paid for goods costing £700. These were recorded as purchases but were never received as they were lost by the carrier responsible for their delivery. The carrier accepted

liability for the loss during March 19X3 and paid full compensation of £700 in April 19X3. No entries had been made in the books in respect of the loss or claim.

5. Bean took goods which had cost the firm £340 for his own use during the year. No entry had been made in the books to record this.

6. The partnership agreement provided that profits and losses should be shared equally between the partners after:

   (a) allowing annual salaries of £2,000 to Bean and £4,000 to Stalk;
   (b) allowing interest of 5% per annum on the balance of each partner's capital account; and
   (c) charging Bean £200 and Stalk £300 interest in drawings.

7. The balances on the capital accounts shall remain unchanged, all adjustments being recorded in the current accounts.

Required:
Prepare the trading, profit and loss and appropriation accounts for the Bean and Stalk partnership for the year to 31 March 19X3 and the balance sheet at that date.

CHAPTER 8

Limited Companies

The three main ways in which business activity is structured within the private sector of the economy were outlined in chapter 1; these are the sole trader, the partnership and the limited company. The accounting practices of sole traders and partnerships have been examined in earlier chapters, and here we turn our attention to the form and content of the accounts of limited companies.

8.1 FORMATION OF 'REGISTERED' COMPANIES

A limited company is formed by registering under the Companies Act 1985, hence the term 'registered' company. Registration is a fairly simple process, but certain formalities must be complied with. It is possible for the individuals wishing to form a limited company to do the work themselves; alternatively they may choose to employ a specialist company registration agent who charges a fee in the region of £150. The following information must be filed with the Registrar of Companies at, or soon after, the registration date:

1. The names and addresses of the first directors.
2. A statement showing the amount of the company's authorised share capital (see chapter 9.1).
3. The address of the company's registered office.
4. The company's memorandum of association and articles of association.

A company must have at least two shareholders whose names and addresses appear in the memorandum to demonstrate the fact that this requirement has been fulfilled. The memorandum also gives the company's name and the nature of its proposed operations which are contained in the 'objects' clause(s).

The articles of association set out the internal rules and regulations of the company which must be observed by both shareholders and management. They deal with such matters as the voting rights of shareholders, the appointment and powers of directors, and the borrowing powers of the company. The Companies Act contains a model set of articles which applies to any limited company not filing articles of its own. The specimen articles also apply to the extent that they are not specifically modified or excluded by any articles which the company files. The model articles are rarely entirely suitable and articles 'tailor made' to the company's individual requirements are usually prepared.

8.2 TYPES OF COMPANY

There are a number of different types of registered company (see Figure 8.1), and the option chosen will depend on the nature and scale of expected business operations.

Figure 8.1

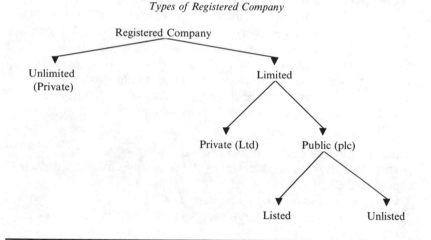

Types of Registered Company

It is first necessary to decide whether the company is to be registered with limited liability or unlimited liability. Usually the main reason for forming a company is to obtain the protection of limited liability for business activities which, by their very nature, are likely to involve a significant element of risk. For this reason unlimited companies are few and far between, and we do not therefore need to consider them further.

There are two basic categories of limited company: the public company and the private company. The public company must include the designatory letters plc after its name, and must have a minimum issued share capital (see chapter 9.1) of £50,000, of which at least one-quarter must be collected at the outset. Private companies must use the designatory letters Ltd and are not allowed to make an issue of shares or debentures to the general public. For both types of company the minimum number of shareholders is two and there is no maximum. Public companies are able to increase the marketability of their shares and debentures by making arrangements for these securities to be listed on the Stock Exchange, but this is a feasible exercise only for very large concerns which are then called listed companies.

Assignment   Students should now work Question 8.1 at the end of this chapter.

8.3   REASONS FOR FORMING A REGISTERED COMPANY

We have seen in chapter 7 that many businesses, initially run by a sole trader, eventually convert into a partnership to take advantage of the additional expertise and/or finance supplied by the new joint-owner. A further possible development of the organisational structure is the conversion of a partnership into a limited company or, where the intermediary stage is by-passed, the direct conversion of a sole trader into a limited company. The advantages of forming a limited company may be summarised as follows:

1. *Limited Liability*   The liability for the company's debts is restricted to the price paid for the shares. This places an effective ceiling on the amount which shareholders can lose should the company get into financial difficulties and be forced to liquidate.
2. *Shares Transferability*   Shareholders wishing to sell all or part of their interest in a limited company are entirely free to adopt this course of action provided a buyer can be found. This will be a relatively straightforward matter in the case of a public company whose shares are listed on the Stock Exchange. In the case of a private company, both finding a buyer and agreeing a price is much more difficult due to the absence of a readily available share valuation.
3. *Perpetual Succession*   The death or retirement of a sole trader naturally results in the business being treated as discontinued, but it is also a legal requirement in the case of partnerships. This outcome can be avoided, however, by the formation of a limited company which, being an artificial person, is not subject to the ills of the flesh. One benefit of continuity is that the reputation and goodwill of a limited company is likely to survive reasonably unimpaired when a director and/or shareholder terminate an involvement with the concern. In

addition, the numerous formalities associated with the cessation of an old partnership and the formation of a new partnership are entirely avoided; all that is required is a fresh entry in the share register.

Balanced against these and other advantages of incorporation must be the additional formalities associated with the formation of a limited company and the publicity and expense incurred during the continuance of its activities described in section 8.1 of this chapter.

8.4   SEPARATION OF OWNERSHIP AND MANAGEMENT

The registered company, which was created in the mid-nineteenth century, helped to transform completely the structure of British industry. The economy had previously been characterised by a very large number of small business units; sole traders and partnerships dominated, with the same individuals providing the bulk of the finance and taking all the major managerial decision, i.e. ownership and management were in the same hands. The essential feature of the registered company is that it has the facility to raise a large amount of capital by attracting finance in small amounts from many individuals. These 'share' holders do not necessarily play any part in running the concern since this job is often delegated to professional managers, i.e. the board of directors. These circumstances produce scope for a separation of the ownership group from the management group.

The extent of the separation varies tremendously, however, depending on the type of company involved. The small family firm, which previously traded as a partnership, may register as a private limited company simply to obtain the protection of limited liability. No other organisational changes need necessarily occur and the owners may continue to act also as the managers. In many private companies there is a looser connection between ownership and management, e.g. many of the shareholders may be members of the family interested in the business only as a source of unearned income, acquaintances of the family or business contacts, and play no part in management. In these circumstances, however, the members of the Board are likely to hold a significant proportion of the total shares issued.

It is in the public limited company, whose shares are listed on the Stock Exchange, that the separation between ownership and management is likely to be most marked; there may well be thousands of shareholders, with only a fraction of the issued share capital owned by members of the Board. Details of the shareholdings in Guinness plc are given in Figure 8.2.

Figure 8.2

Analysis of Shareholdings in Guinness plc, 1988

Category of Shareholder:	Holdings Number	%	Shares Number (mill.)	%
Individuals	84,293	91	153	17
Insurance companies and				
pension funds	748	1	171	19
Banks	2,094	2	10	1
Bank nominees	1,445	1	202	23
Non-bank nominees	2,676	3	207	24
Other corporate holders	1,686	2	140	16
	92,942	100	883	100
Size of Holdings:				
Up to 1,000 shares	53,002	57	26	3
1,001–10,000 shares	37,557	40	96	11
10,001–50,000 shares	1,560	2	31	3
Over 50,000 shares	823	1	730	83
	92,942	100	883	100

Numerically, the private shareholder is most significant, comprising 91% of the investors. However, together they own just 17% of the share capital. The financial institutions account, numerically, for just 4% of the shareholder group, but hold 43% of the shares. A separate section of the annual report shows that the directors own just over six million shares, a substantial figure, but less than 7% of the total issued share capital.

The separation of ownership and management puts the shareholder in a potentially vulnerable position. Money is invested in a company and the shareholder must rely on management to use the resources wisely. The shareholder naturally wishes to know what progress has been made, and it is for this reason that directors are legally required to publish a profit and loss account and balance sheet at least once a year (the Stock Exchange requires listed companies also to publish half yearly results).

Assignment Students should now work Question 8.2 at the end of this chapter.

8.5 CREDITORS' RISK

The introduction of limited liability shifted much of the financial risk associated with business activity from the owner to the creditor because, in the event of failure, the creditor has no automatic right to claim against the owner's personal assets. A careful assessment of the credit-worthiness of a potential customer therefore becomes a greater priority. A thorough examination of the company's financial standing, as exhibited in its balance sheet, is one sensible step in this process, particularly before it is decided to grant credit to a first time customer. And it is for this reason that company law requires companies to make this information publicly available at Companies House (see section 8.6.1 of this chapter).

It is, of course, possible for creditors to take additional steps to protect their investment. Possibilities include:

1. *Personal guarantees* The directors are required to give personal guarantees for business debts. This most commonly happens in the case of a private company, where the directors also own most of the shares, and the practical effect is to remove the protection of limited liability.
2. *Secured loans* The loan is secured against specific assets of the company (see chapter 9.3). The total fund available for the payment of creditors is in this case unchanged, but it is a device which enables particular individuals or institutional lenders to obtain a priority when repayment falls due.

8.6 REGULATIONS

8.6.1 Legal Regulations The affairs of registered companies are regulated by the Companies Acts 1985 and 1989. Students are not required to prepare accounts in accordance with the detailed disclosure requirements of the Act. However, answers should be presented in good form and, for this purpose, a specimen layout is given in Figure 8.3 which complies broadly with legal requirements.

Figure 8.3

Specimen Accounts for a Limited Company

Trading, Profit and Loss and Appropriation Account

	£	£
Turnover		xxx
Less: Cost of sales		xxx
Gross profit		xxx
Less: Distribution costs	xxx	
Administration expenses	xxx	xxx
Net profit before tax		xxx
Less: Corporation tax		xxx
Net profit after tax		xxx
Less: Dividends	xxx	
Transfer to reserves	xxx	xxx
Retained profit for the year		xxx
Retained profit at beginning of year		xxx
Retained profit at end of year		xxx

Balance Sheet

	£	£
Fixed Assets		
Intangible asset: Goodwill		xxx
Tangible assets: Land and Buildings	xxx	
Plant and Machinery	xxx	
Fixtures and Fittings	xxx	xxx
Investments		xxx
		xxx
Current Assets		
Stocks	xxx	
Trade debtors	xxx	
Prepayments	xxx	
Temporary investments	xxx	
Cash at bank	xxx	
	xxx	

	£	£
Less: Current Liabilities		
Debenture loans repayable within one year	xxx	
Unsecured loans repayable within one year	xxx	
Bank loans and overdrafts	xxx	
Trade creditors	xxx	
Taxation	xxx	
Dividends payable	xxx	
Accruals	xxx	
	xxx	
Net Current Assets (Working Capital)		xxx
Total Assets less Current Liabilities		xxx
Less: Non-current Liabilities		
Debentures	xxx	
Unsecured loans	xxx	
Taxation	xxx	xxx
		xxx
Financed by:		
Share capital: Authorised		xxx
Issued*		xxx
Share premium account*		xxx
Revaluation reserve*		xxx
General reserve*		xxx
Retained profit*		xxx
		xxx

Tutorial notes:
1. In the case of fixed assets, figures for original cost (or revalued amount) and accumulated depreciation should be provided.
2. The statements need amendment to take account of the particular circumstances of each company.
3. The items indicated * together comprise shareholders' equity.

Copies of the profit and loss account and balance sheet must be sent to every shareholder and debenture holder at least 21 days before the annual general meeting (AGM). Other interested parties are able to discover the content of a company's annual accounts by taking advantage of the requirement for a copy to be filed with the Registrar of Companies as part of the annual return. These copies are available for public inspection at Companies House in London, Cardiff and, for companies registered in

Scotland, Edinburgh. A payment of £4 must be made for each company file inspected, and the customer is allowed to take away a microfiche which contains copies of the main documents filed and the last few years' published accounts. 'Satellite' offices in Manchester, Birmingham and Leeds provide facilities for obtaining microfiche on an overnight basis.

The accounts filed with the Registrar are abridged versions of the shareholders' accounts in the case of 'small' and 'medium' sized companies as defined by the Act. The reason for this concession is to allow what are, in many cases, small family businesses a measure of confidentiality. A drawback regarding the information available at Companies House is that accounts need not be filed until nine months after the end of the accounting period to which they relate, and many companies even fail to keep to this generous timetable; hence the material is often hopelessly out of date.

8.6.2 Other Regulations The accounting profession issues additional instructions regarding the form and content of published accounts. These instructions are called Statements of Standard Accounting Practice (SSAPs) and they are formally issued by the Accounting Standards Committee on behalf of the accounting profession. Their main purpose is to improve the quality and comparability of published accounts by encouraging companies to employ procedures considered to represent best accounting practice. For example, SSAP 2 specifies the four fundamental accounting concepts which must be followed when preparing published accounts (see chapter 6.5.11). To date (April 1990) 24 SSAPs have been issued.

A final source of regulations is the instructions issued by the Stock Exchange which apply only to public listed companies. Students will be relieved to know that these are entirely outside the 'Introduction to Accounting' syllabus.

8.6.3 The Annual Audit It is a legal requirement for the accounts published by limited companies to be audited. This work is carried out by a professional accountant, who is qualified to carry out the audit function as the result of passing examinations set by professional accounting bodies such as the Institute of Chartered Accountants in England and Wales.

It is the duty of the directors to prepare accounts, annually, and circulate them to shareholders and debenture holders, who use the information presented to them as a basis for assessing the performance of the company in which they have invested. A problem arises because the priorities of management and 'user groups' do not always coincide. For example:

- Management may have as its main objective to ensure survival of the enterprise, whereas the shareholders are concerned with maximising the return on their investment.
- Management may wish to keep the company going, so that they can remain in employment, in circumstances where the creditors would be better advised to withdraw their money before things get worse.

It is therefore the purpose of the audit to carry out an *independent* examination of the accounts in order to assess their reliability. The auditor is appointed by the shareholders and reports to the shareholders. If the auditor is satisfied that the accounts fairly portray the performance and position of the company, a 'clean' audit report will be issued containing the following basic information:

Report of the auditors to the members of AB Ltd
We have audited the accounts set out on pages Y to Z in accordance with approved auditing standards.

In our opinion, the accounts which have been prepared under the historical cost convention, give a true and fair view of the state of affairs of the company at 30 June 1990 and the profit and source and application of funds for the year then ended and comply with the Companies Acts 1985–89.

The first sentence informs the shareholders of the scope of the audit, i.e. that the work done complies with the instructions issued by the professional accounting bodies for the guidance of auditors. The second sentence sets out the auditor's findings. Notice that the auditor does not certify the correctness of the accounts, but instead expresses an opinion on whether they show a true and fair view. This recognises the fact that accounts do not deal with indisputable facts; something which students should be fully aware of having discovered the wide range of asset valuation procedures available to businessmen when measuring profit. However, the audit report indicates that satisfactory procedures have been adopted for the purpose of providing a fair indication of corporate progress.

If the auditor has any reservations regarding the truth and fairness of the accounts, this fact must be referred to in the audit report. Details of any qualification normally precede the second sentence. Where, for example, a report is qualified because provision has not been made for the loss likely to result from the liquidation of a major customer, the following wording is appropriate.

No provision has been made against a debt of £150,000 owing from a customer whose affairs are in the hands of the liquidator. The liquidator has indicated that unsecured creditors are unlikely to receive any payment and, in our opinion, full provision should have been made for the bad debt which is likely to arise. Except for the failure to provide for the amount described above, in our opinion etc.

It will be noticed that nothing has yet been said about the auditor's duty to detect error and fraud. This is because it is not his main job. The auditor's principal duty is to report on the truth and fairness of the accounts but, in order to enable such an assessment to be made, it is obviously necessary to examine the books and records of the company on which the accounts are based. Where error or fraud has occurred, it will quite possibly be discovered during the course of the audit. However, the auditor is not expected to 'pick up' all minor irregularities, as the amount of work involved in checking every transaction would be enormous and probably unjustified. Also, the accountant is not necessarily expected to discover an ingenious fraud which results from the involvement of top management in order to conceal the relevant facts. The auditor is simply required to exercise the degree of skill and care normally associated with a professional person, and will not be held responsible for errors and frauds which remain undiscovered provided this duty is discharged. However, it is to be hoped that such errors and frauds will be discovered, and this is often the case.

We can therefore conclude that the principal duty of the auditor is to express a view on the truth and fairness of the accounts; a secondary obligation is the detection of error and fraud.

Assignment Students should now work Question 8.3 at the end of this chapter.

8.7 REVIEW
After reading the chapter and working the chapter end questions, students should be able to:

- Identify the reasons for forming a registered company.
- Distinguish between different types of registered companies.
- Explain the effect of limited liability on the financial risks taken by shareholders and creditors.
- Explain the different ways in which the accounts of registered companies are regulated.
- Understand the purpose of the annual audit.

8.8 QUESTIONS

Question 8.1
What do you understand by the term 'registered company'? List the different types of limited company and indicate their main characteristics.

Question 8.2
Examine the advantages and disadvantages of operating as a limited company as compared with carrying on business as a sole trader.

Question 8.3
What is the 'annual audit'? Who undertakes this work and what are its main objectives?

CHAPTER 9

Accounting for Limited Companies

This chapter examines a number of important respects in which the accounts of limited companies, introduced in chapter 8, differ from those prepared for sole traders and partnerships.

9.1 SHARE CAPITAL

The memorandum of association contains details of the share capital with which the company is to be initially registered and the division of that share capital into shares of a fixed amount. The figure for the company's registered share capital is described as the 'authorised' share capital, and the face value of each share is called the 'nominal' or 'par' value. A company may be registered, for example, with an authorised share capital of £500,000 divided into 500,000 shares of £1 each. There is no fixed rule regarding the nominal value of each share, though £1 is often used.

There are a number of different categories of share capital; the two most common are ordinary or (equity) shares and preference shares. As the name implies, preference shares are given priority over ordinary shares as regards both payment of the annual dividend and repayment of capital on liquidation.

1. *Dividends* The annual dividend payable on preference shares is fixed, at say 9% per annum, and the dividend is usually paid if profits are sufficient. If profits are insufficient the dividend is lost, unless cumulative preference shares have been issued in which case any arrears must be paid, when trading results improve, before any dividend is paid to the ordinary shareholders. The dividend payable on ordinary shares is entirely at the discretion of the directors; if profits are low and/or the directors wish to retain all profits earned within the company, they may decide to pay no dividend whatsoever.
2. *Capital repayment* On liquidation of the company, the proceeds arising from the disposal of business assets are used to repay sources of finance in the following order:

(a) Outstanding liabilities, e.g. debentures, loans, bank overdrafts and trade creditors.
(b) Preference shareholders, who receive back the nominal value of their investment.
(c) Ordinary shareholders, who receive the balance remaining, as they possess the equity interest in the concern. Where the company is forced into liquidation by financial difficulties, however, there is often nothing left over for the ordinary shareholders.

The directors do not necessarily issue the company's entire authorised share capital at the outset. The figure initially registered represents the total amount the directors expect the company to need in the foreseeable future, i.e. perhaps over the next 10 years. The scale of activity to begin with, however, may be relatively modest and the volume of shares issued should be restricted accordingly.

The method of issuing the shares varies depending on whether the company is private or public. It is likely that the issued share capital of private companies will be acquired entirely by members of the first board of directors, and perhaps also their families and friends. In the case of a large public company, an invitation may be made to the general public to acquire some, if not the whole, of the share capital which the directors plan to issue. In the latter case the shares are advertised in a document, known as the prospectus, the content of which is regulated by company law, and in the case of listed companies, also by the Stock Exchange rules.

9.1.1 Partly Paid Shares Shareholders are not necessarily required to pay immediately the full nominal value of shares acquired. The nominal value may be paid in a number of stages; for example, in the case of a £1 share issued at par, 15p may be payable when the shares are applied for, a further 25p when the shares are issued (called the allotment), and two further instalments, designated 'calls', of 30p each at some future date. Where shares are offered to the general public, it is extremely unlikely for applications to match exactly the number of shares available for issue. If the issue is over-subscribed, one way of dealing with the problem is to issue each subscriber a proportion of the shares applied for. If the issue is under-subscribed it is likely to fail unless the company has taken the precaution of arranging for the issue to be underwritten. The function of the underwriter, often a finance house or an insurance company, is to guarantee the success of an issue by undertaking to subscribe for a new issue of shares to the extent that it is not taken up by the general public. The transaction is in the nature of a speculation; if the issue is popular the underwriter receives his commission and does nothing, but if it fails to attract the required number of subscriptions the underwriter is obliged to acquire shares for which there is little demand and whose price, initially, is likely to fall.

Example 9.1

Griffin Ltd, a newly established private company, is registered with a share capital of £1,000,000 divided into 1,000,000 ordinary shares with a nominal value of £1 each. On 1 January 19X1 400,000 shares are issued at par to members of the board of directors and paid for immediately in cash.

Required:
Prepare the capital section of Griffin's balance sheet as at 1 January 19X1.

Solution

Extracts from the Balance Sheet of Griffin Ltd, as at 1 January 19X1

	£
Share Capital:	
Authorised 1,000,000 ordinary shares of £1 each	1,000,000
Issued 400,000 ordinary shares of £1 each fully paid	400,000

Tutorial note:
The location of these items in a full balance sheet can be seen by referring back to Figure 8.3.

9.2 SHARE PREMIUM ACCOUNT

The initial issue of shares is normally made at par value and if, a few days later, one of the shareholders decides to sell his investment, he is likely to obtain a price not materially different from the issue price. The reason why there is unlikely to be a significant difference between the issue price and the resale price, at this stage, is because the prospects of the company are unlikely to have materially altered during the short space of time which has elapsed since the company was formed. As time goes by the position changes and, assuming the company is successful, the demand for its shares is likely to rise, with the result that the original shareholders are able to demand a price in excess of the nominal value when selling their shares to new investors. The nominal value of each share may be £1 but, depending on the success of the company, its market price may rise to, say, £1.50. It must be recognised, however, that any rise or fall in the market price of the company's shares has no effect on the cash available to the company itself, and the shares continue to be reported in the balance sheet at their nominal value of £1.

The directors may decide, at some later stage, to make a further share issue to help finance an expansion of the company's operations. This additional issue will be made, not at nominal value, but at the best price then obtainable. If the market value of the shares is £1.50, the issue price will be fixed at approximately that figure. An accounting problem arises because of a legal requirement that all share issues, not only the first, must be recorded in the share capital account at their nominal value. This problem is solved by recording any excess of the issue price over nominal value in a share premium account.

Example 9.2

Assume the same facts as in Example 9.1, also that on 31 December 19X5 Griffin Ltd issues, for cash, a further 200,000 ordinary shares at a price of £1.50 each.

Required:
Prepare the capital section of Griffin's balance sheet as at 31 December 19X5.

Solution

Extracts from the Balance Sheet of Griffin Ltd, as at 31 December 19X5

	£
Share Capital:	
Authorised 1,000,000 ordinary shares of £1 each	1,000,000
Issued 600,000 ordinary shares of £1 each fully paid	600,000
Share premium account	100,000

Tutorial note:
The location of the share premium account in a full balance sheet can be seen by referring back to Figure 8.3.

The balance on the share premium account must be treated in the same manner as share capital, which means that no part of it may usually be repaid to the shareholders except on liquidation.

9.3 LOAN CAPITAL AND DEBENTURES

A company's memorandum usually authorises the directors to raise finance by borrowing money as well as by issuing shares. Such loans may be secured or unsecured. A secured loan normally takes the form of a 'debenture', which may be defined as the 'written acknowledgement of a debt usually made under seal'. The security for the loan may take the form of either a fixed charge or a floating charge on the company's assets.

1. *Fixed charge* This is where the asset on which the loan is secured is specified in the debenture deed. Ideally the asset should be one which is likely to appreciate rather than depreciate in value over time, such as land and buildings. As a further protection the company is prevented from selling the charged asset without the debenture holder's express approval.
2. *Floating charge* This is where the debenture is secured on particular categories of assets, e.g. stocks and debtors, or on the assets of the company generally. This form of debenture gives the company greater flexibility, since it is allowed to trade in the assets subject to the floating charge, and their composition may well change on a daily basis.

Debentures are usually issued for a specified period of time, after which they are redeemed. The debenture deed will, however, provide for early repayment in certain circumstances. For example, should the company default on an interest payment, a receiver may be appointed by the debenture holders to take control of the secured assets, sell them, and repay the amount owed. The main differences between debentures, unsecured loans, and share capital are summarised below:

1. Debentures and unsecured loans carry interest at a fixed rate which is payable regardless of profit levels. Dividends, even on preference shares, are payable only if profits are sufficient, and the directors decide to make a distribution which is approved by the shareholders attending the annual general meeting.
2. Interest is an allowable expense in calculating taxable profit; dividends are not an allowable expense.
3. Interest is debited to the profit and loss account; dividends are debited to the appropriation account (see section 9.4 of this chapter).
4. Debentures and unsecured loans are almost always redeemable; share capital is redeemable only in very restricted circumstances.*
5. Debentures enjoy priority of repayment on liquidation. Unsecured loans rank alongside other unsecured creditors, such as trade creditors.

Share capital is repaid, on liquidation, only if resources remain after all other liabilities have been satisfied (see section 9.1 of this chapter).

6. A company may at any time purchase its own debentures in the market; these then remain available for re-issue until cancelled. In certain limited circumstances, a company may purchase its own shares, but these must be cancelled immediately.

7. Unsecured loans and debentures are reported in the balance sheet as a non-current liability and deducted from the balance of total assets less current liabilities (see Figure 8.3). Each year, of course, loans and debentures get closer to their redemption date, and they are eventually re-classified as a current liability when repayable during the forthcoming accounting period. Share capital is reported as part of the shareholders' equity (see Figure 8.3).

* These matters are outside the 'Introduction to Accounting' syllabus, and are covered in the 'Accountancy' core subject of the Associateship examinations.

9.4 THE APPROPRIATION ACCOUNT

Profit is calculated in the trading and profit and loss account; the way in which it is applied is dealt with in the appropriation account. The basic procedure to be followed was demonstrated for partnerships in chapter 7.3; in sections 9.4.1 to 9.4.3 of this chapter, we examine the entries appropriate for the particular circumstances of the limited company.

9.4.1 Corporation Tax Sole traders and partnerships pay income tax on the profits arising from their business activities, whereas the profits of limited companies are subject to corporation tax. The rate of corporation tax differs depending on the level of profits, and is fixed in the Budget. For example, the Finance Act 1990 fixed the rate of corporation tax on profits arising during the year to 31 March 1991 at 25% on profits up to £200,000 and 35% on profits over £1,000,000; a sliding scale, producing an effective marginal tax rate of 37.5% applies between £200,000 and £1,000,000. In the case of a profitable company corporation tax may well represent the largest single cash outflow during an accounting period, and it is therefore of considerable importance.

Corporation tax is levied on taxable profits, and a basic fact which students must grasp is that the figure for *taxable profit* is rarely the same as the profit figure reported in the company's accounts, which is called *accounting profit*. The reason for the difference is that the accountant and the Government have different priorities when measuring profit. A good illustration concerns the treatment of capital expenditure.

1. *Accounting treatment* The aim of the accountant is to produce a profit figure which fairly represents the results of the firm for the year. For example, if it is estimated that an item of plant will last five years and then be worthless, the accountant would consider it appropriate to spread the cost over that period and make a straight line depreciation charge of 20% each year (see chapter 6.3).

2. *Tax treatment* Major priorities of the Government are to ensure equity between taxpayers and to reduce the scope for businessmen to exercise subjective judgment when measuring taxable profit. It is for these reasons that they replace the depreciation charge, which may vary considerably from one company to another, with fixed rates of capital allowance which are also laid down in the Budget. For example, the rate of capital allowance on plant and machinery for the year ended 31 March 1991 was fixed at 25% per annum, applied to the reducing balance.

There are many other adjustments which produce less marked differences between accounting profit and taxable profit. For instance, the cost of entertainment, other than for overseas customers, is disallowed for tax purposes but would naturally be treated as a business cost when accounting profit is computed.

The corporation tax charge for the year is payable nine months after the end of the accounting period to which it relates. It is disclosed in the profit and loss appropriation account as a deduction from net profit; in the balance sheet the amount payable appears as a current liability.

Example 9.3

Adal Ltd was incorporated on 1 January 19X1. It issued 150,000 ordinary shares of £1 each for cash and commenced business on the same day. Plant was purchased immediately for £1,300,000 and expected to possess a four-year life and then be worth £100,000. The company reported a profit of £1,500,000 for 19X1, after charging depreciation of £300,000 (£1,300,000 − £100,000 ÷ 4).

Required:

  (a) A calculation of corporation tax payable for 19X1. For this purpose a writing down allowance of 25% and a corporation tax rate of 35% should be used.

  (b) The appropriation account for 19X1.

Solution

(a)

	£
Accounting profit	1,500,000
Add: Depreciation charge disallowed	300,000
	1,800,000
Less: Capital allowance (£1,300,000 × 25%)*	325,000
Taxable profit	1,475,000
Corporation tax payable £1,475,000 × 35%	516,250

* The balance remaining is carried forward and claimed against profits in future years.

(b)

Profit and Loss Appropriation Account for 19X1

	£
Net profit before tax	1,500,000
Less: Corporation tax	516,250
Net profit after tax	983,750

Tutorial note:

At this level students are not expected to make calculations of taxable profit; this information will be given in the question, where appropriate, as will rates of corporation tax which the Government regularly changes.

9.4.2 Dividends It is the job of the directors to decide how additional resources, generated as the result of profitable trading, are to be employed. There are two options: the money may be either distributed as dividends or retained in the business.

Investors are willing to finance business activity because they expect that, at some future date, the cash returns to them will exceed their initial investment by an amount sufficient to compensate for risk and loss of liquidity. The shareholder of a limited company expects to receive cash returns in two forms, namely dividends and the sales proceeds which arise when the share is finally sold.

Under UK law it is for management to decide how much the firm can afford to pay out in the form of a dividend. At the AGM, shareholders are entitled either to approve the amount proposed by the directors — the usual course of action — or choose to accept a lesser amount; they cannot increase the dividend. The rationale underlying these rules is that the directors are in the best position to judge how much the company can afford, and the shareholders are prevented from insisting on higher payouts which might undermine the financial position of the concern and thereby prejudice the claims of creditors.

Dividends, which are expressed in terms of pence per share, appear as a deduction in the appropriate account. The final dividend is usually paid some months after the end of the financial year, the amount payable being decided upon when the results for the year are known. Where the directors are fairly confident that results will be satisfactory, it is common practice to pay an interim dividend during the financial year.

The directors rarely pay out the entire profits in the form of dividends, and shareholders are usually willing to accept a decision to retain resources within the company because, although they forego immediate income, the expectation is that re-investment will produce greater future returns. Management usually aims for a reasonable balance between distributions and retentions, although in relatively good years the proportion distributed may be rather lower than in poor years when the bulk of the reported profits may be paid out as dividends to demonstrate management's confidence in the future viability of the concern.

Where the current year's profit is insufficient, dividends can be either partly or wholly paid out of undistributed profits brought forward. Where there are accumulated losses brought forward, these must first be made good before a dividend is paid out of the current year's profits.

Example 9.4

Hanbury Ltd has an authorised and issued share capital of £400,000 divided into 800,000 ordinary shares of 50p each. The company made a net profit of £200,000 during 19X1 and, in July of that year, the directors paid an interim dividend of 3p per share. The directors decide to recommend a final dividend of 7p per share, making a total of 10p per share for the year. The retained profit at 1 January 19X1 amounted to £94,000. A provision for corporation tax of £75,000 is to be made on the profits of the year.

Required:
The profit and loss appropriation account of Hanbury for 19X1.

Solution

Profit and Loss Appropriation Account of Hanbury Ltd for 19X1

	£	£
Net profit before tax		200,000
Less: Corporation tax		75,000
Net profit after tax		125,000
Less: Dividends: Paid	24,000 W1	
Proposed	56,000 W2	80,000
Retained Profit for 19X1		45,000
Retained profit at 1 January 19X1		94,000
Retained profit at 31 December 19X1		139,000

W1   3p × 800,000
W2   7p × 800,000

Tutorial note:
Total profit retained and re-invested in the company since it was formed amounts to £139,000 of which £45,000 was retained in the current accounting period.

9.4.3 Provisions and Reserves   A provision is legally defined by the Companies Act 1985, schedule 4, paras 88–9. The definition covers three basic adjustments:

1. The amount written off fixed assets by way of depreciation.
2. The amount written off current assets or investments to reflect the fact that book value exceeds the amount which is ultimately expected to be recoverable. Examples are a provision for bad debts or any provision necessary to reduce stock to net realisable value.
3. The amount set aside to meet a known liability, the amount of which cannot be accurately estimated. This may arise where a company is in breach of contract with an employee but the amount of damages payable is yet to be decided. A second example is a provision for taxation.

A reserve is created by the directors making a discretionary transfer out of profits. The reason for retaining profits, as reserves, may be to help finance expansion, to enable dividends to be declared in a future year when profits are low, to earmark funds for the redemption of share capital or debentures or to meet contingencies unknown at the date of the accounts.

The distinction between provisions and reserves is very important because it affects the measurement of profit and the way financial information is presented in the annual accounts. A provision is a cost of carrying on business activity whereas a transfer to reserve is not. Provisions are therefore charged 'above the line' (in the profit and loss account) and affect reported profits, whereas transfers to reserves are made 'below the line' (in the appropriation account) and leave reported profit unaffected. Clearly it is important for management to identify accurately whether a particular item is in the nature of a provision or a reserve. Equally important, care must be taken when the amount of a provision is estimated, since any under or over provision will directly affect the accuracy of the reported profit figure.

Example 9.5

A company is sued by an employee for unfair dismissal. The company expects the court to allow its former employee damages amounting to £6,000. A provision for this amount is made when computing the reported profit, of £50,000, for 19X1. The court subsequently awards damages of £15,000 on 30 June 19X2.

Required:
Comment on the above information.

Solution

It is clear that the company's liabilities, at 31 December 19X1, have been understated by £9,000 and that profits, for 19X1, have been overstated by a similar figure. If the directors had succeeded in forecasting accurately the damages payable, a profit of £41,000 would have been reported for 19X1 instead of a profit of £50,000. An additional charge of £9,000 must be made in the accounts for 19X2.

In the balance sheet provisions are either:

1. deducted from the value of the asset to which they relate, e.g. depreciation of fixed assets, or
2. included as a current liability, e.g. provision for taxation.

Reserves, on the other hand, remain part of the shareholders' interest and are listed after issued share capital and any balance on share premium account on the face of the balance sheet.

Figure 9.1

Provisions and Reserves

	Nature of item	Location in the Accounts: Profit and Loss Account	Balance Sheet
Provision	Business cost	Above the line	Liability or deducted from asset value
Reserve	Profit retention	Below the line	Part of shareholders' equity

Most of the matters discussed so far in this chapter are contained in Example 9.6 which students should now work before looking at the solution.

Example 9.6

Miskin Ltd commenced business on 1 January 19X2 and the following trial balance was extracted as at 31 December 19X2.

	£	£
Share capital		380,000
8% debentures repayable 19X9		100,000
10% unsecured loan repayable 30 June 19X3		20,000
Tangible fixed assets at cost	480,000	
Gross profit		152,000
Trade debtors	61,500	
Trade creditors		37,870
Bank balance	7,400	
Bad debts written off	320	
Administration and selling expenses	63,200	
Interest paid, 30 June 19X2	5,000	
Interim dividend paid	12,000	
Stock-in-trade at 31 December 19X2	60,450	
	689,870	689,870

The following additional information is provided:

1. The authorised share capital is £500,000 divided into ordinary shares of £1. The balance on the share capital account represents the proceeds from issuing 300,000 shares.
2. A provision for doubtful debts is to be made of 2% on outstanding trade debtors.
3. Depreciation is to be charged on fixed assets at the rate of 4% on cost.
4. The directors propose to recommend a final dividend of 5p per share.
5. Corporation tax of £18,000 is to be provided on the profits for 19X2.
6. A transfer of £10,000 is to be made to dividend equalisation reserve.

Required:
   (a)   A profit and loss account and an appropriation account for 19X2.
   (b)   A balance sheet at 31 December 19X2.

Note:
The accounts should be prepared, as far as possible, in accordance with the format given in Figure 8.3.

Solution

Profit and Loss Account and Appropriation Account for 19X2

	£	£
Gross profit		152,000
Less: Administration and selling expenses	63,200	
Bad and doubtful debts	1,550 W1	
Interest	10,000 W2	
Provision for depreciation	19,200 W3	93,950
Net profit before tax		58,050
Less: Corporation tax		18,000
Net profit after tax		40,050
Less: Dividends: Paid	12,000	
Proposed	15,000 W4	
Transfer to dividend equalisation reserve	10,000	37,000
Retained profit for 19X2		3,050

Balance Sheet at 31 December 19X2

Fixed Assets	£	£
Tangible assets at cost		480,000
Less: Accumulated depreciation		19,200
		460,800
Current Assets		
Stocks	60,450	
Trade debtors	60,270 W5	
Bank	7,400	
	128,120	

Less: Current Liabilities

Unsecured loan repayable 30 June 19X3	20,000	
Trade creditors	37,870	
Taxation due 30 September 19X3	18,000	
Dividend payable	15,000	
Accrual for interest owed	5,000	
	95,870	
Working capital		32,250
Total Assets less Current Liabilities		493,050
Less: Non-Current Liabilities		
8% debentures repayable 19X9		100,000
		393,050

Financed by:
Share Capital:

Authorised 500,000 ordinary shares of £1 each	500,000	
Issued 300,000 ordinary shares of £1 each	300,000	
Share premium account	80,000 W6	
Dividend equalisation reserve	10,000	
Retained profit	3,050	
	393,050	

W1	£320 + (2% of £61,500)	W4	5p × 300,000
W2	£5,000 + £5,000 (1 July–31 Dec 19X2)	W5	£61,500 − £1,230
W3	£480,000 × 4%	W6	£380,000 − £300,000

Assignment   Students should now work Questions 9.1 and 9.2 at the end of this chapter.

9.5 NON-RECURRENT TRANSACTIONS

The profit figure reported in the profit and loss account is used to assess progress and make business decisions. This profit figure relates to a previous accounting period, and its usefulness as the basis for reaching business decisions, such as whether to grant a loan, will depend upon the extent to which past results are a reliable indicator of future profits or losses. The predictive ability of past results will be improved, of course, if a distinction is made between *recurring* and *non-recurring* revenues and expenditures.

Illustration 9.1

The following information is extracted from the accounts of Matlock and Fetlock for 19X8.

	Matlock £000	Fetlock £000
Profit	360	400
Capital invested	1,000	1,000

An examination of the above figures would suggest that Fetlock is the more profitable company. The same amount of money has been invested in each company but, whereas Matlock has generated profits of £360,000, Fetlock has produced profits of £400,000.

However, assume that further investigation discloses that Matlock's profit figure is arrived at after writing off £100,000 for obsolete stock which had been lying, damaged, in a warehouse for a number of years. It could reasonably be concluded that this write-off is of a non-recurring character and that the true profits of Matlock for 19X8 were in fact £460,000 and that it is, in fact, a *more* profitable company than Fetlock.

To deal with this problem SSAP6, entitled 'Extraordinary Items and Prior Year Adjustments', identifies three categories of non-recurring transaction which require separate disclosure in the accounts in order to enable users to assess, more accurately, a company's performance.

9.5.1 Exceptional Items   These are items which result from a company's normal trading activities. However, because of their size or incidence, they require separate disclosure in order to enable the accounts to give a true and fair view. Examples of exceptional items given in SSAP6 include:

1. Redundancy costs relating to a segment of the business which has been rationalised but continues to operate.
2. Reorganisation costs unrelated to the discontinuance of a segment of the business.
3. Amounts transferred to employees' share schemes.
4. Abnormal charges for bad debts and write-offs of stock and work-in-progress.
5. Abnormal provisions for losses on long-term contracts.
6. Surpluses arising on the settlement of insurance claims.

A business segment is defined, for the above purposes, as 'a material and separately identifiable component of a company' normally with its own separate product lines or markets.

Presentation It follows from the fact that these items relate to the ordinary operating activities that they should be included in the accounts 'above the line', i.e. they should be deducted in the profit and loss account before arriving at the figure for net profit before tax (see Figure 8.3). Exceptional items must be separately disclosed, usually as a note to the accounts.

9.5.2 Extraordinary Items These are material items which relate to events or transactions which fall outside the ordinary activities of the company and which are therefore not expected to recur frequently or regularly. Examples identified by SSAP6 include:

1. The discontinuance of a business segment either through termination or disposal.
2. The sale of an investment not acquired with the intention of resale, such as a long-term trade investment in another company.
3. The expropriation of assets, possibly by an overseas government.
4. A change in the basis of taxation.
5. A gain or loss on the disposal of a fixed asset may be treated as either exceptional or extraordinary depending upon the circumstances.

Presentation Because extraordinary items are not associated with normal operations, it is considered desirable to disclose them in a separate section of the profit and loss account (net of related tax), immediately after the calculation of post-tax profits (see Figure 8.3).

9.5.3 Prior Year Adjustments Before the introduction of SSAP6, it was common practice for directors to argue that non-recurring losses were the result of events which occurred in a previous accounting period and should therefore be adjusted against profits brought forward rather than being shown in the profit and loss account. This treatment was considered desirable, by management, for the following reasons:

● It avoided charging the item in the profit and loss account and, thereby, reducing reported profit.
● It avoided giving the item full publicity, by 'tucking it away' in an obscure note to the accounts rather than displaying it on the face of the profit and loss account.

The above practice has been countered by the clear requirement, laid down in SSAP6, for all material non-recurring items to be disclosed in the profit and loss account, appropriately classified as exceptional or extra-ordinary, with just two exceptions:

1. Material adjustments applicable to prior years arising from changes in an accounting policy, e.g. where a company changes from a policy of amortising goodwill over its useful economic life to one of immediate write-off against reserves.
2. The correction of fundamental errors made when preparing an earlier year's accounts, e.g. where an error was made counting stocks resulting in a material under- or over-valuation.

Presentation   Prior year items (net of any related tax) are adjusted against retained profits brought forward from previous years.

Full details of each of the above categories of non-recurrent items must be given in notes to the accounts.

Example 9.7

The following balances relating to 19X7 have been extracted from the books of Padlock Ltd.

	£000
Turnover	10,610
Cost of sales	7,350
Profit on sale of shares in Donnington Ltd	240
Administration expenses	1,200
Distribution costs	170
Retained profit at 1 January 19X7	8,350

It is further discovered that:

1. The shares in Donnington were purchased five years ago with the intention of holding them as a permanent trade investment. The corporation tax estimated to be due on the profit on disposal is £84,000.
2. Partington Ltd, a customer of Padlock Ltd, went into liquidation on 30 June 19X7 and it is expected that the debt outstanding, of £190,000, will prove to be irrecoverable. No provision had been made for the expected loss when the above figures were extracted from the books.

3. Due to an administrative error the bank balance at 31 December 19X6 was included in the accounts at £50,000 instead of £5,000.
4. The corporation tax charge of 19X7, after taking account, where appropriate, of the items referred to in notes 1–3 above, is estimated at £500,000.

Required:
The profit and loss account of Padlock Ltd for 19X7, complying with the provisions of SSAP6.

Solution

Profit and Loss Account of Padlock Ltd for 19X7

	£000	£000
Turnover		10,610
Cost of sales		7,350
Gross profit		3,260
Less: Administration expenses (Note 1)	1,390	
Distribution costs	170	1,560
Net profit before tax		1,700
Less: Corporation tax		500
		1,200
Extraordinary profit (net of tax) (Note 2)		156
		1,356
Retained profit at 1 January 19X7	8,350	
Less: Prior year adjustment (Note 3)	45	8,305
		9,661

Notes to the accounts

1. *Exceptional item*   Administration expenses include a £190,000 bad debt write-off. This amount requires disclosure as an exceptional item because of its size.
2. *Extraordinary item*   During the year the company realised a profit of £220,000 less tax on the sale of an investment.
3. *Prior year item*   A bank balance of £5,000 at 31 December 19X6 was included in last year's accounts, in error, at £50,000.

9.6   REVALUATION RESERVE

The revaluation reserve is an exception to the general rule that reserves are created as the result of transfers from reported profit. Despite determined efforts on the part of successive governments to control inflation, prices have risen almost continuously since 1940. This process has had a significant effect on the usefulness of accounting statements based on the historical cost concept. The major balance sheet items, fixed assets and stocks, are reported at their original cost less, where appropriate, depreciation to comply with this concept. However, fixed assets may have been acquired many years ago when prices were much lower than is the case today; therefore these assets are reported at figures far removed from their current value to the concern. This discrepancy has caused many individuals to question the usefulness of the balance sheet as a statement of a company's financial position, and uneasiness increased with the acceleration in the rate of inflation during the 1970s. The revaluation reserve was developed as a means of restoring an acceptable measure of reality to the corporate balance sheet. The adjustment is quite straightforward:

1. The book value of the fixed asset is increased from historical cost less depreciation to the revalued figure.
2. The surplus arising on revaluation is credited to revaluation reserve which is reported as part of the shareholders' equity in the balance sheet (see Figure 8.3).

The adjustment is entered in the books as follows:

Debit	Credit	With
Revaluation account	Fixed asset at cost account	Historical cost of fixed asset
Provision for depreciation account	Revaluation account	Accumulated depreciation
Fixed asset at revaluation account	Revaluation account	New valuation
Revaluation account	Revaluation reserve	Surplus arising on revaluation

Today many companies revalue their fixed assets from time to time. The fixed assets chosen for this adjustment are, not surprisingly, appreciating assets such as freehold and leasehold properties. For example, Boots plc revalued its properties in 1989, from £249m to £818m. This resulted in a transfer of £569m to revaluation reserve, and more than doubled the figure for shareholders' equity. The benefits considered to result from this action include.

1. The balance sheet more clearly reflects the true commercial reality.
2. Borrowing potential is improved for two reasons. First, the balance sheet displays a stronger asset base. Secondly, lenders are usually unwilling to advance no more than a certain fraction of equity, and so a restatement of asset values enables the equity base to be clearly stated and the loan raising ability to be improved.

Assignment Students should now attempt Questions 9.3 to 9.5 at the end of this chapter.

9.7 LIMITATIONS OF PUBLISHED ACCOUNTS

Accounting statements are used by a variety of different groups as the basis for reaching resource allocation decisions. It is generally agreed that published accounts provide bankers with a useful input for reaching initial loan decisions and for monitoring an advance once it has been made. It is, however, important to recognise that the accounts suffer from the following limitations which must be borne in mind when judging their usefulness.

1. *Subjective Judgment* The published figure for reported profit depends directly on the way in which assets are valued. In many cases there are a number of options available. For example, in the case of fixed assets, depreciation may be charged using a number of different methods, amongst which the straight line method and the reducing balance method are most popular. Having decided which one to use, it is still necessary to choose a depreciation rate, which will in turn depend upon how long the asset is expected to last and what its disposable value is estimated to be. Different businessmen will take different views and different profit figures will result.

2. *Lack of Forecast Information* In reaching a lending decision, the bank's principal concern is to assess what is likely to happen to the company in the future. Published accounts are principally backward looking, however, in that they disclose the profits earned or losses suffered during the most recent accounting period and the financial position at the last balance sheet date. The usefulness of the accounts is therefore dependent on the extent to which past results are likely to be repeated in the future. To some extent, the accounts are a measure of managerial efficiency and, assuming a stable management team, it is quite possible that a company which has been successful in the past will continue to prosper. However, business circumstances change and, as we know, a company which does very well one year may suffer

enormous losses in the following year despite no significant changes in the management structure. This emphasises the need for bankers to obtain regular management accounts showing the up to date position and estimated developments over the forthcoming accounting period.

3. *Out of Date Information*   The published accounts normally become available between three and four months after the end of the accounting period. Assuming the company makes up its accounts on the calendar year basis, those for 19X3 will therefore be published in approximately April 19X4. The information they contain is, therefore, already out of date. The balance sheet sets out the financial position three or four months earlier, while some of the information shown in the profit and loss account relates to transactions entered into in January 19X3, i.e., 15 months earlier. The position gets worse as time goes by. No further accounts will be published until April 19X5.

4. *Historical Costs*   The accounts published by companies are usually based on the historical cost concept. This means that transactions are initially recorded at the price paid to the supplier and that they remain at this figure, suitably adjusted for depreciation in the case of fixed assets, until they are sold. Immediately after the initial transaction occurs, the book value is a reasonable reflection of the asset's true worth but, as time goes by, it becomes a poor measure of the value of assets belonging to the concern. The position naturally gets worse, more quickly, where the rates of inflation are high, but even an annual inflation rate of just 7% causes prices to double in approximately 10 years. The result is that assets are often shown in the balance sheet at figures totally out of line with their real value and therefore useless as a basis for a lending decision.

5. *Undisclosed Assets*   In addition to the fact that some assets are shown at irrelevant figures, some are omitted altogether. For example, goodwill is not recognised in the accounts until it is the subject of an 'arm's length transaction', and even then, it is often written off immediately against reserves (see chapter 6.4). This treatment is justified on the grounds that it is exceedingly difficult to value goodwill in the absence of a market transaction. This is a fair point, but some would argue that it is better to have a subjective measure of the asset's actual worth rather than attributing to it an arbitrary valuation of a zero.

6. *Window Dressing and Off-balance Sheet Finance*   There has been a rapid growth, in recent years, in the use of each of these techniques. They are designed to produce financial statements which conceal the full extent of a company's liabilities and exposure to risk, details of

which are needed if the accounts are to give a true and fair view. The result of the growth of such practices is that there have been many instances of shareholders and creditors extremely surprised to discover the full extent of a company's liabilities when it gets into financial difficulties. What do the terms mean?

Window Dressing   This term covers transactions designed to arrange a company's affairs so that the accounts give a misleading or unrepresentative impression of its financial position. An example would be a loan raised immediately before the year end to improve apparent liquidity.

Off Balance-sheet Finance   This involves funding a company's operations in such a way that, under existing legal requirements and conventions, some or all of the finance does not appear on the face of the balance sheet. An example would be an arrangement whereby a company sells goods with the option to buy them back; the option being constructed so that it is reasonably certain to be exercised. The arrangement may run for months, or even years, during which time the company selling the stock uses the sales proceeds as a form of finance. The stock and the related re-purchase obligation are meanwhile excluded from the balance sheet. The difference between the sales price and the re-purchase price is effectively a finance charge, but it is debited to cost of sales when completion of the transaction occurs. The result of this scheme is that the finance does not appear in the balance sheet and the related 'finance charge' never appears in the profit and loss account. Steps are being taken by the accounting profession to counter the distorting effect of this kind of transaction and help ensure that the accounts reflect the underlying commercial reality.

9.8   REVIEW

After reading the chapter and working the chapter end questions, students should be able to:

- Account for new share issues.
- Appreciate the differences between shares, unsecured loans, and debentures.
- Be familiar with the nature and treatment of corporation tax, dividends, provisions and reserves.
- Understand the nature and purpose of the revaluation reserve and make appropriate entries.
- Be able to prepare, in good form, the final accounts of a limited company.
- Be familiar with the limitations of published accounts.

9.9 QUESTIONS

Question 9.1

(a) Define provisions and reserves and give two examples of each.

(b) Describe how provisions and reserves are (i) accounted for in the profit and loss account and (ii) reported in the balance sheet.

Question 9.2

The following information is provided in respect of the affairs of Newton Ltd, a trading company, for 19X0 and 19X1.

Draft Profit and Loss Account, Year to 31 December

	19X0	19X1
	£000	*£000*
Administration expenses	1,620	1,809
Selling costs	520	572
Distribution costs	140	164
Transfer to general reserve	—	500
Depreciation charge	250	300
Proposed dividend	100	200
Balance of profit	300	60
	2,930	3,605

Draft Balance Sheet, 31 December

	19X0	19X1
Debit balances:	*£000*	*£000*
Stock	724	771
Debtors	570	524
Plant and machinery at cost	1,840	2,650
Cash at bank	92	305
	3,226	4,250
Credit balances:		
Trade creditors	416	480
Provision for depreciation	520	820
General reserve	—	500
Dividend	100	200
Share capital (£1 shares)	1,600	1,600
Profit and loss account	590	650
	3,226	4,250

Required:

(a) Re-draft the above accounts in order to make them more informative. The profit and loss account should show figures for gross profit, net profit and retained profit; the balance sheet should include an appropriate classification of assets and liabilities.

(b)   Comment on the view expressed by one of Newton Ltd's directors that the company should not pay the proposed increased dividend because profits have declined.

Question 9.3
The following trial balance was extracted from the books of Mewday plc as at 31 December 19X9:

	£	£
Share capital authorised and issued, 700,000		
Ordinary shares of £1 each		700,000
15% Debentures repayable 19Y5 (issued 1 Jan 19X5)		250,000
Freehold properties at cost	850,000	
Motor vans:		
Balance 1 Jan. 19X9 at cost	225,000	
Additions (at cost) less proceeds of sale (note c.)	24,000	
Provision for depreciation of motor vans to 1 Jan 19X9		101,200
Stock-in-trade 1 Jan 19X9	206,300	
Balance at bank	96,900	
Bad debts	15,700	
Trade debtors	166,500	
Trade creditors		159,800
Directors' remuneration	60,000	
Wages and salaries	198,700	
Motor expenses	42,300	
Rates	10,500	
Purchases	1,650,000	
Sales		2,350,000
Legal expenses	9,100	
General expenses	86,000	
Debenture interest	37,500	
Profit and loss account: Balance at 1 Jan. 19X9		117,500
	3,678,500	3,678,500

You are given the following information:

(a)   Stock-in-trade at 31 December 19X9, £217,800.
(b)   Rates paid in advance, 31 December 19X9, £2,000.
(c)   On 1 January 19X9 a motor van which had cost £10,000 was sold for £1,000. Depreciation provided for this van up to 31 December 19X8 was £8,250.
(d)   Provide for depreciation of motor vans (including additions) at 20% of cost.
(e)   The figure for legal expenses includes £7,900 in connection with the purchase of a freehold property.

(f) A provision for corporation tax of £90,000 should be made on the profit for the year.

(g) The directors propose to pay a dividend of 12p per share.

Required:
A trading and profit and loss and appropriation account for the year 19X9 and a balance sheet at 31 December 19X9, each presented in vertical format.

Note: Ignore depreciation of freehold properties.

Question 9.4
The following trial balance was extracted from the books of Porchester Ltd on 31 March 19X6.

	£	£
Ordinary share capital (£1 shares)		1,500,000
Retained profit to 1 April 19X5		39,000
10% Debentures repayable 19X9		300,000
Freehold land and buildings at cost	400,000	
Plant and machinery at cost	1,300,000	
Provision for depreciation on plant and machinery at 1 April 19X5		512,000
Debtors and prepayments (including Trade debtors, £360,000)	370,080	
Stock and work-in-progress at 31 March 19X6	984,020	
Bank balance	268,000	
Provision for doubtful debts at 31 March 19X6		15,000
Creditors and accrued expenses		351,500
Gross profit for the year		1,020,800
Administration expenses	216,900	
Selling expenses	150,400	
Bad debts written off	8,700	
General repairs and maintenance	25,200	
Debenture interest to 30 September 19X5	15,000	
	3,738,300	3,738,300

Additional information is provided as follows:

1. The company's freehold property was revalued at £900,000 on 1 October 19X5. The directors have decided to use this figure for the purpose of the accounts.
2. The directors propose to pay a dividend of 5p per share on the ordinary share capital at 31 March 19X6.
3. The company purchased additional plant costing £120,000 on 31 March 19X6. The plant was delivered to the company's premises on that date together with the purchase invoice to be paid within seven

days, but no entry has been made in the books in respect of the transaction.

4. Depreciation is to be provided at 25%, reducing balance, on all plant and machinery owned by the company at the year end, except the plant referred to under 3 above. Ignore depreciation of freehold property.
5. Corporation tax of £150,000, due for payment on 1 January 19X7, is to be provided out of the trading profit for the year.
6. The company's authorised share capital is £2,000,000 divided into ordinary shares of £1 each.

Required:
The profit and loss account and profit and loss appropriation account of Porchester Ltd for the year ended 31 March 19X6, together with the balance sheet at that date. Particular attention should be given to layout, although the accounts need not necessarily be in a form appropriate for publication.

Question 9.5
The trial balance of Southgate plc at 31 December 19X9 was as follows:

	£	£
Ordinary share capital (shares £1 each)		600,000
Freehold property at cost	500,000	
Furniture and equipment at cost	375,000	
Provision for depreciation of furniture and equipment, 1 January 19X9		59,500
Debtors and prepayments	105,000	
Stock and work-in-progress at 31 December 19X9	104,200	
Creditors and accruals		85,300
Balance at bank	72,000	
Gross profit on trading		416,500
Rent and rates	30,000	
Office salaries	142,600	
Advertising costs	21,000	
Transport costs	23,600	
Profit and loss account balance, 1 Jan. 19X9		178,500
Taxation due 1 Jan. 19Y0 on 19X8 profits		103,600
Deposit on new equipment	10,000	
Temporary investment	60,000	
	1,443,400	1,443,400

You are given the following additional information:

1. The company has contracted to purchase new equipment at a cost of £50,000. A deposit of £10,000 was paid during December 19X9 and the remainder will be paid during January when delivery is expected.

2. Depreciation is to be provided on furniture and equipment, other than the new equipment referred to under 1., at the rate of 10% on cost.
3. The figure for rent and rates in the above trial balance covers the 15 months to 31 March 19Y0.
4. During November 19X9 the company's freehold premises were valued at £650,000 by a firm of professional valuers. The company's directors have decided to write the revaluation into the 19X9 accounts and credit the surplus arising to revaluation reserve.
5. Taxation is to be provided at 50% on the company's net profit from trading operations.

Required:
(a) The profit and loss account and appropriation account of South-gate for 19X9 and balance sheet at 31 December 19X9. Each accounting statement should be presented in vertical format.
(b) Your comments on the suggestion, from one director, that the company should pay a dividend of 10p per share on the issued share capital in view of the large bank balance and the fact that no dividend was paid for 19X8.

Note: Ignore depreciation of freehold property.

CHAPTER 10

Decision-Making

10.1 INTRODUCTION

So far, this text has concentrated on how to record and report the financial consequences of past activity. When making decisions, management must look to the future and try to predict the consequences likely to flow from a particular course of action, such as opening a new branch or discontinuing a product line. Accounting techniques can provide an important input to the decision-making process as they can be used to predict the likely outcome if a given plan is followed. An additional benefit of studying how to predict future results is that, by examining the link between future economic activity and its expected financial outcome, additional insight should be gained to help explain how past results have come about.

This chapter:

1. introduces the study and interpretation of cost behaviour; and
2. explains how to forecast cash flows and trading results.

10.2 COST BEHAVIOUR

The decisions which management must take include:

- Whether existing activity should be expanded or reduced.
- Whether a new product should be introduced.
- How existing production techniques could be improved.
- Whether new products should be manufactured or purchased ready made.
- The manufacturing techniques to be used for new products.

In the attempt to maximise profit, all decisions must be viewed according to their impact on profit, and management must be satisfied, before resources are committed, that any proposed activity, or change in existing activity, will add to overall profit. Therefore, when any decisions, such as those outlined above, are under consideration, financial forecasts are needed to show the likely outcomes of alternative courses of action so that the most profitable ones can be adopted. The preparation of forecasts involves an understanding of cost behaviour so that the level of costs likely to result from different actions can be predicted.

It is important to differentiate between the capacity and the output of an organisation:

1. The *capacity* is set by the manner in which production or trading activity is organised. For example, the acquisition of a particular machine sets the maximum output which can be achieved before an additional machine must be bought; similarly, the size of premises used by a shop determines the maximum number of product lines which can be displayed and stored; above a certain level, further space is needed. Therefore, the capacity of the business sets the upper level of activity.
2. The *output* of a firm is the extent to which the available capacity is utilised; the lowest level is zero, and the greatest is the largest amount permitted by available capacity.

Management must decide what the likely output will be and arrange capacity accordingly, bearing in mind that growth may take place. In the long run it may prove cheaper to acquire at the start of the project the additional capacity likely to be needed so as to take advantage of the economies of scale which can result from the use of capital intensive techniques.

10.2.1 Fixed and Variable Costs Business costs may be classified according to how they behave in response to changes in output:

1. *Fixed costs* These remain constant over a range of output and include such items as rent and depreciation. For example, the rent for premises or straight line depreciation charge related to a machine are constant irrespective of whether these assets are being used at full capacity or well below. However, if an output in excess of the existing full capacity is contemplated, then an additional set of fixed costs must be incurred to provide additional capacity.
2. *Variable costs* These vary in direct proportion to output, and include the costs of raw material and manufacturing wages. For example, if no production takes place, then no raw materials have to be purchased, while, at full capacity, the total cost of materials is the number of units produced times the material cost per unit.

Forecast output is unlikely to be achieved exactly in practice, and calculations of the profit expected at different levels of output are helpful in making a decision about whether a new project should be undertaken. This is shown in Example 10.1

Example 10.1

The management of Glass Ltd is considering the possibility of manufacturing a new product which will sell at £15 per unit. Existing capacity is fully utilised, and so a new factory would have to be rented and plant, with a life of 10 years, purchased. The expected costs are:

	£
Annual factory rent	10,000
Purchase price of plant	75,000
Raw material cost per unit	2.10
Labour cost per unit	1.50
Other variable costs	1.00
Fixed costs (excluding rent and depreciation)	6,500

Note: The company depreciates plant on the straight line basis assuming a zero residual value.

Required:
Forecast the profit which will be made from sales of the new product at the alternative annual rates of:
  (a) 2,500 units
  (b) 5,000 units

Solution

Profit Forecasts at Different Sales Levels

	(a)			(b)		
	£	£	£	£	£	£
Sales			37,500			75,000
Fixed Costs:						
Rent	10,000			10,000		
Depreciation	7,500			7,500		
Other	6,500			6,500		
		24,000			24,000	
Variable Costs:						
Raw Materials	5,250			10,500		
Labour	3,750			7,500		
Other	2,500			5,000		
		11,500			23,000	
			35,500			47,000
Profit			2,000			28,000

Tutorial note:
Output has doubled, but profit has increased 14 times.

Another use of forecasts, of the type prepared in Example 10.1 above, is to help decide the method of production; the choice often lies between 'capital intensive' and 'labour intensive' techniques:

1. *Capital intensive* production uses automatic machines, such as the 'robots' seen on car production lines, and requires a large investment in plant with a consequent high level of fixed costs; variable costs are lower as each additional unit produced requires only a small labour input. Additional potential benefits from capital intensive methods are that raw materials are used more efficiently, and therefore cost less per unit, and there is a lower rejection rate at the stage of inspecting the finished product.

2. *Labour intensive* methods use relatively little plant and have low fixed costs, but high variable costs per unit as each additional item produced requires a large input of labour.

Example 10.2

The directors of Hasard Ltd are sure that 10,000 units a year of a newly developed product can be sold at £90 each. They are undecided about how to produce it. The alternatives are:

	Method 1	Method 2
	£	£
Investment in plant with a 10-year life	125,000	750,000
Fixed costs (excluding depreciation)	185,000	200,000
Variable Cost per Unit:		
Raw Materials	35	30
Labour	20	5
Other	6	2

Note: The company calculates depreciation on the straight line basis assuming a zero scrap value.

Required:
Prepare financial statements to show the likely profit from each of the two methods at the expected level of sales.

Solution

Forecast Trading Results

	Method 1			Method 2		
	£	£	£	£	£	£
Sales			900,000			900,000
Fixed Costs:						
Depreciation	12,500			75,000		
Other	185,000			200,000		
		197,500			275,000	
Variable Costs:						
Raw Materials	350,000			300,000		
Labour	200,000			50,000		
Other	60,000			20,000		
		610,000			370,000	
			807,500			645,000
Profit			92,500			255,000

Assignment Students should now work Question 10.1 at the end of this chapter.

Some costs are neither completely fixed nor fully variable; they are termed 'semi-variable'. Although semi-variable costs respond to volume changes, they do not change in direct proportion to them. It is possible for semi-variable costs to remain constant over a relatively small range of activity, and each successive set of costs may differ in price from its predecessor. For example, an increase in manufacturing output creates additional work in the accounts department. The initial load may be carried by an accountant who alone performs all the necessary activities; when his capacity is exceeded, a book keeper may be added to the staff, and then a clerk. Each additional employee, hired to increase the capacity of the accounts department in response to an increase in manufaturing output, adds relatively less to costs as an accountant is paid more than a book keeper, who in turn earns more than a clerk.

Assignment Students should now work Question 10.2 at the end of this chapter.

10.2.2 Contribution Costing A useful technique to apply when examining the way in which fixed and variable costs respond to changes in the level of activity, is to calculate the 'contribution' which each unit sold makes towards fixed costs. Analysis based on this approach assumes that the revenue from each unit is applied first to meet its related variable costs, and any surplus, the contribution, is then set against total fixed costs. Once the fixed costs have been completely recovered, the contribution of each additional unit sold adds to profit. The contribution of each unit is calculated by the formula:

$$\frac{\text{Contribution}}{\text{per Unit}} = \frac{\text{Selling Price}}{\text{per Unit}} - \frac{\text{Variable Cost}}{\text{per Unit}}$$

Example 10.3

Product Z incurs the following variable costs per unit:

	£
Materials	5.00
Wages	4.50
Expenses	1.25

Required:
Calculate the contribution of product Z if its selling price per unit is:
  (a) £12
  (b) £15.

Solution

The total variable cost per unit is:

	£
Materials	5.00
Wages	4.50
Expenses	1.25
Total	10.75

  (a) Contribution = £12 − £10.75 = £1.25
  (b) Contribution = £15 − £10.75 = £4.25

Contribution costing can be applied to the activity of an organisation where a number of departments contribute to overall fixed costs. In these circumstances, the contribution made by each department is the difference between the revenue and costs which it generates. The test to apply when identifying these costs and revenues is that they would no longer arise if the department were to be closed. This is shown in Example 10.4.

Example 10.4

The business of Bits & Co. is divided into three departments of equal size: A, B, and C. The departmental results for 19X7 were (£000):

Departmental Trading Results

	A	B	C	Total
Sales	50	120	180	350
Cost of Goods Sold	25	60	90	175
Gross Profit	25	60	90	175
Departmental Wages	10	20	30	60
	15	40	60	115
Rent (apportioned equally)	20	20	20	60
Profit (Loss)	(5)	20	40	55

Mr Bits is considering closing Department A because it is making a loss. He says it is better to leave the floor space empty than to use it to lose money.

Required:
(a) Prepare a statement to show Mr Bits the effect on total profit if Department A is closed.
(b) Explain to Mr Bits whether Department A should be closed.

Solution

(a)   *Revised Departmental Trading Results (£000)*

	B	C	Total
Sales	120	180	300
Cost of Goods Sold	60	90	150
Gross Profit	60	90	150
Departmental Wages	20	30	50
	40	60	100
Share of Rent*	30	30	60
Profit (Loss)	10	30	40

*Rent and rates shared equally between the remaining departments

(b) The revised departmental trading results show that the plan to close department A is based on a failure to appreciate that all three departments are making a contribution to fixed central costs. Department A should be kept open as it meets 75% of its share of apportioned costs, which will not be avoided if the department is closed. Total profit is reduced by £15,000 if it is not kept open.

Tutorial note:

It is sometimes argued that, because the accounting information which results can lead to wrong decisions, the apportionment of 'joint' overhead costs should not be made. If 'joint' overhead costs are not apportioned, the departmental trading results of Bits & Co. would be presented as follows (£000):

	Department			Total
	A	B	C	
Sales	50	100	200	350
Cost of Goods Sold	25	50	100	175
Gross Profit	25	50	100	175
Departmental Wages	10	20	30	60
Departmental Surplus (contribution)	15	30	70	115
Rent				60
Profit				55

The above presentation highlights the fact that all departments are making a positive *contribution* to general overhead costs which are not controllable at the departmental level.

10.2.3 Break-even Analysis A forecast of sales should be prepared as part of the appraisal of whether a particular project should be undertaken. The volume of anticipated sales sets the capacity which has to be provided and also determines the total value of variable costs. Forecasts cannot be wholly accurate, and so it is usual to examine results based on a number of alternative outcomes. A particularly useful piece of information to know is the volume of sales needed to achieve break-even, which occurs where total costs equal total revenues and neither a profit nor loss is made. Looked at another way, a company breaks even when the contribution from sales is exactly equal to fixed costs. The break-even point is calculated with the formula:

$$\text{Break-even point, measured in units sold} = \frac{\text{Fixed Costs}}{\text{Contribution}}$$

The break-even point in terms of the value of sales can be calculated by multiplying the number of units by the selling price per unit.

The importance of the break-even point is that below it a loss is suffered, and above it a profit is earned. It is, therefore, very important that management selects projects which are likely to achieve at least enough sales to break even.

Example 10.5

The directors of Cumberland Ltd are considering an investment project which is expected to involve the following costs and revenues:

	£
Annual Fixed Costs	100,000
Selling Price per Unit	10
Variable Cost per Unit	7.50

Required:
  (a) Calculate the number of units which have to be sold for the project to break even.
  (b) Calculate the profit or loss which would occur if sales are:
   (i)   1,000 units greater than those needed to break even, and
   (ii) 1,000 less than those needed to break even.

Solution

  (a) Contribution = £10 − £7.50 = £2.50
    Break-even point = $\dfrac{£100,000}{£2.50}$ = 40,000 units

  (b)

	(i) 1,000 less	(ii) 1,000 more
Sales in units	39,000	41,000
	£	£
Contribution (unit sales × 2.5)	97,500	102,500
Fixed Costs	100,000	100,000
Profit (Loss)	(2,500)	2,500

Tutorial note:
An alternative way to calculate the effect of changes in the level of sales on profit is to calculate the increase, or decrease, in the contribution. In this case, the starting profit is zero, and the contribution from sales of 1,000 units = 1,000 × £2.50 = £2,500. Therefore, an increase in sales of 1,000

units gives a profit of £2,500, and a decrease of 1,000 units gives a loss of £2,500.

The certainty with which sales can be forecast may influence the choice of production method and also affect decisions about which products to trade in. Where there is great uncertainty, production methods and products with low break-even points may be chosen to minimise the risk of losses. However, the choice of a method or product with a low break-even point may restrict the total profits which can be earned if high sales are achieved.

Example 10.6

The directors of Trestle Ltd are considering the following alternative methods of manufacturing a new product:

	Method 1	Method 2
	£	£
Plant with a life of 10 years	50,000	150,000
Other annual fixed costs	3,000	3,000
Variable Cost per Unit	7	6.50
Selling Price per Unit	8	8

The plant is expected to have a zero scrap value at the end of its life, and the company uses the straight line method of depreciation.

Method 2 has a lower variable cost because it uses less labour and has lower wastage rates for raw materials.

Required:
  (a) Calculate the break-even point for each method of production.
  (b) Calculate the profit or loss for each method which results from sales levels of 10,000 units, 20,000 units, and 30,000 units.
  (c) What is the greatest loss which might be suffered under each method.
  (d) Advise management on which method should be adopted.

Solution

		Method 1 £	Method 2 £
(a)	Fixed Costs:		
	Depreciation	5,000	15,000
	Other	3,000	3,000
		8,000	18,000
	Contribution	£8 − £7 = £1	£8 − £6.50 = £1.50

	Break-even point	Method 1	Method 2
		$\dfrac{8,000}{1}$ = 8,000 units	$\dfrac{18,000}{1.50}$ = 12,000 units

		Method 1 £	Method 2 £
(b)	*10,000 units*		
	Contribution	10,000	15,000
	Fixed Costs	8,000	18,000
	Profit (Loss)	2,000	(3,000)
	20,000 units		
	Contribution	20,000	30,000
	Fixed Costs	8,000	18,000
	Profit	12,000	12,000
	30,000 units		
	Contribution	30,000	45,000
	Fixed Costs	8,000	18,000
	Profit	22,000	27,000

(c) The greatest loss occurs when there is no contribution (i.e. zero output), and is equal to the fixed costs. Therefore, the maximum loss of Method 1 is £8,000 and of Method 2 is £18,000.

(d) Once Method 2 breaks even, £1.50 is added to profit by every additional unit sold, while Method 1 adds only £1. However, Method 1 breaks even at a lower level of sales. Both methods make the same profit at sales of 20,000 units.

The decision about which method to select therefore rests on expected sales. If 20,000 is the maximum level of expected sales, then Method 1 is better; if sales are expected easily to exceed that level, then Method 2 is better.

Assignment   Students should now work Question 10.3 at the end of this chapter.

Break-even analysis has a number of limitations which mainly arise from its underlying assumptions:

- *Fixed costs* may not be fixed over the full range of output. Before the full capacity of an undertaking is reached, it may be necessary to incur some additional minor fixed costs, such as renting additional storage facilities for raw materials.
- *Variable costs* may not vary in strict proportion with output. For example, as output rises, there may be savings on the cost of raw materials as bulk purchases can be made, but labour costs may rise as overtime has to be worked.
- *Forecast data* are always likely to prove inaccurate.

The possibility of factors like these must be borne in mind when interpreting the results of break-even analysis.

10.3   FORECAST RESULTS

Management is often faced with a number of alternative courses of action, especially when it is considering the long-term development of the company. It is of great assistance to management to prepare forecasts which predict the likely outcome of alternatives so that choices are based on the best information possibly available. Forecasts cannot be completely accurate, as many of the factors which influence actual results, such as the cost of raw materials and the actual demand for the product, are outside the control of management. However, this does not invalidate the exercise of preparing forecasts since the alternative is to make decisions without evaluating the outcome of management's expectations. To prepare forecasts, management must answer such vital questions as:

- How many units do you expect to sell?
- What will be the selling price per unit?
- How much labour will it take to produce each unit?
- How much will each unit of labour cost?

Forecasts bring together the answers to all these questions in accounting statements, and show the expected impact of alternatives on the three key financial matters:

- CASH
- PROFIT
- FINANCIAL POSITION (BALANCE SHEET)

10.3.1 Cash Forecasts   Management must ensure that the company can afford any new project which is under consideration, that is, the company will not run out of cash if a particular plan is followed. Additional external finance, such as a bank overdraft, can be sought if the company's own cash resources are insufficient, but lenders will only be willing to provide funds which are likely to be repaid. The impact of plans on the cash resources of a company can be predicted using a cash forecast, and this is also of great interest to any person or organisation, such as a bank, which is approached for funds. If cash forecasts are not prepared, a company may suddenly find itself short of cash or holding unproductive surplus funds in its bank account. A cash forecast enables a company to foresee a deficit, for which appropriate funding can be sought, or a surplus for which uses can be prepared in advance.

The preparation of a monthly cash forecast involves the identification of the cash flows expected to take place in each month and the calculation of the forecast cash position at the end of each month. The following techniques are used to predict cash transactions:

- *Sales* Cash sales are entered in the forecast as receipts for the month in which they take place. The time lag has to be taken into account for credit sales, for example cash from March sales may be received in April.
- *Purchases* Cash purchases are entered in the month in which they take place. The time lag has to be taken into account for credit purchases, for example cash for October purchases may be paid in November.
- *Regular payments* are entered in the appropriate month, possibly with adjustment for a lag between the date when the expense is incurred and when it is paid.
- *Irregular items,* such as the purchase of fixed assets or the payment of tax, are also entered according to when they arise.

Example 10.7

Hamel runs a shop which makes all of its sales for cash. Forecasts for the first half of 19X6 are:

Sales:	January to March — £25,000 per month.
	April to June — £30,000 per month.
Purchases:	A gross margin of 20% on selling prices is made.
	Every item sold is immediately replaced.
	Suppliers are paid in the month following delivery.
Payments:	Wages and other expenses £4,000 per month.
	Drawings £1,000 per month.
	Delivery van cost £7,000; van delivered on 1 January
	and paid for in February.
Opening Balances:	Owed to suppliers £16,000
	Cash £1,000

Ignore interest on any overdraft which may arise.

Required:
  (a) Calculate the value of monthly purchases.
  (b) Prepare a cash forecast for Hamel for the first six months of 19X6 which shows the cash balance at the end of each month.
  (c) Comment on the position shown by the forecast.

Solution

  (a)

	Sales	Purchases (sales - 20%)
	£000	£000
January	25	20
February	25	20
March	25	20
April	30	24
May	30	24
June	30	24

  (b)

	Jan £	Feb £	March £	April £	May £	June £	Total £
CASH IN:							
Sales	25,000	25,000	25,000	30,000	30,000	30,000	165,000
CASH OUT:							
Purchases	16,000	20,000	20,000	20,000	24,000	24,000	124,000
Wages and other expenses	4,000	4,000	4,000	4,000	4,000	4,000	24,000
Drawings	1,000	1,000	1,000	1,000	1,000	1,000	6,000
Delivery Van . .		7,000					7,000
	21,000	32,000	25,000	25,000	29,000	29,000	161,000

Opening balance	1,000	5,000	(2,000)	(2,000)	3,000	4,000	1,000
+ Cash In . . .	25,000	25,000	25,000	30,000	30,000	30,000	165,000
− Cash Out . .	21,000	32,000	25,000	25,000	29,000	29,000	161,000
Closing Balance	5,000	(2,000)	(2,000)	3,000	4,000	5,000	5,000

(c) The purchase of the van creates a cash deficit in February and March, but this is made good from trading cash inflows by April. The bank should be approached for a temporary loan; an overdraft would be best. By the end of June the business is accumulating a cash surplus which will continue to increase if trade stays at the same level. Thought should be given to how any permanently spare cash is to be used.

Tutorial note:
The use of a columnar layout, as shown in the solution to part (b) of the example, is recommended because:

● It saves time as the descriptions of cash flows do not have to be repeated for each month.
● Errors are less likely to occur as any inconsistent entries are more easily identified.
● It aids comparison throughout the period covered by the forecast of the individual elements of cash flow.

Assignment Students should now work Question 10.4 at the end of this chapter.

10.3.2 Forecast Trading and Profit and Loss Account and Balance Sheet The preparation of a trading and profit and loss account and balance sheet from the cash account, and opening and closing values for assets and liabilities, was explained in chapter 3 in the context of past results. Once the cash forecast has been prepared, the same techniques may be applied to prepare a forecast trading and profit and loss account and balance sheet.

Example 10.8

The balance sheet of Hamel at 31 December 19X5 was:

Balance Sheet

	£	£
FIXED ASSETS		
Premises		10,000
CURRENT ASSETS		
Stock	18,500	
Cash	1,000	
	19,500	
CURRENT LIABILITIES		
Trade Creditors	16,000	
		3,500
		13,500
CAPITAL		13,500

Hamel expects to undertake the transactions given in Example 10.7 above during the first six months of 19X6. You may assume that the monthly cash forecast has been prepared which gives a summary of cash transactions in the 'Total' column.

The van is expected to have a life of five years and a zero scrap value at the end of that time. Hamel uses the straight line method to calculate depreciation.

Required:
Prepare Hamel's forecast trading and profit and loss account for the six months to 30 June 19X6 and a balance sheet at that date.

Solution

Forecast Trading and Profit and Loss Account

	£	£
Sales		165,000
Less: Cost of Goods Sold (W1)		132,000
Gross Profit		33,000
Wages	24,000	
Depreciation ($0.5 \times 7,000/5$)	700	
		24,700
Net Profit		8,300

Balance Sheet

	£	£
FIXED ASSETS		
Premises		10,000
Van	7,000	
Less: Depreciation	700	
		6,300
		16,300
CURRENT ASSETS		
Stock	18,500	
Cash	5,000	
	23,500	
CURRENT LIABILITIES		
Trade Creditors (June purchases)	24,000	
		(500)
		15,800
CAPITAL		
Opening balance		13,500
Plus: Profit		8,300
		21,800
Less: Drawings		(6,000)
		15,800

Working (W1)

Purchases = Payments − opening creditors + closing creditors

Purchases = 124,000 − 16,000 + 24,000 (June purchases) = 132,000

The level of stock has remained unchanged, and so purchases and cost of goods sold have the same value.

Assignment   Students should now work Question 10.5 at the end of this chapter.

10.4   REVIEW

After reading this chapter and working the chapter end questions, students should be able to:

● Differentiate between: the capacity and output of an undertaking; and fixed and variable costs.

- Calculate the costs resulting from different levels of activity.
- Analyse the results of decisions based on contribution costing.
- Calculate and interpret the break-even point and be aware of the limitations of break-even analysis.
- Prepare and interpret forecast results.

10.5 QUESTIONS

Question 10.1

Rock Ltd manufactures a single product which passes through two separate processes, designated X and Y, in two separate factories; all products must pass through both processes before they are ready for sale.

Rock's summary revenue account for 19X5 is as follows:

	£
Process X	
Raw materials	20,000
Wages	30,000
Depreciation	12,000
Rent	8,000
Transfer to process Y	70,000
Process Y	
Raw materials	10,000
Wages	40,000
Depreciation	12,000
Rent	8,000
Cost of production	140,000
General expenses	36,000
Net profit	24,000
Sales (100,000 units)	200,000

There are no stocks of any type at the beginning or at the end of the year.

There is a heavy demand for the product. Production costs and selling price are to be maintained at the same level as in 19X5.

Consideration is being given to three proposals for increasing production as follows:

(i) The expansion of manufacturing capacity at both factories. The cost of rent and the depreciation charge will in both cases be double that for 19X5; materials consumed and wage rates would continue for both factories at the same unit cost as for 19X5.

(ii) The purchase of the additional Process X components from an outside source at a price of 80p per unit. Expansion of manufacturing capacity at factory Y on the same terms and the same cost as for proposal (i).

(iii) The purchase of the additional finished goods from an outside source at 180p per unit and their sale at 200p per unit. No additional capacity would be required.

General expenses will increase in all cases at the rate of £2,000 per additional 25,000 units sold.

Required:
Prepare a financial statement for management which shows the forecast *additional* profit under each of the three proposals if outputs and sales increase by (a) 25,000 units and (b) 50,000 units.

Question 10.2
Glen Eagles is the proprietor of a small but long-established manufacturing business which has consistently made an annual profit of £20,000. The financial results of the business have shown little change in recent years, and the financial position has been very stable, supported by the fact that annual drawings have generally been lower than profit. The expectation is that there will be little change over the next few years and that the level of profit will be maintained.

Eagles has recently been invited by Troon Ltd to increase his production to meet an export demand in a market where the prospects of development and increased sales are very substantial. Additional plant with a life of 10 years, and a zero residual value at the end of that period, will be needed for such an expansion. Machines which will produce 46,000 items per annum are available at a cost of £36,000 each.

The selling price per item is £1, and the variable costs of manufacture for the export market will be 55p per item. Additional general expenses will amount to £10,000 for the first £46,000 increase in sales, but will fall to £4,000 for each £46,000 block of additional sales above the first £46,000.

Eagles has no private resources. The existing liquid resources of the business would cover any additional working capital required, and also provide £10,000 towards the capital cost of the new project. A bank is willing to lend up to £100,000 to Eagles at an interest rate of 15% per annum.

An alternative proposal is made to Eagles. Troon Ltd offers him £120,000 in cash for his entire business and is prepared to retain his services as a manager on a 10-year contract at a salary of £14,000 per annum plus an additional £3,000 per annum for each £46,000 increase in turnover.

Eagles can expect to invest the proceeds of the sale of his business to earn interest of 10% per annum.

Required:
- (a) Statements reporting on the profit likely to be received from overseas sales at the rate of £46,000, £92,000 and £138,000 per annum respectively.
- (b) Prepare a report to Eagles which shows the results of the alternative courses of action open to him.

Question 10.3
During 19X4 Feather Ltd sold 60,000 units of a product and made a net profit of £20,000. The contribution to fixed costs and profit per unit was £2, and the selling price was £5 per unit. The variable costs per unit are expected to increase by £0.10 for 19X5 and fixed costs in 19X5 are expected to be £4,500 greater than in 19X4; apart from these changes, trading conditions are expected to remain the same.

Required:
- (a) Prepare the summary profit and loss account for 19X4, showing sales, variable costs, fixed costs, and profit.
- (b) Calculate the break even level of sales for 19X4 in terms of units and £s.
- (c) Calculate the break even level of sales for 19X5 in terms of both units and £s.

Question 10.4
Grant commences business on 1 January 19X6 and introduces £20,000 cash as capital. He also borrows £8,000 from his brother at 10% per annum interest, payable half yearly in June and December. He makes the following estimates about the first six months of 19X6:

Fixed assets	£20,000 purchased for cash in January
Sales	£12,000 per month. Two months' credit to be given to customers
Purchases	£16,000 in January and £8,000 per month thereafter. Suppliers will allow one month's credit
Expenses	£800 per month average, excluding interest, payable in the month in which they are incurred
Drawings	£200 per month

Required:
Prepare a cash forecast for the business of Grant for the first six months of 19X6 which shows the cash balance at the end of each month.

Question 10.5

Required:
Use the information in Question 10.4 to prepare Grant's forecast trading and profit and loss account for the six months to 30 June 19X6 and his balance sheet at that date.

The fixed assets are to be depreciated at the rate of 20% per annum on cost, and Grant calculates selling prices of goods by adding 50% to their cost price.

Grant expects that the interest on the forecast overdraft will cost £300 and be paid in July.

CHAPTER 11

Performance Assessment: Ratio Analysis

11.1 INTRODUCTION

It is widely accepted that the maximisation of profit is a major business objective, and it is part of management's job to devise an effective means of achieving this ambitious aim. The link between growth in output and profitability was established in section 10.2 of chapter 10, and it is because sales and profit usually increase together that management often follows a policy of expansion. Management must, however, recognise that there exists an effective constraint on the rate of expansion, and this limitation is the quantity of cash available at any point in time. If management pursues a policy of expansion without first taking steps to ensure that suffcient cash is available for this purpose, the consequence will be, at the very least, financial embarrassment and, at worst, bankruptcy or liquidation.

It is therefore important for management to plan carefully future business developments, and this planning process should concentrate attention on two separate, but related, areas:

- Profitability.
- Financial stability.

Each area is of equal importance, and any tendency to emphasise one aspect to the exclusion of the other is likely to produce unfavourable repercussions. For instance, pre-occcupation with financial stability is likely to discourage innovation. Constant changes in consumer demand is a fact of business life, and the failure of management to anticipate, or at least respond to, these changes will result in a decline in the demand for the company's products to a level where the business is no longer viable. On the other hand, investment in a project which promises high profits in the near future, without first attempting to assess whether the company can afford the project, is equally ill advised. Recognition of the importance of financial stability should not cause management to ignore the need for profit, but it will cause management to follow a policy of long run rather than short run profit maximisation.

A proper assessment of business performance must therefore focus attention on the adequacy of both profit and cash. This is done with the use of ratio analysis which expresses one figure as a ratio or percentage of another; the objective is to disclose significant relationships and trends which are not immediately evident from an examination of the individual balances appearing in the accounts. To be meaningful, the ratios must relate two figures which are linked by an identifiable economic relationship. For example, profit is related to sales, and so expressing net profit as a percentage of sales is more illuminating than simply stating the value of profit, say £6m (see section 11.2 of this chapter).

The usefulness of an accounting ratio is enhanced if it is compared with others. There are three options available:

1. Comparison with results achieved by the same company during previous accounting periods (trend analysis). The banker is in a position to require figures for previous years as a condition for considering a loan request, and so should not have any trouble obtaining the necessary information. A limitation of trend analysis is that it provides little useful guidance about whether a business is doing as well as it should. For example, comparison may show that the current year's results are better than last year's, but last year's may have been disastrous and this year's very bad.

2. Comparison with the results of other companies (inter-firm comparison). It is important to discover how well a firm is performing relative to others as this throws light on the efficiency of management and the concern's long-term prospects. However, care should be taken when carrying out comparisons to ensure that the firms are in the same line of business and the results are not distorted by the application of different accounting policies.

3. Where companies set predetermined standards or budgets, it is useful to compare actual performance with these predictions. This type of information is not publicly available, but the banker should be able to obtain access to it. One drawback is that, although performance might be in line with the budget, it might still not represent an adequate level of achievement.

A number of accounting ratios are used when analysing accounts to build up a profile of the organisation. It is rare for all the ratios to point in the same direction, and so too much emphasis must not be attached to a single figure. This chapter now examines the main accounting ratios.

11.2 PROFIT RATIOS

The study of break-even analysis in chapter 10.2.3 showed that the amount of profit depends on the level of sales. It is useful, when assessing performance, to examine not only the absolute figure for profit, but also the relative profitability of different options. This is done by calculating the gross profit and net profit ratios. These ratios are used either to interpret past results or to assist the process of making decisions where the choice lies between a number of alternatives.

11.2.1 Gross Profit Margin (Ratio) This ratio compares gross profit with sales. It is calculated, as a percentage, using the formula:

$$\text{Gross Profit Margin} = \frac{\text{Gross Profit}}{\text{Sales}} \times 100$$

In the case of a trader, who buys and sells goods without processing them further, the ratio is expected to remain constant when sales levels change as the entire cost of goods sold is a variable cost.

Example 11.1

The sales, cost of goods sold and gross profit of Printer Ltd for 19X4 and 19X5 were:

	19X4 £	19X5 £
Sales	162,000	196,000
Cost of Goods Sold	121,500	147,000
Gross Profit	40,500	49,000

Required:
Calculate the gross profit margin for each year.

Solution

The gross profit margin for each year is:

19X4

$$\frac{40,500}{162,000} \times 100$$

$$= 25\%$$

19X5

$$\frac{49,000}{196,000} \times 100$$

$$= 25\%$$

The constant gross profit margin calculated in Example 11.1 results from the fact that for each additional unit sold, an extra unit is purchased, and prices, both for buying and selling, are unchanged. In practice, the margin does not always remain stable for reasons which include the following:

- Increased purchases may enable bulk purchase discounts to be obtained. This gives a lower average unit cost and therefore increases the gross profit margin.
- Prices may be reduced to enable more units to be sold. This reduces the gross profit margin, but, provided sufficient extra units are sold, total gross profit may still increase.

The gross profit margin of *manufacturers* varies with changes in the level of activity even where there are no price changes. This is because manufacturing expenses include some fixed costs and, as production increases, the fixed costs are spread over a greater number of units with the result that the total cost per unit falls.

Example 11.2

Yale Ltd incurs annual fixed manufacturing costs of £75,000 and a variable manufacturing cost per unit of £5. Each unit sells for £10. 20,000 units were produced and sold in 19X1 and 25,000 in 19X2. There were no opening or closing stocks in either year.

Required:
   (a)   Calculate the average fixed manufacturing cost per unit.
   (b)   Calculate the company's total gross profit and gross profit margin for each year.
   (c)   Comment on the results prepared in answer to parts (a) and (b).

Solution

(a)   19X1   19X2

Average Fixed Manufacturing $\dfrac{£75,000}{20,000} = £3.75$ $\dfrac{£75,000}{25,000} = £3$
      Cost per Unit

(b)

	£	£	£	£
Sales		200,000		250,000
Fixed Costs	75,000		75,000	
Variable Cost	100,000		125,000	
		175,000		200,000
Gross Profit		25,000		50,000

Gross Profit Margin

$$\frac{£25,000}{£200,000} \times 100 \qquad \frac{£50,000}{£250,000} \times 100$$

$$= 12.5\% \qquad\qquad = 20\%$$

(c)   An increase in sales of 25% has resulted in an increase in gross profit of 100% and in the gross profit margin of 60%. This is because the average fixed cost per unit has fallen from £3.75 to £3.00.

The interpretation of the gross profit margin of a manufacturer is also affected by the possibility of changes in purchase or selling prices which accompany a change in the rate of activity as described above for traders. Other unit cost changes may result from increased activity, for example overtime, which is paid at a higher rate, may have to be worked.

11.2.2   Net Profit Percentage (Ratio)   The net profit percentage compares net profit with sales and is expressed as a percentage. It is calculated by the formula:

$$\text{Net Profit Percentage} = \frac{\text{Net Profit}}{\text{Sales}} \times 100$$

The expenses charged against gross profit to calculate the net profit can be either fixed or variable with respect to sales. For example, interest paid on debentures is fixed provided that no further loans are taken out, while delivery costs are likely to respond to changes in the level of sales. Therefore, the net profit percentage of both traders and manufacturers changes as a result of an increase or decrease in sales. It is anticipated that increased sales, which spread the fixed costs over a greater output, will be accompanied by an increase in the net profit percentage, while decreased sales will be reflected by a fall in the percentage. Both the gross profit and net profit percentages may be affected by changes in prices unrelated to the level of sales, for example if the price of raw material rises, the effect on the percentages depends on the extent to which the increase can be passed on to the firm's customers.

Example 11.3

Crackle is a trader who buys and sells goods. His trading results for 19X6 and 19X7 were:

Summarised Trading Results

	19X6 £	19X7 £
Sales	80,000	100,000
Cost of Goods Sold	60,000	75,000
Gross Profit	20,000	25,000
Expenses	10,000	12,000
Net Profit	10,000	13,000

There were no opening or closing stocks in either year. The cost of goods which Crackle sells rose by 10% on 1 January 19X7.

Required:
 (a) Calculate Crackle's gross profit margin and net profit percentage for 19X6 and 19X7.
 (b) Comment on the changes in the percentages calculated in part (a).

Solution

(a)

	19X6	19X7
Gross profit margin	$\dfrac{20,000}{80,000} \times 100 = 25\%$	$\dfrac{25,000}{100,000} \times 100 = 25\%$
Net profit percentage	$\dfrac{10,000}{80,000} \times 100 = 12.5\%$	$\dfrac{13,000}{100,000} \times 100 = 13\%$

 (b) The gross profit margin has remained constant at 25%, and so we can conclude that Crackle has been able to pass on the 10% increase in costs to his customers. The growth in the value of sales is due not only to the price rise, but also to an increase in the volume of sales. If sales had simply risen in line with the price rise, they would have been only £80,000 + 10% = £88,000.

 The value of sales has grown by 25%, while expenses have increased by only 20% (perhaps some of them are fixed costs). As a result, the net profit percentage has increased from 12.5% to 13%.

Changes in the gross profit margin also affect the net profit percentage, and, to examine the relative impact of items charged in the profit and loss account, it is useful to express them all as a percentage of sales.

Example 11.4

Stamp Ltd, a trading company, did not increase its selling prices between 19X6 and 19X7, but the cost of the goods it sells rose 1.25% on 1 January 19X7. Its trading and profit and loss accounts for 19X6 and 19X7 were:

Summarised Trading and Profit and Loss Accounts

	19X6	19X7
	£	£
Sales	50,000	60,000
Cost of Goods Sold	40,000	48,600
Gross Profit	10,000	11,400
Rent	1,200	1,200
Other Expenses	2,000	2,400
	3,200	3,600
Net Profit	6,800	7,800

Required:
    (a) Prepare statements for 19X6 and 19X7 in which all costs, the net profit and the gross profit are expressed as percentages of sales.
    (b) Comment on the results shown in the statement prepared in part (a).

Solution

    (a)

	19X6	19X7
	%	%
Sales	100.0	100.0
Cost of Goods Sold	80.0	81.0
Gross Profit	20.0	19.0
Rent	2.4	2.0
Other Expenses	4.0	4.0
	6.4	6.0
Net Profit	13.6	13.0

(b) The gross profit has risen, but the gross profit margin has fallen by 1% as a result of the rise in the cost of goods it sells (if this had not risen, cost of goods sold would have been £48,000; 1.25% × 48,000 = 600, representing the price rise). Rent is a fixed cost, and its impact has fallen from 2.4% to 2% and other expenses have remained constant at 4%; the net result is a fall in the total profit and loss account costs from 6.4% to 6%. The overall impact is a fall in the net profit percentage of 0.6%, although the amount of net profit has risen. If the gross profit margin could have been maintained by passing on the price rise to customers, the net profit percentage would also have risen.

Assignment Students should now work Question 11.1 at the end of this chapter.

11.3 RETURN ON CAPITAL EMPLOYED (ROCE)

The amount of profit earned by a business is important but, in order to assess the relative performance of a number of businesses, or even the performance of the same business over a number of years, it is necessary to examine the figure for profit in relation to the amount of money invested (capital employed) in the business. This is done by calculating the Return on Capital Employed (ROCE) using the formula:

$$\text{Return on Capital Employed} = \frac{\text{Net Profit*}}{\text{Capital Employed}} \times 100$$

Tutorial note:
* The net profit *before* or the net profit *after* tax can be used in this calculation. Whichever approach is used, it must be applied consistently.

Example 11.5

The following information is provided for 19X1.

	Company A £	Company B £
Net profit	100,000	150,000
Capital employed	500,000	1,500,000

Required:
(a) Calculate the return on capital employed for each company.

(b)   Comment on the comparative results achieved by these companies from the point of view of a prospective investor.

Solution

(a)   Company A $= \dfrac{\pounds100,000}{\pounds500,000} \times 100 = 20\%$

Company B $= \dfrac{\pounds150,000}{\pounds1,500,000} \times 100 = 10\%$

(b)   Company A has reported a profit of £100,000 whereas company B has reported a profit of £150,000. Company B has therefore generated 50% more profit than company A. However, the ROCE figures make it clear that, contrary to the initial impression, company A is the better proposition for a prospective investor. Company B earns a profit which is 50% higher but, to achieve this, three times the level of investment is required. When profit is related to the amount invested we find that company A earns a return of 20% compared with 10% by company B, i.e. on every £1 invested in company A a return of 20p is earned, whereas on every £1 invested in company B a return of 10p is earned.

11.3.1   Calculation of Capital Employed   Capital employed is the amount of money invested in the business. The two most common methods of calculating capital employed are as follows:

- *Owners' capital employed (net assets)*   This is the amount invested by the owner or owners. It is the balance on the sole trader's capital account, the aggregate of the balances on the partners' capital and current accounts or, in the case of a limited company, the ordinary shareholders' capital plus share premium account, retained profits and any balances on reserve accounts. Using an asset-based approach, owners' capital employed is alternatively calculated by taking total assets and deducting non-ownership liabilities.

- *Total capital employed (gross assets)*   This is found by adding together all sources of finance, i.e. capital, non-current liabilities and current liabilities. The alternative calculation adds together the balance for each category of asset belonging to the business.

Owners captal employer
Capital Employed = net assets
ord capital employed = all sources f financ ind holder

Example 11.6

The following balances were extracted from the books of Compass Ltd at 31 December 19X2.

	£
Fixed assets	130,000
Ordinary share capital	100,000
Share premium account	20,000
10% loan repayable 19X8	50,000
Trade creditors	25,000
Current assets	105,000
Revaluation reserve	12,000
Proposed dividend	10,000
Retained profit	18,000

Required:
    (a)   Prepare the balance sheet of Compass Ltd at 31 December 19X2, presented in horizontal format.
    (b)   Calculate the figures for:
        (i)   Owners' capital employed.
        (ii)   Total capital employed.

Solution

(a)   *Balance Sheet of Compass Ltd at 31 December 19X2*

	£		£
Fixed assets	130,000	Ordinary share capital	100,000
Current assets	105,000	Share premium account	20,000
		Revaluation reserve	12,000
		Retained profit	18,000
			150,000
		10% loan repayable 19X8	50,000
			200,000
		Current liabilities	
		Trade creditors	25,000
		Proposed dividend	10,000
	235,000		235,000

(b)   (i)   Owners' capital employed = £150,000
      (ii)   Total capital employed = £235,000

11.3.2   Matching Profit with Capital Employed   The profit figure used for the purpose of calculating ROCE differs depending on the version of capital employed under consideration.

- *Owners' capital employed*— Use net profit reported in the accounts.
- *Total capital employed* — Use net profit before deducting any interest charges, including interest on any bank overdraft.

These calculations are used for different purposes: the former calculation measures the return earned for investors on the amount they have invested in the enterprise, while the latter calculation directs attention to the efficiency with which management utilises the total resources at its disposal.

Example 11.7

Assume the same facts as for Example 11.6. In addition, the summarised profit and loss account of Compass Ltd for 19X2 is as follows:

Profit and Loss Account of Compass Ltd for 19X2

	£	£
Gross profit		100,000
Less: Administrative costs	54,000	
Selling and distribution costs	17,000	
Interest on long-term loan	5,000	76,000
Net profit		24,000
Less: Dividends		10,000
Retained profit for 19X2		14,000
Retained profit at 1 January 19X2		4,000
Retained profit at 31 December 19X2		18,000

Required:
- (a)   Calculations of the return on:
  - (i)   Owners' capital employed.
  - (ii)   Total capital employed.
- (b)   Comment on the different results revealed by these calculations.

Solution

(a)   (i)   Owners' capital employed: Return $= \dfrac{24,000}{150,000} \times 100 = 16\%$

(ii)   Total capital employed: Return $= \dfrac{29,000^*}{235,000} \times 100 = 12.3\%$

* £24,000 (net profit) + £5,000 (all interest charges)

(b) The rate of return earned on total capital employed is 12.3%; looked at another way, the directors of Compass have managed to achieve a return of 12.3% on the total resources at their disposal. The return earned on the owners' capital employed is significantly higher, at 16%. There are two reasons for this:

1. Compass benefits from 'free' finance amounting to £35,000, consisting of the dividend not yet due (£10,000) and trade credit (£25,000), and it is for this reason that businessmen usually take the maximum amount of finance offered by suppliers.

2. The directors have raised some loan capital at a favourable rate of interest, i.e. the £50,000 loan repayable in 19X8 attracts interest at the rate of 10% per annum and, because the return earned on total capital employed is higher, the surplus accrues to the ordinary shareholders who are, as a result, better off. This will not always happen; if the return on total capital employed is *below* 10%, the providers of loan finance must still be paid their 10%, and the 'loss' is suffered by the ordinary shareholders. Management should therefore raise loan capital only if it is reasonably confident that the return earned will exceed that payable to loan creditors.

The rates of return, calculated in this section, are based on capital employed at the *year end*. Profit arises throughout the 12-month period, however, and a more precise calculation is made by using *average* capital employed during the year. Because the information needed to calculate average capital employed is rarely provided, and because absolute accuracy is not a priority, it is perfectly acceptable to use the year end figure which usually produces a close enough approximation.

Assignment Students should now work Question 11.2 at the end of this chapter.

11.4 WORKING CAPITAL

A business must be able to meet its debts as they fall due to maintain its creditworthiness. For this desirable state of affairs to exist, a business must have an adequate balance of working capital, which is calculated with the formula:

Working Capital = Current Assets − Current Liabilities

A secure financial position is illustrated in Example 11.8.

Example 11.8

The following balances were extracted from the books of Campion Ltd as at 31 December 19X1.

	£
Share capital	100,000
Reserves	75,000
Taxation due 30 September 19X2	10,000
Trade creditors	15,000
Balance of cash at bank	5,000
Fixed assets at cost less depreciation	150,000
Stock	22,000
Trade debtors	23,000

Required:
Calculate Campion's working capital balance at 31 December 19X1.

Solution

Calculation of working capital:	£	£
Current assets: Stock		22,000
Trade debtors		23,000
Bank balance		5,000
		50,000
Less: Current Liabilities: Trade creditors	15,000	
Taxation payable	10,000	25,000
Working capital		25,000

The above calculation shows that Campion is able to pay its current liabilities out of resources made available by the conversion of current assets into cash and, in addition, it shows that £25,000 remains after the necessary payments have been made. The fact that business activity is continuous means that additional purchases will be made during January 19X2 and more sales will also occur, consequently the £25,000 surplus will never actually arise in a single lump sum. Nevertheless, the working capital calculation provides a useful indication of the company's ability to meet its short-term debts as they fall due for payment, i.e. it focuses attention on the solvency position of the firm.

11.4.1 Working Capital Ratio The significance which can be attached, in isolation, to the balance for working capital is, however, limited. A figure of £25,000 suggests financial stability in the case of a small business, such as Campion, but probably not in a much larger enterprise. In another company, the deduction of current liabilities amounting to, say, £975,000 from current assets of £1,000,000 would also show a working capital balance of £25,000 but, in view of the much larger scale of short-term commitments, it would probably be regarded as a totally inadequate financial 'cushion'. It is for this reason that users of accounting statements pay more attention to the working capital (or current) *ratio,* which examines the proportional relationship between current assets and current liabilities. It is calculated as follows:

$$\text{Working capital ratio} = \frac{\text{Current Assets}}{\text{Current Liabilities}} : 1$$

The working capital ratio of Campion is as follows:

$$\text{Working capital ratio} = \frac{£50,000}{£25,000} : 1$$

$$= 2 : 1$$

The purpose of the working capital ratio is to help assess the solvency position of a business, and the question which therefore naturally arises is 'What is an acceptable ratio?' Unfortunately it is not possible to be dogmatic, since much depends on the nature of the trade in which the company is engaged. It may be assumed, for the purpose of illustration, that Campion is a trading company which purchases and sells goods on credit, also that the company receives from suppliers the same period of credit that it allows to customers; 30 days is the normal credit period, although the exact duration is unimportant because, provided a company allows customers, on average, the same period of credit as is granted by its suppliers, the amount of money due from customers will be received in time for the creditors to be paid as their debts fall due. Because Campion sells goods on credit, however, none of the money presently tied up in stock will be converted into cash in time to pay the current liabilities as they mature. It is true that some stock will be sold in the next few days, but it will be at least a further 30 days before the cash is collected from the customer. It will be even longer before the remaining stock is converted into cash. The conclusion which arises from this analysis is that the working capital ratio must be sufficiently high to accommodate the inclusion of stock amongst the current assets. If stock comprises no more than 50% of total current assets, as is the case at Campion, an adequate ratio of current assets to current liabilities is in the region of 2:1.

In practice a ratio of 2:1 is conventionally regarded as the acceptable norm. It cannot be emphasised too strongly, however, that this is a broad generalisation which should be treated with great caution. For example, companies in certain sectors of the economy turn stock into cash very quickly and, for them, a ratio of well below 2:1 may be quite acceptable. This state of affairs usually exists in the retail trade where sales are made mainly for cash. In circumstances where resources are tied up in stock for a much longer time period, as happens in the construction industry, a working capital ratio of perhaps 4:1 may be regarded as normal.

11.4.2 Working Capital Requirements and Dividend Policy Dividends are declared on the basis of profits earned, but a payment can be made only if cash is available for this purpose. When deciding whether a dividend should be paid and, if so, how much, the directors take account of the company's current financial position and future commitments. Their aim is to ensure that, as far as possible, the shareholders receive an adequate return on their investment; also that the financial position is not undermined as a result of the payment made.

Example 11.9

The summarised balance sheets of Galston Ltd as at 31 December 19X5 and 19X6 are as follows:

	19X5		19X6	
	£	£	£	£
Fixed assets at cost		303,000		367,500
Less: Accumulated depreciation		124,500		157,500
		178,500		210,000
Current Assets				
Stock	37,500		75,000	
Debtors	34,500		43,500	
Bank	18,000		1,500	
	90,000		120,000	
Less: Current Liabilities	45,000		55,500	
		45,000		64,500
		223,500		274,500

Financed by:	£	£
Share capital	150,000	150,000
Retained profit at 31 December 19X5 . .	73,500	73,500
Profit for 19X6	—	51,000
	223,500	274,500

The figure of current liabilities as at 31 December 19X5 includes a proposed dividend of £7,500 for the year to that date. No decision has been taken yet about the dividend to be paid for 19X6, and nothing is included in the 19X6 balance sheet for such a dividend.

The directors are considering the dividend that should be paid for 19X6 in the light of the excellent results for that year.

Required:
   (a)   Calculate Galston's working capital and working capital ratio as at 31 December 19X5 and 31 December 19X6.
   (b)   Calculate the maximum dividend that should be declared for 19X6 if the working capital ratio at 31 December 19X6 is to be the same as at 31 December 19X5.
   (c)   A brief discussion of the financial policy pursued by the directors of Galston Ltd in 19X6.

Solution

(a)   31 December

	19X5	19X6
	£	£
Current assets	90,000	120,000
Less: Current liabilities	45,000	55,500
Working capital	45,000	64,500
Working capital ratio	2:1	2.16:1

(b)   31 December 19X6:

	£
Current assets per balance sheet ....:	120,000
Current liabilities, assuming a working capital ratio of 2:1 (120,000/2)	60,000
Current liabilities per balance sheet	55,500
Maximum permissible dividend	4,500

(c)   The directors have made an additional net investment of £31,500 in fixed assets, but this is amply covered by the retained profts of £46,500 (£51,000 minus maximum permissible dividend of £4,500) and the working capital ratio has been maintained at 2:1. The financial policy pursued by the directors appears a little less sound when we look at the cash position. The heavy investment in stock has been at the expense of cash; debtors have also increased but at a rate which is not unreasonable in relation to the other changes.

11.5 LIQUIDITY RATIO

The purpose of the liquidity ratio is similar to the working capital ratio, in that it is designed to assess the ability of a business to meet its debts as they fall due. The calculation is as follows:

$$\text{Liquidity ratio} = \frac{\text{Liquid assets}}{\text{Current liabilities}} : 1$$

It is a more rigorous test of solvency than the working capital ratio, because it omits the current assets which are unlikely to be converted into cash in time to meet liabilities falling due in the near future. The ratio is for this reason sometimes described as the 'acid test' of solvency. Non-liquid current assets which must therefore be left out of the calculation include stock (unless sales are made on the cash basis, in which case stock is also a liquid asset) and any trade debts not receivable in the near future, because customers have been allowed an extended period of credit.

The liquidity ratio of Campion (Example 11.8) is as follows:

$$\text{Liquidity ratio} = \frac{£23,000 + £5,000}{£25,000} : 1$$

$$= 1.1:1$$

This calculation shows that Campion Ltd has sufficient liquid assets to cover its current liabilities. A ratio of 1:1 is generally considered desirable in practice and, on the whole, this is a fair test. However, students should be aware of the fact that the conventional method of calculation can understate the short-term financial position of the firm because, although current assets are carefully examined and less liquid items excluded, the same distinction is not made in the case of current liabilities. Normally all current liabilities are included, despite the fact that some of the amounts outstanding, particularly taxation, may not be payable for a number of months. In Campion's case, current liabilities include taxation which is not due for payment until 30 September 19X2, nine months after the balance sheet date. A more realistic calculation of the liquidity ratio should therefore exclude taxation as well as stock.

$$\text{Liquidity ratio} = \frac{£23,000 + £5,000}{£15,000} : 1$$

$$= 1.9:1$$

The conventional approach to the calculation of the liquidity ratio, which includes all current liabilities, is consistent with the accounting concept of 'prudence' but may, in certain circumstances, be a little misleading.

Assignment Students should now work Question 11.3 at the end of the chapter.

11.6 GEARING
Long-term funds are derived from two sources:

- equity (share capital plus reserves)
- loans.

It is quite likely that only shares are issued when a company is formed, but it is usual for loans to be raised at some later date. There are many reasons for issuing loan capital. For instance, the owners might want to increase their investment, but avoid the risks attaching to share capital; they can do this by making a secured loan. Alternatively, management might require additional funds which the shareholders are unwilling to provide, and so a loan is raised instead. In either case, the effect is to introduce an element of gearing, or leverage, into the capital structure of the company.

There are numerous ways of measuring gearing, and the debt/equity ratio is one which is commonly used. For the purpose of calculating this ratio, debt can be calculated in either of two ways:

1. *Debt defined as long-term loans*

$$\text{Debt/equity ratio} = \frac{\text{Long-term loans*}}{\text{Shareholders' equity}} \times 100$$

Tutorial note:
* This figure includes any preference shares outstanding as these carry a fixed rate of return.

2. *Debt defined as total borrowings*
   The banker, when assessing risk, wants to examine *total* borrowings in relation to the equity base. In these circumstances, it is useful to extend

equity – shareholdings

Debt/equity × 100
(*Total*)

the definition of debt when calculating the debt/equity ratio, and so the ratio is calculated with the following formula:

$$\underline{\text{Total debt/equity ratio}} = \frac{\text{Total financial debt*}}{\text{Shareholders' equity}} \times 100$$

Tutorial note:
* This includes loans from directors and bank overdrafts which, although technically of a short-term nature, are a permanent source of finance for many businesses.

Example 11.10

long term loan.
Total financial debt.

Required:
Calculate the gearing (debt/equity) ratio of Compass Ltd from the information given in Example 11.6.

Solution

$$\text{Gearing ratio} = \frac{50,000 \text{ (Loan)}}{150,000 \text{ (Shareholders' equity)}} \times 100 = 33\%$$

The use of loans has direct implications for the profit left for ordinary shareholders after all expenses, including interest on the loans, have been met. Expansion is often financed using loans so as to 'gear up' the rate of return for shareholders, but this can only be achieved if the trading profit earned from investing the additional funds exceeds the cost of the interest payable in return for borrowing the funds.

Three features of loan finance, compared with share capital, which must be remembered when it is used by limited companies are:

1. The interest charge is allowed as a deduction from profit *before* corporation tax is calculated; dividends are paid out of the profit left *after* corporation tax has been deducted. This is clear from the fact that interest is charged in the profit and loss account while dividends are shown in the appropriation account.
2. The interest on loans is a fixed cost and has to be paid irrespective of the amount of profit made; it still has to be paid even if losses are occurring. This contrasts with the dividends payable to shareholders which can

only be paid out of profits, and do not have to be paid if the company cannot afford them.
3. The rate of interest on loans is usually fixed; dividends can vary according to the amount of profit made and how much of this the directors decide the company can afford to pay out.

Example 11.11

The directors of Rotblat Ltd are planning to undertake a new project which calls for a total investment of £1m in fixed assets and working capital. They plan to finance this with a long-term loan carrying interest at the rate of 12% per annum. The finance director forecasts that in the first year after the project is undertaken a profit before interest and tax of £150,000 will be made from the project, while in the second year a profit of £300,000 will be made.

The company pays corporation tax at the rate of 25%.

Required:
   (a) Calculate the 'surplus' profit, if any, expected to accrue to the company's shareholders in each of the first two years if the loan is raised and the project undertaken.
   (b) Comment on the results of the first two years from the viewpoint of the company's shareholders.

Solution

(a)

	Year 1 £	Year 2 £
Profit before interest and tax	150,000	300,000
Less: Interest (£1m x 12%)	120,000	120,000
	30,000	180,000
Less: Corporation tax at 25%	7,500	45,000
Surplus	22,500	135,000

(b) The profit made by the project doubles over the two years, but the surplus for the shareholders in the second year is £135,000 compared with £22,500 in the first year; this is a sixfold increase. The disproportionate increase is due to the fact that the interest payable on the loan is a fixed cost which does not vary with activity or profit.

As was shown above in Example 11.11, the shareholders of a geared company reap disproportionate benefits when earnings before interest and tax increase, and this will be reflected in the ROCE ratio. The converse is also true, and a geared company is likely to find itself in severe financial difficulties when trading results are poor; the extent of these difficulties is determined by the amount of gearing. It is not possible to specify an optimal level of gearing for all companies, but, as a general rule, gearing should be low in those industries where demand is volatile and profits are likely to fluctuate.

Assignment   Students should now work Questions 11.4 and 11.5 at the end of this chapter.

11.7 REVIEW
After reading the chapter and working the chapter end questions, students should be able to:

- Understand the need of companies for profitability and financial stability.
- Understand that, to be meaningful, results must be considered on a comparative basis.
- Be able to calculate and interpret the following ratios: gross profit to sales; net profit to sales; return on capital employed; working capital ratio; liquidity ratio; and the debt/equity (gearing) ratio.
- Understand the restraints which working capital and liquidity requirements create.

11.8 QUESTIONS

Question 11.1
The summarised profit and loss account of Sannoy Ltd 19X5 is as follows:

	£		£
Expenses	50,400	Sales	56,000
Net profit	5,600		
	56,000		56,000

Two alternative plans for 19X6 have been prepared and they are under consideration. The plans are:

PLAN 1	£
An investment in plant costing	16,000
Sales expected to increase to	84,000
Anticipated total expenses (including depreciation)	76,440

PLAN 2

An investment in plant costing	36,000
Sales expected to increase to	112,500
Anticipated total expenses (including depreciation)	103,500

Required:
- (a) Summary profit and loss accounts for 19X6 showing the results of Plan 1 and Plan 2 as they would appear if the forecasts are exactly achieved.
- (b) A comparison of the financial results to be expected under each of the two plans, both between themselves and with respect to the results of 19X5, including calculations of the net profit percentages.

Question 11.2

The summarised trading and profit and loss account of Rubber Ltd for 19X1 and its summarised balance sheet at 31 December 19X1 are as follows:

Trading and Profit and Loss Account for 19X1

	£		£
Cost of sales (variable)	126,000	Sales	180,000
Gross profit	54,000		
	180,000		180,000
Expenses (fixed)	39,000	Gross profit	54,000
Net profit	15,000		
	54,000		54,000

Note: A dividend of £10,000 is proposed for 19X1.

Balance Sheet as at 31 December 19X1

	£		£	£
Fixed assets	113,000	Share capital		100,000
Current assets	70,000	Retained profit ...		50,000
				150,000
		Current Liabilities:		
		General	23,000	
		Dividend	10,000	33,000
	183,000			183,000

The company could expand production to a sales level of £225,000 with no increase in fixed expenses, and the cost of sales would remain the same percentage of sales as for 19X1.

Required:
  (a) Calculate the gross profit margin, net profit as a percentage of sales and the return on capital employed for 19X1.
  (b) A calculation of the additional sales that would have been necessary to increase the return on capital employed by $2\frac{1}{2}\%$.

Note: For the purpose of the answer, capital employed is to be interpreted as issued capital plus retained profit on 31 December.

Question 11.3
The following information has been extracted from the accounts of Lock Ltd, a wholesale trading company.

Balances at 31 December

	19X1	19X2
	£000	£000
Fixed assets	500	550
Trade debtors	125	150
Cash at bank	25	—
Proposed dividend	20	60
Overdraft	—	20
Trade creditors	80	100
Stocks	150	200

Results for the year to 31 December

	19X1	19X2
	£000	£000
Sales	2,000	3,000
Cost of sales	1,000	1,450
Overhead costs	800	1,300

Required:
  (a) A statement showing the return on capital employed, the value of working capital, the working capital ratio and the liquidity ratio. Your answer should be presented in the following form:

	19X1	19X2
Return on Capital Employed	—	—
Working Capital	—	—
Working Capital Ratio	—	—
Liquidity Ratio	—	—

  (b) A brief discussion of the implications of the information calculated above.

Note: For the purpose of your calculations, capital employed is defined as shareholders' equity.

Question 11.4

Town Ltd and Country Ltd are companies engaged in the same kind of business. Past experience indicates that profits, before deducting loan interest, are likely to fluctuate up to 50% above or below those made in 19X1, for which year the following information is provided:

	Town £000	Country £000
Shareholders' equity	3,500	2,000
15% Debentures repayable in 19X9	500	4,000
Profit for 19X1 before loan interest	600	900

Required:

(a) Calculate the return on the owners' capital employed of each company for 19X1.

(b) Calculate the return on the owners' capital employed for profits 50% above and below the 19X1 levels.

(c) Comment briefly on the effect of the different capital structures of the two companies.

Note: Ignore taxation.

Question 11.5

The following information is obtained in connection with the affairs of two companies, manufacturing specialised metal products, in respect of the year ended 31 December 19X5.

	Metalmax Ltd £000	Precision Products Ltd £000
Sales	800	950
Adminstration expenses	30	30
Selling expenses (including promotional costs)	45	60
Plant and machinery at cost	360	360
Depreciation to 31 December 19X4	110	110
Current assets	240	400
Trade creditors	120	320
Share capital (£1 ordinary shares)	200	200

It is also established that both companies incur variable costs of sales, excluding depreciation, of 80% on sales. Depreciation should be charged at 15% on the cost of machinery. Reserves may be treated as the balancing figure in the balance sheets.

Required:
  (a) Summary trading and profit and loss accounts for the year ended 31 December 19X5 and balance sheets at that date for each company in vertical format to facilitate comparison.
  (b) A comparison of the profitability of the two companies during 19X5 and of their respective financial positions at the end of the year. Relevant accounting ratios should be used to support the discussion.

Notes:
1. Within the current asset totals are included balances in respect of stocks and work-in-progress as follows:

Mctalmax Ltd	£120,000
Precision Products Ltd	£200,000

2. Ignore taxation.

CHAPTER 12

Performance Assessment: Funds Flow

12.1 THE STATEMENT OF SOURCES AND APPLICATIONS OF FUNDS

A company's balance sheet sets out its financial state at a particular point in time, while the profit and loss account reports the financial effects of those transactions which occur during the year and directly impinge upon the calculation of profit, i.e. revenues and expenses. Other transactions involving flows of resources, such as an issue of shares or debentures, or the purchase of a fixed asset are not reported in the profit and loss account since they are *capital* as opposed to *revenue* transactions. These events, which often involve significant amounts of money, are of interest to the users of accounts, and a report called the 'Statement of Sources and Applications of Funds', often abbreviated to the 'Statement of Funds', was developed to provide information on these flows. It is a requirement that limited companies include a Statement of Source and Applications of Funds in their annual accounts.

- *Definition* The statement of funds sets out, in an orderly manner, the sources of finance which have been raised and generated by a business during the year and the ways in which those funds have been applied.

- *Objective* The purpose of the statement of funds is to provide some insights into the financial policy pursued by management during the year, and the likely effect of that policy on the financial position of the company.

The various sources of finance available to businesses, and the ways in which they are employed, are examined in the next two sections. The construction of the statement is then examined in section 12.1.3 of this chapter.

12.1.1 Sources of Funds It is management's job to ensure that there is a satisfactory balance between long-, medium- and short-term finance. The main sources of finance and the periods for which they are available are listed below.

1. *Owner's capital* This is the amount invested by the owner(s) in the business and is long-term finance.
2. *Debentures and loans* In the case of debentures, the advance is normally made on a long-term basis, for between 10 and 40 years. The duration for which loans are made depends on the terms of the agreement between the borrower and the lender.
3. *Hire purchase and extended credit* These are useful ways for a company to spread the heavy cost of a new fixed asset. The finance is either short-term, where the instalments are all payable within one year, or a mixture of short- and medium-term, where they extend beyond a 12-month period.
4. *Trade credit from suppliers* This is short-term finance, although new creditors will replace those currently paid, thus ensuring a more or less permanent source of finance in this form.
5. *Taxation and dividends payable* These are liabilities but, until the payment is made, the cash may be used by the company. They are therefore short-term finance.
6. *Bank overdraft* This is, in theory, a short-term source of finance, although in practice it is employed on a long-term basis by many businesses.
7. *Sale of fixed assets* The cash inflow from the sale of fixed assets is available for management to invest on a long-term basis.
8. *Funds generated from operations* During the course of trading activity a company generates revenue, principally in the form of sales receipts, and incurs expenditure comprising a wide range of different outlays, some of which result in an outflow of funds in the current accounting period and others which do not. Most outlays fall into the first category, e.g. expenditure on purchases of materials, wages, salaries and rent. There are, however, a small number of items, the most important of which is depreciation, which are charged against profit but do not result in a current outflow of funds.

The purpose of the depreciation charge is to reflect the fact that sales revenue has benefitted, during the period under review, from the acquisition of fixed assets which occurred in a previous accounting period. The effect of making the charge is to reduce reported profit and ensure that an equivalent amount of cash is retained within the business, which may be used, in due course, to help finance replacement of the asset when it is worn out. It is therefore necessary to add back the depreciation charge to the reported profit figure to identify total funds generated from operations, i.e.

Funds generated from operations = Profit + Depreciation

Some of the profit is usually paid out in the form of dividends, of course, but the remainder is retained and is available for investment on a long-term basis.

Students often find it difficult to grasp the fact that the depreciation charge is *represented* by an equivalent *inflow* of cash. The link is demonstrated in Example 12.1.

Example 12.1

The balance sheet of Pencil Ltd, which purchases and sells goods for cash, is as follows at 31 December 19X1.

Balance Sheet at 31 December 19X1

	£	£
Fixed assets at cost		1,800
Less: Depreciation		540
		1,260
Current Assets		
Stock	400	
Cash	200	
		600
		1,860
Less: 10% loan repayable 19X7		500
		1,360
Financed by:		
Share capital		1,000
Retained profit		360
		1,360

During 19X2 cash sales and cash purchases amounted respectively to £4,000 and £2,500. The stock level remained unchanged during the year and £600 was *paid out* for wages and other operating expenses. In addition, loan interest was paid on 31 December 19X2, and depreciation of £240 was charged on fixed assets.

Required:

(a) The cash account for 19X2.

(b) The trading and profit and loss account for 19X2.

(c) The balance sheet at 31 December 19X2.

(d) A calculation of funds generated from operations during 19X2, i.e. profit + depreciation.

Solution

(a)   *Cash Account for 19X2*

	£		£
Opening balance	200	Purchases	2,500
Sales	4,000	Wages etc.	600
		Interest	50
		Closing balance	1,050
	4,200		4,200

(b)   *Trading and Profit and Loss Account for 19X2*

	£	£
Sales		4,000
Opening stock	400	
Purchases	2,500	
Less: Closing stock	(400)	
Cost of goods sold		2,500
Gross profit		1,500
Wages etc.	600	
Interest	50	
Depreciation	240	
		890
Net profit		610

(c)   *Balance Sheet at 31 December 19X2*

	£	£
Fixed assets at cost		1,800
Less: Depreciation		780
		1,020
Current Assets		
Stock	400	
Cash	1,050	
		1,450
		2,470
Less: 10% loan repayable 19X7		500
		1,970

Financed by: £
Share capital   1,000
Retained profit   970
                                                            _____
                                                             1,970

(d)

Funds generated from operations:

	£
Profit	610
Depreciation	240
Funds from operations	850

Tutorial note:

The cash balance has increased from £200 to £1,050 and the cash account shows, in detail, how this increase of £850 has been brought about. The profit and loss account shows a profit figure of £610, and this is less than the increase in the cash balance because a 'non-cash' item of expenditure, i.e. depreciation £240, has been debited to the profit and loss acount. It therefore follows that to reconcile the opening cash balance with the closing cash balance it is necessary to add the figure for 'funds generated from operations', profit + depreciation, to the opening cash figure.

	£
Opening cash balance	200
Add: Funds generated from operations	850
Closing cash balance	1,050

A note of warning A common misconception is that the depreciation charge *produces* an inflow of cash, and that cash inflows can be increased by raising the amount of the charge. This is entirely wrong. Cash is generated from trading transactions, and the depreciation charge is merely a 'book entry' which earmarks a proportion of funds generated from operations for retention within the business. If the depreciation charge, in the above example, is increased from £240 to £400, profit falls from £610 to £450 and funds generated from operations remain unchanged at £850 (depreciation £400 + profit £450). An effect of raising the charge is, however, to earmark a *larger* quantity of funds for retention within the business; although later in the asset's life, charges and retentions will be correspondingly lower because the balance which remains to be written off is reduced by £160.

Example 12.2

Assume the same facts as appear in the solution to Example 12.1.

Required:
Calculate the closing cash balance of Pencil, on 1 January 19X3, in each of the following circumstances:
  (a)   The entire profit of £610 is paid out as dividends on 1 January 19X3.
  (b)   The depreciation charge is amended to £400 and the entire profit of £450 is paid out as dividends on 1 January 19X3.

Note: No other transactions occur on 1 January 19X3.

Solution

	(a)	(b)
	£	£
Cash balance at 31 December 19X2	1,050	1,050
Less: Dividends	610	450
Cash balance at 1 January 19X3	440	600

Tutorial note:
The increase in the depreciation charge, under (b), reduces the maximum dividend payable by £160 and, as a result, the balance of cash which remains is £160 higher, at £600.

In practice, the change in the cash balance is rarely entirely due to funds generated from operations. There are numerous other transactions which cause it to change, e.g. new plant is purchased or additional shares issued.

12.1.2   Applications of Funds   The sources of funds, described in the previous section, may be applied in the following ways:

1.   *Purchase of fixed assets*   This is a long-term investment.
2.   *Repayment of loan capital*   To maintain a secure base of long-term finance, the loan repaid will usually be replaced by a new issue of either long-term loans or shares; alternatively the repayment may be financed out of profits earned and retained in the business, provided they have not already been used for another purpose.

3. *Payment of tax and dividends* These payments are claims against profit earned during the year.

4. *Investment in stocks* This is a short-term investment in the sense that the stock is sold after a relatively short interval, although it will then probably be replaced by new purchases.

5. *Credit allowed to customers* Again a short-term investment, but where new debts replace those currently paid.

The main sources and applications of funds, discussed above, are summarised in Figure 12.1.

Figure 12.1

Checklist of Sources and Applications of Funds

	Sources	Applications
Capital and loans raised	/	
Capital and loans repaid		/
Increase in current asset balances (e.g. stock, debtors, bank)		/
Decrease in current asset balances	/	
Increase in current liability balances (e.g. creditors, overdraft, dividends and tax payable)	/	
Decrease in current liability balances		/
Funds generated from operations (positive)	/	
(negative)		/
Provisions for tax and dividends		/

12.1.3 Constructing a Statement of Funds The statement of funds was defined, in section 12.1 of this chapter, as one which sets out the sources of finance which have been raised and generated by a business during the year and the way in which those funds have been applied. Since the balance sheet shows the accumulated sources of finance and the way in which that money has been spent up to a particular point in time, most of the information required to prepare a statement of funds can be obtained by deducting the balances appearing in the opening balance sheet from those appearing in the closing balance sheet.

Illustration 12.1

The following information is provided for Ruler Ltd:

| | Balance Sheets 31 December | | | | Differences | |
| | 19X3 | | 19X4 | | Source | Application |
	£000	£000	£000	£000	£000	£000
Fixed Assets						
Machinery at cost		320		470		150
Less: Accumulated depreciation		150		192	42	
		170		278		
Current Assets						
Stock	86		107			21
Trade debtors	53		75			22
Bank	12		64			52*
	151		246			
Less: Current Liabilities						
Trade creditors	46		61		15	
Working capital	—	105	—	185		
		275		463		
Less:						
12% loan repayable 19X9 .		—		140	140	
		275		323		
Financed by:						
Share capital		200		220	20	
Retained profit		75		103	28	
		275		323	245	245

Tutorial note:
* The increase in the cash balance is shown as an application because it represents extra cash made available during the year which has not yet been invested in business assets or used for any other purpose.

The above worksheet shows sources of funds, totalling £245,000, and the ways in which those funds have been applied. The statement of source and application of funds (see Illustration 12.2 below) arranges these items in two groups:

1. Sources and applications of funds which *cause* working capital to increase or decrease. These are further divided into:

(i)　funds generated from operations; and

(ii)　funds from other sources.

2.　Changes in the various items which make up working capital, i.e. in Illustration 12.1, stocks, debtors, cash, and trade creditors.

Illustration 12.2 shows the statement of source and application of funds of Ruler Ltd from Illustration 12.1 based on this division.

Illustration 12.2

Ruler Ltd
Statement of Sources and Applications of Funds for 19X4

SOURCES OF FUNDS		£000	£000
Profit			28
Add: item not involving an outflow of funds			
Depreciation			42
Funds generated from operations			70
Funds from other sources:			
Share issue		20	
Loan		140	
			160
			230
APPLICATIONS OF FUNDS			
Purchase of machinery			150
INCREASE IN WORKING CAPITAL			80
CHANGES IN WORKING CAPITAL ITEMS			
Decrease in working capital (Sources)			
Trade creditors		(15)	
Increases in working capital (Applications)			
Stock		21	
Trade debtors		22	
Bank		52	80

The above statement shows that Ruler raised long-term finance, amounting to £230,000 during 19X4, made up of funds from operations, £70,000, and from other sources £160,000. From this, £150,000 was invested long term, in new machinery, and the surplus, of £80,000, increased working capital from £105,000 to £185,000 (see balance sheet figures). The second part of the statement gives details of changes in the various items which make up the balance of working capital. Current assets have increased, in total, by £95,000 (£21,000 + £22,000 + £52,000). This has been partly financed by additional credit from suppliers, £15,000, with the remaining £80,000 provided from longer-term sources.

Assignment Students should now work Questions 12.1 and 12.2 at the end of this chapter.

Ruler Ltd is a simplified example; in addition to analysing the changes revealed by comparing the opening and closing balance sheet, it is normally necessary also to take account of information contained in the profit and loss account and in the notes to the accounts to build up some of the figures for inclusion in the statement of funds. For example, assume that we are also told that the directors of Ruler paid an interim dividend of £15,000 during July 19X4. The profit for 19X4 becomes:

	£000
Retained profit for 19X4	28
Add: Interim dividend	15
Total profit for 19X4	43

In the statement of funds, profit of £43,000 should be shown as a source of funds and the dividend paid, of £15,000, as an application of funds. A second common complication occurs when a company sells *and* purchases fixed assets during the year. In these circumstances the work sheet shows only the 'net' change, and it is useful to build up a fixed asset schedule which shows gross changes during the year.

Example 12.3

The following information is extracted from the balance sheet of Staple Ltd at 31 December.

Fixed Assets	19X0	19X1
Motor vehicles at cost	40,000	57,500
Less: Accumulated depreciation	22,700	31,600
	£17,300	£25,900

On 1 July 19X1, Staple sold a motor vehicle for £750. The machine had cost £6,000 some years ago, and accumulated depreciation at 31 December 19X0 was £4,900. The company's policy is to charge a full year's depreciation in the year of purchase and none in the year a vehicle is sold.

Required:
  (a) Calculate the net changes in the fixed asset at cost and accumulated depreciation balances during the year.
  (b) Calculate additions to fixed assets during the year and depreciation charged.
  (c) Show details to be included in the statement of funds concerning the motor vehicles.

Solution

(a)

Fixed Assets	19X0	19X1	Differences	
	£	£	Source	Application
Motor vehicles at cost	40,000	57,500		£17,500
Less: Accumulated depreciation .	22,700	31,600	£8,900	

(b)

	Cost	Depreciation
	£	£
Net increases	17,500	8,900
Add: Sales	6,000	4,900
Additions/Charge for the year . .	23,500	13,800

Tutorial note:
The fact that the changes over the year in the two account balances, Motor Vehicles at Cost and Accumulated Depreciation, are due to two separate movements, one an increase and the other a decrease, is shown if the related ledger accounts are completed. The double entry for the disposal of the vehicle is entered in a Disposal of Motor Vehicle Account from which the balance is transferred to the profit and loss account.

Motor Vehicles at Cost

		£			£
1.1.X1	Balance b/d	40,000	1.7.X1	Disposal account . .	6,000
31.12.X1	Additions	23,500	31.12.X1	Balance c/d	57,500
		63,500			63,500

Accumulated Depreciation

		£			£
1.7.X1	Depreciation	4,900	1.1.X1	Balance b/d	22,700
31.12.X1	Balance c/d	31,600	31.12.X1	Profit and loss A/c	13,800
		36,500			36,500

Disposal of motor vehicle

		£			£
1.7.X1	Motor vehicle A/c ..	6,000	1.7.X1	Cash	750
			1.7.X1	Acc. depreciation	4,900
			31.12.X1	Profit and loss A/c .	350
		6,000			6,000

(c)

Sources: Depreciation charged £13,800

Loss on sale of vehicle 350*

Sales proceeds 750

Applications: Purchase of motor vehicles 23,500

Tutorial note:
* The book value of the motor vehicle at the date of sale was £1,100 (£6,000 cost − £4,900 depreciation). The vehicle was sold for £750, and this produced a loss of £350 which is debited to the profit and loss account to make up for the fact that insufficient depreciation has been charged. Like depreciation, the loss on sale is a non-cash expense and must be added back to profit to produce the figure for funds generated from operations. Any profit on sale, credited to the profit and loss account, must likewise be deducted from profit, as the entire sales proceeds appear in the statement under the heading 'funds from other sources'.

Assignment   Students should now work Question 12.3 at the end of the chapter.

12.2   FINANCIAL POLICY
Section 12.1 of this chapter drew attention to the fact that the purpose of the statement of funds is to provide some insights into the financial policy pursued by management during the year, and the effect of that policy on the financial position of the company. To interpret the information contained in the statement, the user should bear in mind the matters discussed in sections 12.2.1 and 12.2.2 below.

12.2.1   Financing Long-Term Investment   It is management's job to ensure that sources and applications of funds are properly matched, i.e. short-term finance should only be committed for a short period of time while long-term investment must be paid for out of long-term finance. For example, the purchase of a fixed asset should be paid for by raising a long-term loan, or shares, or by retaining profits permanently within the business. The reason for this is that a company is likely to suffer acute financial embarrasment if it attempts to finance the purchase from, say, a bank overdraft. The new acquisition is expected to generate sufficent revenue to cover its cost and produce an adequate balance of profit, but this process will probably take a number of years and short-term finance will have to be repaid long before it is complete.

12.2.2 Over-Trading Over-trading is a condition which arises when a company attempts to do too much too quickly and, as a result, fails to maintain a satisfactory balance between profit maximisation and financial stability. Usually it occurs when a company rapidly expands its scale of business activities but fails first to make available sufficent long-term finance for this purpose. Where a company has over-traded, some or all of the following financial consequences will be apparant from an examination of its balance sheet:

- A sharp increase in expenditure on fixed assets.
- A decrease in the balance of cash, and perhaps the emergence of a bank overdraft.
- The structure of the current assets becomes less liquid, probably because the proportion of current assets 'tied up' in stock increases dramatically.
- A sharp increase in creditors caused by the company's inability to pay debts as they fall due.
- An inadequate working capital ratio.

The actual *causes* of over-trading are clearly demonstrated in the statement of funds which shows how much long-term finance has been made available during the year, the extent to which it covers long-term applications, and the effect of developments on the working capital of the business.

Example 12.4

Madoc is confused and worried and has come to you for advice. He tells you that, although he made a bigger profit in 19X7 than in 19X6, and has also made less drawings, he does not seem to be any better off and is finding difficulty in paying his creditors.

The balance sheets of Madoc's business at the end of 19X6 and 19X7 are shown below:

Balance Sheets at 31 December

	19X6		19X7	
	£	£	£	£
Machines at cost		10,000		20,500
Less: Accumulated depreciation		3,000		5,500
		7,000		15,000
Current assets				
Stock	1,700		4,900	
Debtors	1,800		3,700	
Bank	3,500		400	
	7,000		9,000	
Less: Current liabilities				
Creditors	3,000		10,000	
Working capital		4,000		(1,000)
		11,000		14,000
Financed by:				
Capital				
Opening balance		12,000		11,000
Add: Net profit		5,000		7,000
Less: Drawings		(6,000)		(4,000)
Closing balance		11,000		14,000

Required:

Explain the situation to Madoc, and support your explanation with an appropriate numerical statement. Briefly advise Madoc on future policy.

Tutorial note:

Students should first prepare a worksheet as in Illustration 12.1, although this can be omitted with practice, as is done in this case.

Solution

Statement of Funds for 19X7

SOURCES OF FUNDS	£	£
Net profit		7,000
Add: Depreciation (5,500 − 3,000)		2,500
Funds generated from operations		9,500
APPLICATIONS OF FUNDS		
Drawings	4,000	
Purchase of fixed assets	10,500	14,500
REDUCTION IN WORKING CAPITAL		(5,000)
CHANGES IN WORKING CAPITAL ITEMS		
Increases in working capital:		
Increase in stocks	3,200	
Increase in debtors	1,900	
Decreases in working capital:		
Increase in creditors	(7,000)	
Decrease in bank balance	(3,100)	(5,000)

The cause of Madoc's confusion is that he mistakenly believes that profit produces an equivalent increase in the bank balance. This may happen, in certain circumstances, but only if no additional investment takes place. The above statement of funds shows that Madoc has invested heavily in additional fixed assets, and there have also been substantial increases in stocks and debtors. In total, these outlays significantly exceed funds generated from operations; the result is that the bank balance has fallen dramatically and the amount owed to creditors has more than trebled.

Madoc is in a very difficult financial position, as a result of over-trading, and it is important that he undertakes no further investment at this stage. He should also keep drawings to a minimum and use future profits to reduce his firm's reliance on short-term credit.

Assignment   Students should now work Question 12.4 at the end of this chapter.

12.3   LINKING TOGETHER FUNDS FLOW ANALYSIS AND RATIO ANALYSIS

Accounting ratios, such as the gross profit percentage, net profit percentage, and the return on capital employed, can be used to assess the profit performance of a company during an accounting period. Comparisons with earlier years and the performance of other businesses provide useful yardsticks for assessing whether or not an improvement has occured and for gauging whether or not results are as good as they could be. Additional ratios may be calculated as a basis for assessing the company's solvency position at particular points in time; the most useful ratios for this purpose are the working capital ratio and the liquidity ratio. The statement of funds complements these calculations by helping to explain how improvements in a company's financial position have been brought about or why a deterioration has occurred. Example 12.5 illustrates how the two forms of financial analysis may be employed, alongside one another, to gain an understanding of the financial performance and position of a business enterprise. In addition, it shows how the annual accounts, although relating to a *past* time period, may be used as a basis for estimating likely future prospects.

Example 12.5

Expansion Ltd is a private company which has carried on copper mining activities for a number of years. At the beginning of 19X2 the company purchased a small established tin mine at a cost of £350,000; production commenced at once. Tin extracted from the new mine in 19X2 amounted to 600 tons, this is expected to increase to 900 tons by 19X8 and then decline gradually. Finance for the new mine was partly provided by a two-year loan of £300,000 repayable by equal monthly instalments.

The summarised balance sheets for 19X1 and 19X2 are as follows:

	19X1		19X2	
Fixed Assets				
Mines at cost	465,000		815,000	
Less: Depreciation	150,000	315,000	190,000	625,000
Plant & equipment at cost	213,250		263,250	
Less: Depreciation	56,200	157,050	75,200	188,050
		472,050		813,050
Current Assets				
Stocks of tin & copper	143,100		169,000	
Debtors	86,250		118,250	
Cash at bank	44,100		1,800	
	273,450		289,050	
Less: *Current Liabilities*				
Trade creditors & accrued expenses	63,000		138,100	
Short-term loan	—		150,000	
	63,000		288,100	
Working capital		210,450		950
		682,500		814,000
Financed by:				
Share capital		500,000		500,000
Profit & loss account		182,500		314,000
		682,500		814,000

The net profit earned during 19X2 was £181,500 (19X1 £103,000) of which £50,000 (19X1 £25,000) was paid out in dividends. Turnover increased from £1,060,000 in 19X1 to £1,500,000 in 19X2.

Required:

Examine the financial policies pursued by the directors of Expansion Ltd during 19X2 and comment on proposals to develop further by acquiring an additional site in the early months of 19X3. You should use a statement of funds and relevant accounting ratios to suppport your analysis.

Solution

Examination of Solvency

Statement of Funds for 19X2

SOURCES OF FUNDS	£	£
Profit		181,500
Add: Depreciation: Mine		40,000
Plant		19,000
		240,500
APPLICATIONS OF FUNDS		
Purchases: Mine	350,000	
Plant	50,000	
Dividend	50,000	450,000
DECREASE IN WORKING CAPITAL		(209,500)
CHANGES IN WORKING CAPITAL ITEMS		
Decreases in working capital		
Bank	(42,300)	
Trade creditors	(75,100)	
Short-term loan	(150,000)	
Increases in working capital		
Stocks	25,900	
Debtors	32,000	(209,500)

Ratios	19X1	19X2
Working capital ratio	4.3:1	1:1
Liquidity ratio	2:1	0.4:1

The company had surplus funds at the end of 19X1 and so decided to expand. It financed the remainder of the expansion with a two-year loan to be repaid out of funds generated from operations. The financial position at the end of 19X2 is weak due to the failure to raise sufficent long-term finance to meet the cost of the investment programme.

Examination of Profitability

Ratios	19X1	19X2
Net profit percentage	9.7%	12.1%
Return on Total Capital Employed	13.8%	16.5%
Return on Owners equity	15.1%	22.3%

A significant improvement in profitability has occurred, which might be expected to continue with further increases in output from the new mine. The company has paid a good dividend.

Conclusions and Prospects

Expansion has been funded out of short-term finance and the financial position at the end of 19X2 is weak. This is risky and an element of over-trading has undoubtedly occured. However, the project is profitable and it seems that the company will recover on the basis of funds generated from operations which, in 19X2, amounted to £240,500. Further expansion appears undesirable at present; there should be a delay of a year to 18 months. If this is not possible, the company should raise medium-/long-term finance to cover the cost of the additional site.

Assignment Students should now work Question 12.5 at the end of the chapter.

12.4 REVIEW
After reading this chapter, and working the chapter end questions, students should:

- Be able to define and understand the objective of the Statement of Sources and Applications of Funds (Statement of Funds).
- Know the sources from which funds are obtained and the applications to which they can be put.
- Be able to construct a Statement of Funds.
- Understand the calculation of funds generated from operations as Profit plus Depreciation.
- Be able to interpret the results revealed by a Statement of Funds.
- Understand the need to balance long-term applications with long-term sources of funds.
- Be able to recognise 'over-trading'.
- Be able to interpret a set of final accounts and review a firm's prospects using ratio and funds flow analysis.

12.5 QUESTIONS

Question 12.1

The following are the draft balance sheets of Dividers Ltd as at 31 December 19X2 and 19X3.

	19X2 £	19X3 £		19X2 £	19X3 £
Fixed assets at cost	25,000	30,000	Share capital	20,000	20,000
Less: Accumulated			Reserves (profit and		
depreciation . . .	5,000	6,500	loss account) . . .	10,000	15,000
	20,000	23,500			
Stock	11,000	17,000	Debentures, 19X9 .	1,000	800
Debtors	5,000	6,000	Trade creditors . . .	6,000	7,500
Cash at Bank	1,000	—	Overdraft	—	3,200
	37,000	46,500		37,000	46,500

There were no disposals of fixed assets during 19X3, and no dividends were paid.

Required:

(a) A statement showing the value of current assets, current liabilities and working capital, together with the working capital ratio at 31 December 19X2 and 19X3. Your answer should be presented in the following form:

	19X2	19X3
Current assets	—	—
Current liabilities	—	—
Working capital	—	—
Working capital ratio	—	—

(b) A statement of funds for 19X3.

(c) Comment briefly on the changes that have taken place in Dividers Ltd's working capital during 19X3.

Question 12.2

The balance sheets of Southall Ltd at 31 December 19X1 and 31 December 19X2 are as follows:

	19X1		19X2	
Fixed Assets:	£	£	£	£
Plant at cost	52,000		70,000	
Less: Depreciation	16,500	35,500	22,700	47,300
Transport at cost	10,000		10,000	
Less: Depreciation	3,600	6,400	4,800	5,200
		41,900		52,500
Current Assets:				
Stock	10,200		12,600	
Debtors	8,300		13,700	
Bank	4,900		—	
	23,400		26,300	
Less: Current Liabilities:				
Trade creditors	5,100		5,800	
Bank overdraft	—		1,300	
	5,100		7,100	
Working capital		18,300		19,200
		60,200		71,700
Financed by:				
Share capital		50,000		54,000
Profit and loss account		10,200		17,700
		60,200		71,700

Required:

A statement of funds for 19X2.

Question 12.3

The following balances relate to the affairs of Tufton Ltd as at 31 March 19X0 and 31 March 19X1.

	19X0 £	19X1 £
Share capital	500,000	500,000
Retained profit	395,800	527,100
10% Debentures	200,000	300,000
Creditors	179,800	207,500
Proposed Dividend	50,000	60,000
Bank Overdraft	—	36,900
	1,325,600	1,631,500
Plant at cost	658,300	796,900
Less: Depreciation	263,500	371,600
	394,800	425,300
Freehold property at cost	300,000	350,000
Stock	327,100	608,300
Debtors	265,700	247,900
Cash at Bank	38,000	—
	1,325,600	1,631,500

During the year to March 19X1, plant with a written down value of £202,500 was sold for £169,500. This plant had originally cost £390,000.

Required:

A statement of source and application of funds for the year to 31 March 19X1. You should prepare a worksheet and show the build up of your figures for profit, purchases of plant and equipment and depreciation charged.

Question 12.4

The following information is provided for Sharpener Ltd:

Balance Sheets 31 December

		19X4		19X5
Fixed Assets:	£	£	£	£
Cost		650,000		680,000
Less: Accumulated depreciation .		176,500		203,700
		473,500		476,300
Current Assets				
Stock	126,400		127,500	
Trade debtors	97,700		95,000	
Bank balance	23,600		—	
	247,700		222,500	
Less: Current Liabilities				
Trade creditors	72,900		87,100	
Proposed dividend	44,000		44,000	
Bank overdraft	—		37,900	
	116,900		169,000	
Working capital		130,800		53,500
Less: 6% Debentures		604,300		529,800
repayable 19X9		100,000		20,000
		504,300		509,800
Share capital		400,000		400,000
Retained profit		104,300		109,800
		504,300		509,800

During 19X5 the directors offered to repay the debentures, and this invitation was accepted by the majority of the debenture holders.

Required:

(a)   A statement of funds for 19X5.

(b)   A brief explanation for the decline in the bank balance based on the information contained in the statement.

Question 12.5

The following information relates to the affairs of General Engineering plc.

Balance Sheets 31 December

	19X7 £000	19X7 £000	19X8 £000	19X8 £000
Plant at cost less depreciation . .		2,600		2,760
Property at cost less depreciation		800		700
Investments at cost		300		250
		3,700		3,710
Current Assets:				
Stock and work-in-progress . .	900		2,120	
Debtors	660		700	
Short-term loans and deposits				
at bank	290		620	
	1,850		3,440	
Current Liabilities:				
Creditors	520		720	
Proposed final dividend	400		400	
	920		1,120	
Working capital		930		2,320
		4,630		6,030
Less: Long-term loan (12%) . . .		—		300
		4,630		5,730
Financed by:				
Issued share capital		2,000		2,500
Share premium account		—		200
Retained profit		2,630		3,030
		4,630		5,730

Extracts from the Profit and Loss Account for 19X8

	£000
Trading profit for the year after charging all costs, including depreciation of plant, £250,000 and depreciation of property, £100,000	700
Interest and dividends received, less interest paid	20
Net profit from ordinary activities	720
Add: Profit from the sale of an investment	80
	800
Less: Proposed dividend	400
Retained profit for the year	400
Retained profit at 1 January 19X8	2,630
Retained profit at 31 December 19X8	3,030

During 19X8 investments which had cost £50,000 some years earlier were sold for £130,000.

Required:
  (a) A statement of funds for the year to 31 December 19X8.
  (b) A discussion of the change in the financial position of General Engineering between the end of 19X7 and the end of 19X8. You are not required to examine the profitability of the firm, but should use the working capital and liquidity ratios to help assess financial developments.

Note: Ignore taxation.

APPENDIX

Solutions to Questions

Solution 1.1

Business.   Transactions (ii), (iii) and (iv).
Personal.   Transaction (i).
Part business/part personal.   Transaction (v).

Solution 1.2

(a)   *Balance Sheet of John's Business, 1 April 19X2*

	£		£
Cash at bank	4,000	Capital	4,000

(b)   *Balance Sheet of John's Business, 2 April 19X2*

	£		£
Cash at bank	4,600	Capital	4,000
		Loan from John's father	600
	4,600		4,600

(c)   *Balance Sheet of John's Business, 4 April 19X2*

	£		£
Cash at bank	4,600	Capital	4,000
Cash in hand	150	Loan from John's father	600
		Loan from Peter	150
	4,750		4,750

Solution 1.3

(a)   *Balance Sheet of Roger's Business, 1 September 19X3*

	£		£
Cash at bank	1,200	Capital	1,200

(b)   *Balance Sheet of Roger's Business, 2 September 19X3*

	£		£
Machine	750	Capital	1,200
Bank (£1,200 + £1,000)	2,200	Endridge Local Authority . . .	1,000
		Creditors	750
	2,950		2,950

(c)   *Balance Sheet of Roger's Business, 3 September 19X3*

	£		£
Machines (£750 + £1,820). . .	2,570	Capital	1,200
Stock	420	Endridge Local Authority . . .	1,000
		Creditors	750
		Bank overdraft	
		(£2,200 − £1,820 − £420)	40
	2,990		2,990

(d)   *Balance Sheet of Roger's Business, 4 September 19X3*

	£		£
Machines	2,570	Capital	1,200
Stock (£420 + £215)	635	Endridge Local Authority . . .	1,000
		Creditors (£750 + £215)	965
		Bank overdraft	40
	3,205		3,205

Solution 1.4

(a)

Balance Sheet of Jeff's Business, 2 October 19X5

	£		£
Machine	2,200	Capital	5,300
Stock (£2,870 − £360)	2,510	Add: Profit (£80 + £75)	155
			5,455
Debtors (£800 + £315)	1,115		
Bank (£120 + £200)	320	Trade creditors	690
	6,145		6,145

(b)

Balance Sheet of Jeff's Business, 3 October 19X5

	£		£
Machinery	2,200	Capital	5,455
		Trade creditors	
Stock (£2,510 + £190)	2,700	(£690 + £190)	880
Debtors (£1,115 − £150)	965		
Bank (£320 + £150)	470		
	6,335		6,335

(c)

Balance Sheet of Jeff's Business, 4 October 19X5

	£		£
Machines (£2,200 + £600)	2,800	Capital	5,455
		Trade creditors	
Stock	2,700	(£880 − £75)	805
Debtors	965	Bank overdraft	
		(£470 − £75 − £600)	205
	6,465		6,465

Solution 1.5

(a)

Balance Sheet of Daley at 31 December 19X1

	£		£
Business premises	9,000	Capital (balancing figure)	13,450
Stock	5,250	Loan from Weakly	3,000
Trade debtors	3,340	Trade creditors	2,890
Cash	1,750		
	19,340		19,340

(b)   *Balance Sheet of Daley at:*

SOURCES OF FINANCE	Jan. 1 £	Jan. 2 £	Jan. 3 £	Jan. 4 £	Jan. 5 £	Jan. 6 £	Jan. 7 £
Capital	13,450	13,450	13,450	13,450	13,450	13,450	13,450
Add: Profit					180	180	180
Less: Drawings							(100)
					13,630	13,630	13,530
Loan from Weakly	3,000	3,000	3,000	3,000	3,000	2,000	2,000
Trade creditors	3,390	3,390	2,720	2,980	2,980	2,980	2,980
	19,840	19,840	19,170	19,430	19,610	18,610	18,510
ASSETS							
Business premises	9,000	9,000	9,000	9,000	9,000	9,000	9,000
Typewriter	500	500	500	500	500	500	500
Stocks	5,250	5,250	5,250	5,510	5,160	5,160	5,060
Trade debtors	3,340	3,150	3,150	3,150	3,150	3,150	3,150
Cash	1,750	1,940	1,270	1,270	1,800	800	800
	19,840	19,840	19,170	19,430	19,610	18,610	18,510

Solution 1.6

TRANSACTION	ASSETS = £	CAPITAL £	+ LIABILITIES £
1	+ 2,000 =	+ 2,000	0
2	+ 3,000 =	0	0
	− 3,000 =		
3	+ 800 =	0	+ 800
4	+ 5,000 =	0	+ 5,000
5	− 750 =	0	0
	+ 750 =		
6	− 1,000 =	+ 400	0
	+ 1,400 =		
7	− 220 =	0	− 220
8	+ 350 =	0	0
	− 350 =		
9	+ 60 =	0	+ 60
10	− 100 =	− 100	0

Solution 1.7

Balance Sheet at 31 December 19X1

	A	B	C	D	E	F
SOURCES OF FINANCE	£	£	£	£	£	£
Capital at 1 January 19X1	2,500	2,000	3,000	4,000	3,800	7,400
Add: Profit	1,000	3,200	1,400	5,700	2,300	7,000
Less: Drawings	(800)	(3,000)	(1,000)	(4,900)	(2,500)	(4,500)
	2,700	2,200	3,400	4,800	3,600	9,900
Current Liabilities	750	400	600	1,300	1,700	2,100
	3,450	2,600	4,000	6,100	5,300	12,000
ASSETS	£	£	£	£	£	£
Fixed assets	1,800	1,750	2,800	4,200	3,700	8,500
Current assets	1,650	850	1,200	1,900	1,600	3,500
	3,450	2,600	4,000	6,100	5,300	12,000

Solution 1.8

(i) *Accounting.* This is a system for recording and reporting business transactions, in financial terms to interested parties who use this information as the basis for decision-making and performance assessment.

(ii) *Entity concept.* It is assumed, for accounting purposes, that the business entity has an existence separate and distinct from owners, managers and other individuals with whom it comes into contact during the course of its trading activities. The assumption requires business transactions to be separated from personal transactions and accounting statements to concentrate upon the financial position of the firm and its relationship with outsiders.

(iii) *Balance sheet.* This is a financial statement which shows, on the one hand, the sources from which a business has raised finance and, on the other, the ways in which those monetary resources are employed. The balance sheet sets out the financial position at a particular moment in time and has been colourfully described as an instantaneous financial photograph of a business.

(iv) *Realisation concept.* This assumes that profit is earned or realised when the sale takes place. The justification for this treatment is that a sale results in the replacement of stock by either cash or a legally enforceable debt due from the customer.

(v) *Trade credit.* This is the period of time which elapses between the dates goods are supplied and paid for.

(vi) *Trading cycle, credit transactions.* This is a series of transactions which begins with the delivery of stock from suppliers. The stock is then sold and delivered to customers resulting in a profit being realised or a loss incurred. Next, cash is collected from customers and the cycle is completed by paying suppliers the amount due.

(vii) $A = C + L$. This formula expresses the balance sheet relationship between sources of finance and assets where —

A = Assets.
C = Capital invested by the owners, including retained profits.
L = Liabilities.

The balance sheet must always balance because all assets appearing on the left-hand side of the balance sheet must be financed, and the various sources employed appear on the right.

(viii) *Owner's capital.* This is the amount of the initial investment in the concern, to which is added any further injections of capital plus profit earned, and from which is deducted drawings made by the owner for personal use.

(ix) *Money measurement concept.* Assets are reported in the balance sheet only if the benefit they provide can be measured or quantified, in money terms, with a reasonable degree of precision.

(x) *Fixed assets.* These are purchased and retained to help carry on the business. Fixed assets are not sold in the normal course of business and their disposal will usually occur only when they are worn out, e.g. machinery.

(xi) *Current assets.* These are assets which are held for resale or conversion into cash, e.g. stock-in-trade and trade debtors.

(xii) *Current liabilities.* These are debts payable within 12 months of the balance sheet date, e.g. trade creditors and a bank overdraft.

(xiii) *Gross assets.* These are the total assets belonging to a business entity and therefore include both fixed assets and current assets.

Solution 1.9

Current liabilities: (iv) (ix).
Current assets: (ii) (vii).
Fixed assets: (i) (iii)
Items not indicated:

(v) *Capital investment.* This is reported in the capital section, i.e. the first item on the sources of finance side of the balance sheet.

(vi) *Pearl necklace and gold wristwatch.* These are the personal belongings of Mrs Greasy and must be excluded from the balance sheet.

(viii) *Loan.* This is a non-current liablity and is reported between the capital and current liability sections of the balance sheet.

(x) *Shop.* This must be excluded from the balance sheet since it belongs to the property company.

Solution 1.10

Balance Sheet of C. Forest at 31 Dec. 19X3

	£	£		£	£
Fixed Assets			Opening capital		52,380
Leasehold premises .		25,000	Add: Profit		12,600
Plant and machinery		26,500	Less: Drawings		(10,950)
		51,500			54,030
			Loan repayable 19X9		9,000
Current Assets			*Current Liabilities*		
Stock-in-trade	14,200		Loan repayable 19X4	2,500	
Trade debtors	14,100		Trade creditors	10,600	
Cash-in-hand	270	28,570	Bank overdraft	3,940	17,040
		80,070			80,070

Solution 2.1

(a) Gross assets, £6,700.

Net assets, £6,500 (gross assets £6,700 − liabilities £200).

Working capital, £4,500 (current assets £4,700 − current liabilities £200).

(b)

Transaction	Profit	Net Assets	Gross Assets	Working Capital
	£	£	£	£
1	NIL	NIL	NIL	NIL
2	NIL	Increase, £500	Increase, £500	Increase, £500
3	Decrease, £100	Decrease, £100	Decrease, £100	Decrease, £100
4	NIL	Decrease, £50	Decrease, £50	Decrease, £50
5	NIL	NIL	Increase, £150	NIL
6	NIL	NIL	NIL	Decrease, £700

Solution 2.2

(a)   Calculation of capital by deducting liabilities from assets:

Statement of Assets, Liabilities and Capital at 30 June 19X4

	£	£
ASSETS		
Fixed Assets		9,850
Stocks		4,270
Debtors		1,450
Cash at bank		570
Cash-in-hand		30
		16,170
Less: Liabilities		
Loan	3,000	
Trade creditors	1,890	4,890
Capital		11,280

(b)   Calculation of profit on the basis of the increase in capital:

	£
Closing capital	11,280
Less: Opening capital	10,330
Profit	950

(c)   *Balance Sheet at 30 June 19X4*

	£	£
Fixed Assets		9,850
Current Assets		
Stocks	4,270	
Debtors	1,450	
Cash at bank	570	
Cash-in-hand	30	
	6,320	
Less: Current Liabilities		
Trade creditors	1,890	
Working capital		4,430
		14,280
Financed by:		
Opening capital		10,330
Add: Net profit		950
Closing capital		11,280
Loan		3,000
		14,280

Solution 2.3

(a)   Calculation of capital by deducting liabilities from assets.

Statement of Assets, Liabilities and Capital at 31 Dec. 19X8

	£	£
Assets		
Fixed assets		15,930
Stock		6,536
Debtors		4,864
		27,330
Less: Liabilities		
Bank overdraft	2,492	
Creditors: Goods	4,236	
Expenses	168	6,896
Capital		20,434

(b)   Calculation of profit.

	£
Closing capital	20,434
Less: Opening capital	23,496
Reduction in capital	(3,062)
Add: Drawings	10,800
Profit	7,738

Note: Drawings have exceeded profit by £3,062 (£10,800 − £7,738) and capital has therefore fallen by this amount.

(c)   *Balance Sheet at 31 Dec. 19X8*

	£	£
Fixed assets		15,930
Stock	6,536	
Debtors	4,864	
	11,400	
Less: Current Liabilities		
Creditors: Goods	4,236	
Expenses	168	
Bank overdraft	2,492	
	6,896	
Working capital		4,504
		20,434
Financed by:		
Opening capital		23,496
Add: Profit		7,738
		31,234
Less: Drawings		10,800
Closing capital		20,434

Solution 2.4

(a) Calculation of capital.

Statement of Assets, Liabilities and Capital at 31 Dec. 19X3 and 19X4

	19X3 £	19X3 £	19X4 £	19X4 £
Gross Assets				
Fixed assets		9,000		12,144W1
Stocks		2,650		3,710
Trade debtors		5,200		5,600
Bank balance		—		50
		16,850		21,504
Less: Liabilities				
Trade creditors	1,710		1,210	
Bank overdraft	360	2,070	—	1,210
Capital		14,780		20,294

Calculation of profit	£
Closing capital	20,294
Less: Opening capital	14,780
Increase in capital	5,514
Add: Drawings	8,100W2
Less: Capital introduced	(600)
Profit	13,014

Workings:
W1 £9,000 + £3,144 = £12,144
W2 (£150 × 52) + £300 = £8,100

(b)   *Balance Sheet at 31 Dec. 19X4*

	£	£		£	£
Fixed assets		12,144	Opening capital		14,780
			Add: Net Profit		13,014
			Additional capital		
			investment		600
					28,394
Current Assets:					
Stocks	3,710		Less: Drawings–cash	7,800	
Trade debtors	5,600		–stock	300	8,100
Bank balance	50	9,360			20,294
			Current Liabilities		
			Trade creditors		1,210
		21,504			21,504

Solution 3.1

£

(a) (i)   Cash collected in respect of: credit sales   41,750
                                    cash sales   12,350

           Receipts from customers   54,100

     (ii) Receipts from customers   54,100
           Less: Opening debtors . . . .   (12,650)
           Add: Closing debtors   11,780

           Sales   53,230

     (iii) Payments to suppliers   36,590
           Less: Opening creditors . . . .   (6,540)
           Add: Closing creditors   8,270

           Purchases   38,320

     (iv) Opening stock   9,150
           Add: Purchases   38,320
           Less: Closing stock . . . .   (9,730)

           Cost of goods sold   37,740

(b)   *Trading Account for 19X3*

	£		£
Purchases	38,320	Sales	53,230
Add: Opening stock	9,150		
Less: Closing stock	(9,730)		
Cost of goods sold	37,740		
Gross profit	15,490		
	53,230		53,230

Tutorial note: It is conventional practice to show the calculation of cost of goods sold on the face of the trading account, but not the calculations of purchases and sales.

Solution 3.2

(a)   *Trading and Profit and Loss Account*
                         Year ended 30 September 1989

	£	£
Sales		65,588W1
Less: Cost of Sales:		
Purchases	35,650W2	
Add: Stock 30/9/88	931	
	36,581	
Less: Stock 30/9/89	1,240	35,341
Gross Profit		30,247
Less: Expenses:		
Wages	10,398	
Rent and rates	6,676W3	
Heating and lighting	1,411W4	
Bank charges	314	
Sundry trade expenses	1,792	
Depreciation: lease	1,210	
equipment	1,422	23,223
		7,024
Add bank deposit interest		428
Net profit for the year		7,452

(b)   *Balance Sheet as at 30 September 1989*

Fixed Assets	£	£
Leasehold shop at cost	12,100	
Less: Aggregate depreciation	9,360	2,740
Shop equipment at cost	19,634	
Less: Aggregate depreciation	13,007	6,627
		9,367
Current Assets		
Stock	1,240	
Debtors	241	
Prepaid expenses	824	
Cash at bank: deposit account	6,912W5	
current account	835	
	10,052	
Current Liabilities		
Creditors	786	
Accrued expenses	210	
	996	9,056
		18,423

Capital Account

Balance brought forward	17,518	
Add: Net profit for year	7,452	
	24,970	
Less: Drawings	6,547	18,423

W1   60,205 (takings) + 5,500 (cash drawings) + 241 (closing debtors) − 358 (opening debtors)

W2   37,014 (payments) + 786 (closing creditors) − 2,150 (opening creditors)

W3   7,500 (payments) − 824 (prepaid)

W4   1,201 (payments) + 210 (accruals)

W5   6,412 (opening balance) + 500 (transfer from current account)

Solution 3.3

(a)   *Balance Sheet at 30 April 1987*

	£	£
Fixed Asset		
Taxi at cost		10,500
Current Assets		
Fares outstanding	312	
Prepayments	453	
Bank	34	
	799	
Current Liabilities		
Creditors	209	
Net current assets		590
		11,090
Capital investment		11,090

(b)   *Profit and Loss Account for Year to 30 April 1988*

	£	£
Fares and tips		20,038W1
Less: Operating expenses		10,347W2
		9,691
Advertising revenue	200	
Less: Depreciation of sign	130W3	70
		9,761
Less: Hire charges	540	
Advertising	192	
Trade subscription	75	
Bank charges . . . . :	48	
Depreciation of taxi	2,625W4	3,480
Net profit . . . . :		6,281

Balance Sheet at 30 April 1988

	£	£
Fixed Asset		
Taxi and illuminated sign at cost		11,020
Less: Accumulated depreciation		2,755
		8,265
Current Assets		
Fares outstanding	587	
Prepayments	531	
Bank	981	
	2,099	
Current Liabilities		
Creditors	317	
Net current assets		1,782
		10,047
Capital investment at 1 May 1988		11,090
Add: Net profit		6,281
Less: Drawings		(7,324) W5
		10,047

W1   16,013 (banked) + 3,750 (cash drawings, 75 × 50) + 587 (closing debtors) − 312
      (opening debtors)
W2   10,317 (payments) + 453 (opening prepayments) + 317 (closing creditors) − 531
      (closing prepayments) − 209 (opening creditors)
W3   520 × 25%
W4   10,500 × 25%
W5   3,147 (personal expenses) + 427 (foreign currency) + 3,750 (cash drawings)

Solution 3.4

(a)   *Balance Sheet of Stondon at 31 Dec. 19X3*

	£	£		£	£
Fixed Assets			Capital (A − L) . . .		9,947
Furniture and fittings		800	*Current Liabilities*		
Motor van at cost			Trade creditors . . .	3,586	
less depreciation		2,500	Bank overdraft . . .	782	4,368
		3,300			
Current Assets:					
Stock	6,891				
Trade debtors	4,124	11,015			
		14,315			14,315

(b)

	£
Capital at 31 December 19X3	9,947
Less: Capital at 31 December 19X2	7,940
Increase in capital	2,007
Add: Drawings	12,840
	14,847
Less: Capital introduced	4,200
Net profit for 19X3	10,647

(c)   *Trading and Profit and Loss Account for 19X3*

	£	£
Sales (25,067 × 4)		100,268(4)
Less: Purchases (by difference)	76,708 (8)	
Add: Opening stock	5,384 (7)	
Less: Closing stock	(6,891)(6)	
Cost of goods sold		75,201(5)
Gross profit		25,067(3)
Less: Running expenses		14,420(2)
Net profit		10,647(1)

Note: The numbers in brackets indicate the order in which the trading and profit and loss account is reconstructed.

Solution 4.1

Cash Account

	£		£
Balance b/d	550	Wages	2,000
Sales	10,000	Vehicle repairs	300
		Petrol	250
		Rent	1,400
		Purchases	4,000
		Salaries	1,000
		Balance c/d	1,600
	10,550		10,550

Sales

		£
	Cash	10,000

Wages and Saleries

	£		£
Cash: wages	2,000		
Cash: salaries	1,000		

Motor Expenses

	£		£
Cash: repairs	300		
Cash: petrol	250		

Rent

	£		£
Cash	1,400		

Purchases

	£		£
Cash	4,000		

Solution 4.2

Sales: Department A

	£		£
		Debtors	12,500
		Cash	10,000

Sales: Department B

	£		£
		Debtors	22,000
		Cash	11,000

Debtors

	£		£
Balance b/d	15,000	Cash	35,000
Sales	32,000	Discounts allowed	1,500
		Balance c/d	10,500
	47,000		47,000

Cash

	£		£
Debtors	35,000		
Sales	23,500		

Discounts Allowed

	£	£
Debtors	1,500	

Notes:

1. The identification of the sales made by each department enables management to monitor their progress and performance individually.
2. The values entered for sales in the cash account and debtors account are the totals of the sales of the two departments; this saves recording the debit impacts separately which, in an organisation with a large number of activities to monitor separately, would save a significant number of entries and hence time.

Solution 4.3

Journal Entries — Commencer

Transaction Number		Debit £	Credit £
1	Cash	4,000	
	Capital		4,000
2	Cash	1,000	
	Loan		1,000
3	Plant	3,000	
	Cash		3,000
4	Purchases	1,250	
	Cash		1,250
5	Purchases	1,400	
	Creditors		1,400
6	Debtors	1,100	
	Sales		1,100
7	Cash	600	
	Debtors		600
8	Creditors	750	
	Cash		750
9	Wages	180	
	Cash		180

Note: The above entries can be checked to the 'T' accounts given in the solution to Example 4.2.

Solution 4.4

(a)   £

Profit in draft balance sheet   26,500
Computer wrongly recorded . . . .   + 6,000
Depreciation on computer . . . .   − 2,000
Purchases not recorded . . . .   − 3,000
Prepaid rates . . . .   + 800
Bad debt . . . .   − 200
Bank charges . . . .   − 300

Adjusted profit   27,800

(b)   *Revised Balance Sheet*

                                                                    £   £

FIXED ASSETS
At cost (200,000 + 6,000)   206,000
Less: Depreciation (20,000 + 2,000)   22,000
                                                                               184,000 ·

CURRENT ASSETS
Stock   38,700
Prepayment   800
Debtors (42,800 − 200)   42,600
                                                                    82,100

CURRENT LIABILITIES
Trade creditors (47,400 + 3,000)   50,400
Bank overdraft (7,600 + 300)   7,900
                                                                    58,300

WORKING CAPITAL   23,800
                                                                               207,800

Financed by:
Capital introduced   180,000
Profit for year   27,800
                                                                               207,800

Solution 4.5

(a)

Cash Book

	£		£
Balance b/d	293	Cheque 085	117
Jones	825	Returned cheque	782
Excelsior dividend	35	Moon Insurance	375
Balance c/d	218	Bank charges	97
	1,371		1,371
		Balance b/d	218

(b)

Bank Reconciliation Statement

	£	£
Balance per cash book		− 218
Outstanding cheques:		
Johnson	257	
Thames Water	110	
		+ 367
		+ 149
Outstanding lodgements:		
Victor	178	
Watson	35	
		− 213
Balance as per bank statement		− 64

(c) Cheque 085, which appears on the bank statement, seems to have been omitted from the cash book; investigation should be made to find out why.

    The returned cheque, presumably from Fisherman, means that, for some reason — possibly lack of funds, it has not been met by the drawer's bank. Action should be taken to ensure that the debt is settled, and no further goods supplied on credit to Fisherman until this matter has been resolved.

    The payments to Moon Insurance and for bank charges, derived from the bank statement and entered in the cash book, should be verified to ensure that they are correct.

    It should be verified in the future that all the outstanding items in the bank reconciliation statement have been properly cleared.

Note: It is necessary to combine debits shown in the cash book to agree them with entries in the bank statement. For example, the £903 paid in on 2 September comprises £517 from Ajax, £72 from Bertram, and £314 from Chorlton.

Solution 5.1

(a)

Item	Location	Comment
Sales	Trading Account	Revenue
Purchases	Trading Account	Expense
Returns inwards	Trading Account	Reduces sales
Returns outwards	Trading Account	Reduces purchases
Stock 1 January 19X9	Trading Account	Charged against sales
Capital at 1 January 19X9	Balance Sheet	Liability to ownership
Cash at bank	Balance Sheet	Asset
Debtors	Balance Sheet	Asset
Creditors	Balance Sheet	Liability
Premises	Balance Sheet	Asset
Wages	Profit & Loss Account	Expense
Discounts received	Profit & Loss Account	Sundry revenue
Rent and rates	Profit & Loss Account	Expense
Delivery costs	Profit & Loss Account	Expense
Cash drawings	Balance Sheet	Reduces capital
Heat and light	Profit & Loss Account	Expense
General expenses	Profit & Loss Account	Expense

(b)

*Trading and Profit and Loss Account
for the Year to 31 December 19X9*

	£	£
Sales		130,000
Less: Returns inwards		250
		129,750
Opening stock	15,000	
add: Purchases	80,000	
less: Returns outwards	(150)	
Closing stock	(17,750)	
Cost of goods sold		77,100
Gross profit		52,650
Discounts received		300
		52,950
Wages	17,300	
Rent and rates	3,000	
Delivery	2,750	
Heat and light	3,500	
General expenses	2,750	
		29,300
Net profit		23,650

Balance Sheet at 31 December 19X9

	£	£
Premises		8,000
Stock	17,750	
Debtors	15,400	
Cash	3,100	
	36,250	
Less: Creditors	5,000	
		31,250
		39,250
Financed by:		
Capital at 1 January		27,600
Profit for year		23,650
		51,250
Less: Drawings		(12,000)
Capital at 31 December		39,250

Solution 5.2

Trading and Profit and Loss Account
for the Year to 30 April 19X8

	£	£
Sales		108,920
Opening stock	9,470	
add: Purchases	72,190	
less: Closing stock	(9,960)	
Cost of goods sold		71,700
		37,220
Depreciation	3,000	
Wages	14,330	
Rent and rates	1,000	
Other costs	4,590	
		22,920
Net profit		14,300

Balance Sheet at 30 April 19X8

	£	£
FIXED ASSETS		
At cost		35,000
Less: Accumulated depreciation (12,500 + 3,000)		15,500
		19,500
CURRENT ASSETS		
Stock	9,960	
Debtors	7,350	
Cash	1,710	
	19,020	
CURRENT LIABILITIES		
Less: Creditors	6,220	
		12,800
		32,300
Financed by:		
CAPITAL		
At 1 May		30,350
Profit for year		14,300
		44,650
Less: Drawings		(12,350)
At 30 April		32,300

Solution 5.3

The most direct way to answer this question and comply with the requirement to show workings is to draw up the ledger account for each type of expense and extract the required information from them.

Insurance Account

19X8		£	19X8	£
1 Jan	Balance b/d	1,350	31 Dec Balance c/d W1	1,530
June	Cash	3,060	Profit and Loss*	2,880
		4,410		4,410

Rates Account

19X8		£	19X8	£
1 Jan	Balance b/d	870	31 Dec Balance c/d W2	1,170
March	Cash	2,340	Profit and Loss*	4,380
Sept	Cash	2,340		
		5,550		5,550

Gas Account

19X8		£	19X8		£
March	Cash	2,550	1 Jan	Balance b/d	1,800
June	Cash	2,520	31 Dec	Profit and Loss*	10,020
Sept	Cash	1,830			
Dec	Cash	2,880			
31 Dec	Balance c/d W3	2,040			
		11,820			11,820

*Balancing figure

Workings

W1   The payment made in June covers 12 months, of which only half will pass before 31 December 19X8. The prepayment is therefore £3,060 ÷ 2.

W2   The payment made in September covers six months, of which only half will pass before 31 December 19X8. The prepayment is therefore £2,340 ÷ 2.

W3   The gas consumed during December 19X8 will not be paid for until 19X9 and so an accrual equal to its value has to be made.

  (a)   The sums to be charged in the profit and loss account for the year to 31 December 19X8 are:

    Insurance £2,880

    Rates £4,380

    Gas £10,020.

  (b)   The amounts to appear in the balance sheet at 31 December 19X8 and their manner of presentation are:

    Insurance £1,530   This is a prepayment and will be included in current assets.

    Rates £1,170   This is a prepayment and will be included in current assets.

    Gas £2,040   This is an accrual and will be included in current liabilities.

Solution 5.4

(a)

Debtors Account

	£		£
Balance b/d	156,937	B Clyde — bad debt	560
		M Poppins — bad debt	227
		Balance c/d	156,150
	156,937		156,937

Bad Debts Account

	£		£
Balance b/d	750		
Debtors — B Clyde	560		
Debtors — M Poppins	227	Profit and loss	1,537
	1,537		1,537

Provision for Doubtful Debts

	£		£
Balance c/d	4,248	Balance b/d	2,600
		Profit and loss*	1,648
	4,248		4,248

	£
*Comprises:	
S Wars	340
M Express	78
B Mann	80
Increase in general provision (3,750 − 2,600)	1,150
	1,648

(b) Balance Sheet Extract

	£
Debtors	156,150
Less: Provision for doubtful debts	4,248
	151,902

Solution 5.5

*Trading and Profit and Loss Account for the
Year to 31 December 19X6*

	£	£
Sales		234,481
Stock 1 January	32,193	
Purchases	164,770	
	196,963	
Less: Goods taken as drawings	(1,250)	
Stock 31 December	(34,671)	
Cost of goods sold		161,042
Gross Profit		73,439
Profit on sale of van		500
		73,939
Rent and rates (3,000 − 300)	2,700	
General expenses	7,263	
Wages (26,649 + 271)	26,920	
Bad debts (693 + 104)	797	
Depreciation	7,000	44,680
Net Profit		29,259

Balance Sheet at 31 December 19X6

	£	£	£
Fixed Assets			
Freehold land and buildings			114,000
Motor Vans at cost (37,500 − 2,500 + 1,500)		36,500	
Less: Depreciation (15,450 + 7,000 − 1,500)		20,950	
			15,550
			129,550
Current Assets			
Stock		34,671	
Debtors	20,911		
Less: Provision for doubtful debts (876 + 104)	980		
		19,931	
Prepaid rent and rates		300	
Cash		32,728	
		87,630	
Less: Current Liabilities			
Creditors	13,006		
Accrued wages	271		
		13,277	
Working Capital			74,353
			203,903

Capital

At 1 January		193,894
Profit for 19X6		29,259
		223,153
Less: Drawings: Cash	18,000	
Stock	1,250	
		19,250
		203,903

Solution 5.6

(a)   *S. Top — Journal*

	Debit £	Credit £
1. Plant and machinery	2,750	
Repair to machinery		2,750
Transfer of purchase of lathe wrongly recorded		
2. Repairs	350	
Manufacturing wages		350
Transfer of repair costs wrongly recorded		
3. Bad debts	1,290	
Debtors		1,290
Irrecoverable debt due from J. Jones written off		
4. Drawings	200	
Rates		200
Transfer of S. Top's private electricity bill		
5. Purchases	1,500	
Creditors		1,500
Goods received but not recorded at year end		
6. Provision for depreciation	1,000	
Machinery		1,000
Fully depreciated machine scrapped during year		
7. Drawings	150	
Purchases		150
Goods taken for S. Top's personal use		
8. Delivery	125	
Purchases		125
Transfer of delivery cost wrongly recorded		

(b)   *Statement of Effect of Adjustments on Profit*

	Decrease Profit £	Increase Profit £
1. Expense capitalised		2,750
3. Increase in bad debts	1,290	
4. Expense charged to owner		200
5. Increase in purchases	1,500	
7. Purchases charged to owner		150
		3,100
	2,790	2,790
Net increase in profit		310

Solution 5.7

(a) Workings

Age of debt	Value £	Doubtful Debts %	Doubtful Debts £
1 month	24,906	1	249
1–2 months	8,476	3	254
2+ months	1,826	5	91
	35,208		594

(i) Balance Sheet Extract

	£
Debtors	35,208
Less: Provision for doubtful debts	594
	34,614

(ii) Provision for Doubtful Debts Account

	£		£
Balance c/d	594	Balance b/d	450
		Profit and loss	144
	594		594

£144 will be debited to the profit and loss account in the year to 30 June 1989.

(b)

Loan Account

1989		£	1989		£
1 May	Cash	275	1 April	Cash	5,000
31 May	Balance c/d	4,800	30 April	April Interest	75
		5,075			5,075
1 June	Cash	272	31 May	Balance b/d	4,800
30 June	Balance c/d	4,600		May Interest	72
		4,872			4,872
1 July	Cash	269	30 June	Balance b/d	4,600
31 July	Balance c/d	4,400	June	June Interest	69
		4,669			4,669

Interest Account

1989		£			£
30 April	Loan Interest	75			
31 May	Loan Interest	72			
30 June	Loan Interest	69			
31 July	Interest Accrued c/d	66	31 July	Profit and loss ...	282
		282			282

The charge for interest in the profit and loss account will be £282, and the balance sheet will show the outstanding loan at £4,400 and accrued interest, a current liability, of £66.

(c)   Workings

Telephone Account

		£			£
Oct 88	Cash	138	1 Sept	Balance b/d	92
Jan 89	Cash	94			
Apl 89	Cash	93			
Jul 89	Cash	144			
Aug 89	Balance c/d*	112	Aug 89	Profit and loss** ..	489
		581			581

  * 2/3 × £168 (the bill for 3 months to the end of September).
** Balancing figure.

Note that when using 'T' accounts as part of 'workings', it is not necessary to prepare them in great detail; all that is needed is sufficient to enable the examiner to see how figures have been arrived at.

(i)   The profit and loss account charge will be £489.

(ii)   The accrual in the balance sheet, shown as a current liability, will be £112.

Solution 5.8

Manufacturing, Trading and Profit and Loss Accounts
for the Year to 31 March 19X6

	£	£	£
Raw materials: Opening stock		12,000	
add: Purchases		40,000	
less: Closing stock		(14,000)	
Consumed		38,000	
Production wages		30,000	
Prime cost		68,000	
Depreciation		7,000	
Rent		4,800	
Light, heat and power		9,000	
Overheads		17,500	
		106,300	
Work-in-progress: at 1 April 19X5		2,000	
at 31 March 19X6		(7,000)	
Manufacturing cost of goods completed Transferred to Trading Account		101,300	
Sales			209,500
Transfer from manufacturing		101,300	
Add: Stock at 1 April 19X5		11,500	
Less: Stock at 31 March 19X6		(13,800)	
Cost of goods sold			99,000
Gross profit			110,500
Administration expenses:			
Rent	1,600		
Light, heat and power	3,000		
Expenses	12,500		
Salaries	15,000		
Hire of equipment	7,000		
Postage and telephone	5,350		
		44,450	
Finance costs:			
Bank charges	1,250		
Loan interest	3,000		
		4,250	
Delivery costs:			
Van hire	5,000		
Wages	17,000		
Petrol, etc	3,000		
		25,000	
			73,700
Net profit			36,800

Balance Sheet at 31 March 19X6

FIXED ASSETS	£	£	£
At cost			70,000
Less: Accumulated depreciation			21,000
			49,000
CURRENT ASSETS			
Stocks:			
Raw materials		14,000	
Work-in-progress		7,000	
Finished goods		13,800	
		34,800	
Debtors		20,000	
		54,800	
CURRENT LIABILITIES			
Overdraft	10,000		
Creditors	5,000		
		15,000	
			39,800
			88,800
Long–term loan			30,000
			58,800
Financed by:			
CAPITAL			
At 1 April 19X5			50,000
Profit for year			36,800
			86,800
Less: Drawings			28,000
			58,800

Solution 6.1

The fundamental rule is that stock should be valued at the *lower* of cost and net realisable value, taking each item or groups of similar items separately.

Valuation of stock calculated as follows:

Product	Cost	NRV	Lower of cost and NRV
A	2,400	2,760	2,400
B	1,290	740	740
C	3,680	750	750
D	2,950	4,760	2,950
E	6,280	9,730	6,280
Value of stock			13,120

Solution 6.2

(a) *Quantity of units in stock*

	19X8 £	19X9 £
Opening balance	—	300
Production	12,000	21,000
Less: Sales	(11,700)	(12,900)
Closing balance	· 300	8,400

(b) (i) *Marginal cost basis*

$$\frac{\text{Marginal cost of production}}{\text{Number of units produced}} \times \text{number of units in stock}$$

$$19X8: \frac{\pounds240,000 \text{ W1}}{12,000} \times 300 = \pounds6,000$$

$$19X9: \frac{\pounds420,000 \text{ W1}}{21,000} \times 8,400 = \pounds168,000$$

(ii) *Total cost basis*

$$\frac{\text{Total cost of production}}{\text{Number of units produced}} \times \text{number of units in stock}$$

$$19X8: \frac{\pounds312,000 \text{ W1}}{12,000} \times 300 = \pounds7,800$$

$$19X9: \frac{\pounds514,500 \text{ W1}}{21,000} \times 8,400 = \pounds205,800$$

W1	19X8 £	19X9 £
Materials consumed	108,000	186,000
Manufacturing wages	132,000	234,000
Marginal cost	240,000	420,000
Manufacturing expenses	72,000	94,500
Total cost	312,000	514,500

(c) 19X8: The total cost stock valuation is £1,800 higher than the marginal cost valuation due to the inclusion of a proportion of manufacturing expenses. The use of the total cost basis, rather than the marginal cost basis, for valuing closing stock will therefore cause cost of sales to be £1,800 lower and reported profit to be £1,800 higher.

19X9: The total cost basis again produces a significantly higher closing stock valuation. In assessing the effect on profit, however, one must also take into account the opening stock valuation, and bear in mind the fact that the higher figure brought forward under the total cost method *increases* the charge for the year. The closing stock valuation, using the total cost basis, is £37,800 (£205,800 − £168,000) higher than the marginal cost valuation, compared with an opening total cost valuation which is £1,800 higher. Therefore the net effect of using the total cost basis, for 19X9, is to produce a profit figure which is £36,000 (£37,800 − £1,800) higher.

Solution 6.3

(a) Units of stock on hand: 235 (purchases) − 155 (sales) = 80

Valuation of stock:	£
75 units at £30	2,250
5 units at £25	125
80	2,375

(b) Calculation of cost of goods sold (balancing item):

	£
Opening stock	0
Add: Purchases	5,750W1
Less: Closing stock	2,375
Cost of goods sold	3,375

(c) Calculation of gross profit:

	£
Sales	6,260W2
Less: Cost of goods sold	3,375
Gross profit	2,885

W1 *Purchases*	Units	Price	£
January: 8	100	20	2,000
13	60	25	1,500
17	75	30	2,250
	235		5,750

W2 *Sales*			
January: 14	125	40	5,000
22	30	42	1,260
	155		6,260

Solution 6.4

(a) There are two main tests:

    (i) Expenditure which enhances the ability of the firm to earn profits is capital, whereas expenditure designed merely to maintain the existing level of operations is revenue.

    (ii) Capital expenditure is incurred on the purchase of assets which are expected to possess a useful life which extends over a number of accounting periods; moreover, it is not intended to sell these assets in the normal course of business. Revenue expenditure is incurred in aquiring goods and services which are consumed in a short space of time. A correct allocation is important, because otherwise profit and asset values are wrongly reported. For example, the misallocation of capital to revenue causes both profit and gross assets to be understated.

(b) (i) Revenue. This is a normal repair to make good wear and tear.

    (ii) Capital. Hourly capacity is increased.

    (iii) Capital. This is part of the cost of acquiring the new asset.

    (iv) Capital. This increases the firm's productive capacity.

    (v) Capital. This expenditure is needed to make the plant ready for use.

Solution 6.5

(a)

Bank Account for 19X3

	£		£
Bank balance 1.1.19X3	19,400	General expenses	2,500
Receipts	76,500	Cost of properties	85,250
		Legal expenses on purchases .	2,550
		Legal expenses on sales	1,250
		Improvements	1,780
		Closing balance	2,570
	95,900		95,900

(b)   *Profit and Loss Account for 19X3**

	£	£
Sales		107,750
Less: Cost of properties sold:		
No. 1	30,250	
3 36,250 + 1,000 + 260	37,510	
4 24,000 + 750 + 1,000	25,750	
	93,510	
Selling expenses	1,250	
General expenses	2,500	
		97,260
Net profit		10,490

Balance Sheet at 31 December 19X3

	£		£
Properties on hand:		Opening capital	79,000
2	29,350	Profit	10,490
5 25,000 + 800 + 520 ...	26,320		
	55,670		
Bank balance	2,570		
Debtors	31,250		
	89,490		89,490

	£	£
* An alternative presentation:		
Sales		107,750
Opening stock	59,600	
Purchases (including legal expenses, on purchase, and improvements)	89,580	
Closing stock	(55,670)	93,510
Gross profit		14,240
Less: Legal expenses on sales	1,250	
General expenses	2,500	3,750
Net Profit		10,490

Solution 6.6

(a)

Year	(i) Straight line		(ii) Reducing balance	
	Charge £	Book value £	Charge £	Book value £
19X1	3,800 W1	16,200	9,000 W2	11,000
19X2	3,800	12,400	4,950	6,050
19X3	3,800	8,600	2,723	3,327
19X4	3,800	4,800	1,497	1,830
19X5	3,800	1,000	830	1,000
	19,000		19,000	

W1 Straight line: (£20,000 − £1,000) ÷ 5 = £3,800.
W2 Reducing balance: 45% of net book value.

(b) Depreciation charge is lowest and reported profit highest using the following methods.

19X1 — Straight line.
19X2 — Straight line.
19X3 — Reducing balance.
19X4 — Reducing balance.
19X5 — Reducing balance.

Over the entire five-year period each method produces exactly the same effect on reported profit as the total charge amounts to £19,000.

Solution 6.7

		£	£
(a)	Goodwill:		
	Price paid		120,000
	Less: Net assets acquired:		
	Fixed assets	71,500	
	Stocks	20,000	
	Debtors	10,000	
		101,500	
	Deduct trade creditors	5,000	96,500
			23,500
(b)	Goodwill at cost		23,500
	Less: Amount written off		4,700 W1
			18,800

W1 23,500 ÷ 5

Solution 6.8

Examples are:
(a)   Insurance premiums received before the period covered by the insurance; rents received before the rental period.
(b)   Cash sales of goods; sale of goods on credit where the cash is collected in the same accounting period.
(c)   Collection of customers' accounts in the period following the sale; receipt of interest after the period to which it relates.
(d)   Prepayment of insurance premiums or rent.
(e)   Payments for office salaries and telephone charges in the period in which they are used (debit entry is to an expense account).
(f)   Payment of suppliers' accounts outstanding at the year end; payment for rent accrued at the year end.

Solution 6.9

(a)   *Trading Account for 19X1*

		£	£
Sales			100,000
Less: Opening stock		10,000	
Purchases		80,000	
Closing stock		(11,000)	
Cost of goods sold			79,000
Gross profit			21,000

(b)   The effect of the revision is to reduce gross profit and, therefore, net profit by £3,000.

Solution 6.10

(a)   *Revised Profit and Loss Account of Deer Ltd for 19X1*

	£000	£000
Sales		600
Less: Prime costs	800	
Factory expenses	200	
	1,000	
Deduct closing stock	600 W1	
Cost of goods sold	400	
General expenses	100	500
Net profit		100

(b)   *Forecast Profit and Loss Accounts of Deer Ltd for 19X2*

	Prime cost		Total cost	
	£000	£000	£000	£000
Sales		2,100		2,100
Less: Opening stock	480		600	
Prime costs	800		800	
Factory expenses	—		200	
	1,280		1,600	
Deduct closing stock	160		200	
	1,120		1,400	
Factory expenses	200		—	
General expenses	100	1,420	100	1,500
		680		600

W1 300,000 ÷ 500,000 × 1,000

(c) Total cost is an acceptable basis for valuing stock; indeed, it is the method favoured for external reporting purposes by SSAP 9. Provided the resulting valuation is not less than net realisable value, there is no reason why it should not be used.

   The use of a different valuation basis does not, of course, alter the underlying financial facts but it can affect the allocation of profit between consecutive accounting periods. Use of the total cost basis, which relates manufacturing costs to output rather than time, will produce higher profits than the marginal (prime) cost basis when production exceeds sales. Under (a) above, three-fifths of the fixed costs (£200,000) are added to the value of closing stock and this converts a reported loss of £20,000 into a reported profit of £100,000. The situation is reversed when sales exceed production, see (b) above.

   The company's bank manager no doubt will be aware of the effect of differing accounting policies on reported profit and should not be unduly impressed by a revised method which places an improved appearance on the underlying facts. Nevertheless, use of the marginal cost approach, when output exceeds sales, will unduly deflate profits where there is a ready market for the goods manufactured. In such circumstances use of the total cost basis is fully justified.

Solution 7.1

Appropriation Account

	£	£		£	£
Salaries: Jack	10,000		Profit		42,000
Jill	7,500		Interest of drawings:		
Jane	5,000		Jack	600	
		22,500	Jill	450	
			Jane	400	
Interest on Capital:					1,450
Jack	3,600				
Jill (W1)	2,700				
Jane	4,800				
		11,100			
Residue: Jack	3,940				
Jill	3,940				
Jane	1,970				
		9,850			
		43,450			43,450

Workings
W1 12% × 20,000 (opening capital) + 12% × 5,000 x .5 (capital introduced half way through the year) = 2,700.

Solution 7.2

(a) *Appropriation Account*

	£		£
Share of Profit:		Profit	42,000
Jack	14,000		
Jill	14,000		
Jane	14,000		
	42,000		42,000

(b) In the absence of an agreement to the contrary, the provisions of the Partnership Act 1890 apply. The profit is divided equally between the partners and there are no charges for salaries or interest.

Solution 7.3

Current Accounts

	Ice £	Cube £		Ice £	Cube £
Drawings:			Balance b/d	30,000	20,000
Cash	12,500	14,000	Share of profit	22,500	22,500
Car disposal a/c .	1,500				
Transfer to					
capital account . . .	20,000	10,000			
Balance c/d	18,500	18,500			
	52,500	42,500		52,500	42,500

Capital Accounts

	Ice £	Cube £		Ice £	Cube £
Balance c/d	70,000	70,000	Balance b/d	50,000	60,000
			Transfer from		
			current account	20,000	10,000
	70,000	70,000		70,000	70,000

Solution 7.4

Trading and Profit and Loss Account
Year to 31 December 19X4

	£	
Sales (200,000 + 6,400 + 5,460)		211,860
Purchases: 160,000 (bank)		
2,500 (cash)		
3,800 (creditors)		
− 2,260 (drawings)		
	164,040	
Less: Closing stock	9,200	
Cost of goods sold		154,840
Gross profit		57,020
Less:		
Rent and rates (3,500 − 100)	3,400	
Light and heat (1,260 + 140)	1,400	
Depreciation (19,000 − 3,000)/5	3,200	
Wages	17,000	
Petrol	2,000	
Maintenance	1,000	
Advertising	900	
		28,900
Net Profit		28,120
Appropriation:		
Minute	14,060	
Second	14,060	
		28,120

Balance Sheet at 31 December 19X4

	£	£	£
Van: Cost			19,000
Depreciation			3,200
			15,800
Current Assets:			
Stock		9,200	
Debtors		5,460	
Prepaid rent		100	
Cash		5,240	
		20,000	
Current Liabilities:			
Trade creditors	3,800		
Accrued light and heat	140		
		3,940	
Working Capital			16,060
			31,860

	Second	Minute	
Capital Accounts	20,000	20,000	40,000
Current Accounts			
Profit	14,060	14,060	
Drawings: Cash	(18,000)	(16,000)	
Stock	(1,000)	(1,260)	
	(4,940)	(3,200)	(8,140)
			31,860

Solution 7.5

Trading and Profit and Loss Account
for the Year to 31 March 19X3

	£	£
Sales		150,000
Opening stock	30,000	
Purchases	110,000	
Goods lost	(700)	
Stock drawings	(340)	
Closing stock	(40,000)	
Cost of goods sold		98,960
Gross profit		51,040
Depreciation	1,500	
Wages (14,500 + 500)	15,000	
Rent (5,000 − 1,000)	4,000	
Expenses	3,000	
Heat and light	1,200	
Delivery	5,300	
		30,000
Net Trading Profit		21,040
Appropriation:		
Interest on drawings:		
Bean		200
Stalk		300
		21,540
Salaries:		
Bean	2,000	
Stalk	4,000	
		6,000
		15,540
Interest:		
Bean	1,500	
Stalk	500	
		2,000
		13,540
Residue:		
Bean	6,770	
Stalk	6,770	
		13,540

Balance Sheet at 31 March 19X3

	£	£	£
Fixed Assets			6,000
Less: Depreciation			1,500
			4,500
Current Assets:			
Stock		40,000	
Debtors		14,000	
Debtor for goods lost		700	
Prepaid rent		1,000	
Cash		4,500	
		60,200	
Current Liabilities:			
Creditors	11,500		
Accrued Wages	500		
		12,000	
Working Capital			48,200
			52,700

	Bean	Stalk	
Capital	30,000	10,000	40,000
Current Accounts:			
Balance 1 April 19X2	3,000	5,000	
Interest on drawings	(200)	(300)	
Drawings: Cash	(7,000)	(9,000)	
Stock	(340)	—	
Interest on capital	1,500	500	
Salaries	2,000	4,000	
Share of residue	6,770	6,770	
	5,730	6,970	12,700
			52,700

Solution 8.1
A registered company is formed by filing certain information with the registrar of companies and paying specified fees. The information to be filed is laid down in the Companies Act. Registration is a fairly simple process and it is possible for an individual wishing to form a limited company to do the work personally; alternatively the services of a specialist company registration agent may be engaged.

There are a number of different types of registered company, and the choice will depend on the nature and scale of expected business operations.

Unlimited Company   Here the shareholders accept unlimited liability for the debts of the company. Since the main reason for forming a company is to obtain the protection of limited liability, unlimited companies are few and far between.

Limited Company   The shareholders' liability for a company's debts is limited to the amount of their investment. If the company fails, the claims of creditors are restricted to the assets belonging to the business.

Public Limited Company   This type of limited company must include the designatory letters 'plc' after its name, and must have a minimum issued share capital of £50,000, of which at least one-quarter must be collected at the outset. The public company may offer shares to the general public.

Private Limited Company   This type of company must use the designatory letters 'Ltd' and is not allowed to make an issue of shares or debentures to the general public. Private companies are usually, but by no means always, family firms simply seeking to obtain the protection of limited liability.

Listed Company   The marketability of a public company's shares and debentures can be improved by making arrangements for these securities to be listed on the Stock Exchange. This is a feasible exercise only for very large concerns.

Solution 8.2

The advantages and disadvantages of forming a limited company may be summarised as follows.

Advantages:

Limited Liability   The liability for the company's debts is restricted to the price paid for the shares. This places an effective ceiling on the amount which shareholders can lose should the company get into financial difficulties and be forced to liquidate.

Share Transferability   Shareholders wishing to sell all or part of their interest in a limited company are entirely free to adopt this course of action provided a buyer can be found. This will be a relatively straightforward matter in the case of a public company whose shares are listed on the Stock Exchange. In the case of a private company, both finding a buyer and agreeing a price is much more difficult due to the absence of a readily available share valuation.

Perpetual Succession   The death or retirement of a sole trader naturally results in the business being treated as discontinued. This outcome can be avoided, however, by the formation of a limited company which, being an artificial person, has an indefinite life-span. One benefit of the continuity which results is that the reputation and goodwill of a limited company is likely to survive reasonably unimpaired when a director and/or shareholder terminates an involvement with the concern.

Disadvantages:
Costs Certain documentation must be filed with the registrar at the outset. The formalities involved are time-consuming, although it is possible to engage the services of a company formation agent to do much of the work at an approximate cost of £150. The company must, annually, have its accounts audited and file an annual return, each of which involves further cost.

Publicity Limited companies are required to prepare annual accounts for the shareholders and also for filing with the registrar of companies, where they are open to public scrutiny.

Solution 8.3

The annual audit involves an independent examination of the accounts prepared by the directors of a limited company for its shareholders and debenture holders. It is a legal requirement for this work to be done. This work is carried out by a professional accountant, who is qualified to fulfil the audit function as the result of having passed examinations set by a professional accounting body such as the Institute of Chartered Accountants in England and Wales.

The objectives of the audit are as follows:

1. To carry out an *independent* examination of the accounts in order to assess their reliability. The auditor is appointed by the shareholders and reports to the shareholders. If the auditor is satisfied that the accounts fairly portray the performance and position of the company, a 'clean' audit report will be issued. If the auditor has any reservations regarding the truth and fairness of the accounts, this fact must be referred to in the audit report.

2. To detect error and fraud. In order to enable the auditor to report on the truth and fairness of the accounts, it is necessary to examine the books and records of the company on which the accounts are based. Where error or fraud has occurred, it will quite possibly be discovered during the course of the audit. However, the auditor is not necessarily expected to 'pick up' minor irregularities as the amount of work

involved in checking every transaction would be enormous and probably unjustified. Also, the accountant is not necessarily expected to discover an ingenious fraud which results from the involvement of top management in order to conceal the relevant facts. The auditor is simply required to exercise the degree of skill and care normally associated with a professional person and will not be held responsible for errors and frauds which remain undiscovered provided this duty is discharged. However, it is expected that such errors and frauds will usually be discovered.

Solution 9.1

(a) *Provisions* These are balances set aside to meet known liabilities, the amount of which cannot be ascertained with substantial accuracy. Examples: Provisions for bad debts and depreciation.

Reserves These are transfers made out of profits to meet no specific liability presently known to the directors of the company. Examples: Reserves for contingencies and the equalisation of dividends.

(b) (i) Provisions are a cost of operating the business and appear as a deduction in arriving at profit for the year, i.e. they are charged 'above the line'. Reserves appear as appropriations of reported profit, i.e. they are deducted 'below the line'.

(ii) In the balance sheet, provisions appear either as a deduction from the asset to which they relate or as a current liability; reserves appear as part of the shareholders' equity.

Solution 9.2

(a)

Profit and Loss Account

	19X0 £000	19X1 £000
Gross profit	2,930	3,605
Less: Administration expenses	1,620	1,809
Selling costs	520	572
Distribution costs	140	164
Depreciation charge	250	300
	2,530	2,845
Net profit	400	760
Less: Proposed dividend	100	200
Transfer to general reserve	—	500
	100	700
Retained profit for the year	300	60
Add: Retained profit at 1 January	290	590
Retained profit at 31 December	590	650

Balance Sheet at 31 December

	£000	19X0 £000	£000	19X1 £000
Plant and machinery at cost		1,840		2,650
Less: Depreciation		520		820
		1,320		1,830
Current Assets:				
Stock	724		771	
Debtors	570		524	
Bank	92		305	
	1,386		1,600	
Current Liabilities:				
Creditors	416		480	
Dividend	100		200	
	516		680	
Working capital		870		920
		2,190		2,750
Financed by:				
Share capital		1,600		1,600
General reserve		—		500
Profit and loss account		590		650
		2,190		2,750

(b) The revised accounts show that the *retained* profit is much lower in 19X1, but the *net* profit earned is almost twice as high as in 19X0. The draft accounts do not distinguish between *charges* against profit and *appropriations* of profit, and the revised accounts show that the lower retained profit is principally due to the large transfer to general reserve which was not made in the previous year. The fact that profits have substantially increased fully justifies the directors' decision to increase the dividend to £200,000. A further point which should be considered is whether there is sufficient cash available to finance the proposed distribution. However, there is £305,000 in the bank account and this suggests that the company will have no difficulty in meeting the dividend payment when it falls due.

Solution 9.3

Trading and Profit and Loss Account for 19X9

	£	£
Sales		2,350,000
Less: Opening stock	206,300	
Purchases	1,650,000	
Closing stock	(217,800)	
Cost of goods sold		1,638,500
Gross profit		711,500
Less: Director's remuneration	60,000	
Wages and salaries	198,700	
Motor expenses	42,300	
Rates	8,500 W1	
Legal expenses	1,200 W2	
General expenses	86,000	
Bad debts	15,700	
Loss on sale of motor van	750 W3	
Depreciation of motor vans	48,000 W4	
Debenture interest	37,500	498,650
Net profit before tax		212,850
Corporation tax		90,000
Net profit after tax		122,850
Less: Proposed dividend		84,000
Retained profit for the year		38,850
Retained profit at the beginning of the year		117,500
Retained profit at the end of the year		156,350

Balance Sheet as at 31 December 19X9

	£	£	£
Fixed Assets			
Freehold properties at cost			857,900 W5
Motor vans at cost		240,000 W4	
Less: Accumulated depreciation		140,950 W4	99,050
			956,950
Current Assets			
Stock		217,800	
Debtors		166,500	
Rates paid in advance		2,000	
Bank		96,900	
		483,200	
Less: Current Liabilities			
Trade creditors	159,800		
Corporation tax	90,000		
Dividend	84,000	333,800	149,400
Total assets less current liabilities			1,106,350
Less: 15% Debentures, repayable 19Y5 . . .			250,000
			856,350
Financed by			
Authorised share capital			700,000
Issued ordinary shares of £1 each			700,000
Retained profit			156,350
			856,350

W1 10,500 − 2,000 (prepaid).
W2 9,100 − 7,900 (capitalised).
W3 1,750 (book value) − 1,000 (sales proceeds).
W4

	Cost	Depreciation
	£	£
Motor vans		
Balance at 1 January	225,000	101,200
Sales	(10,000)	(8,250)
Additions	25,000	
Charge for year, 20% of £240,000		48,000
	240,000	140,950

W5 850,000 + 7,900 (legal expenses).

Solution 9.4

Profit and Loss Account year ended 31 March 19X6

	£	£
Gross Profit		1,020,800
Less: Administration expenses	216,900	
Selling expenses	150,400	
Bad debts written off	8,700	
General repairs and maintenance	25,200	
Debenture interest	30,000	
Depreciation	197,000 W1	628,200
Net profit before tax		392,600
Corporation tax		150,000
Net profit after tax		242,600
Less: Proposed dividend		75,000
Retained profit for the year		167,600
Retained profit at 1 April 19X5		39,000
Retained profit at March 19X6		206,600

Balance Sheet as at 31 March 19X6

	£	£	£
Fixed Assets			
Freehold land and buildings at valuation			900,000
Plant and machinery at cost		1,420,000 W2	
Accumulated depreciation to April 19X5	512,000		
Charge for current year	197,000	709,000	711,000
			1,611,000
Current Assets			
Stock and work-in-progress		984,020	
Debtors and prepayments	370,080		
Less: Provision for doubtful debts	15,000	355,080	
Bank balance		268,000	
		1,607,100	
Less: Current Liabilities			
Creditors and accrued expenses		471,500 W2	
Debenture interest outstanding		15,000	
Proposed dividend		75,000	
Corporation tax due 1 Jan. 19X7		150,000	
		711,500	
Net current assets			895,600
Total assets less current liabilities			2,506,600
Less: 10% Debentures repayable 19X9			300,000
			2,206,600

Financed by:	£
Ordinary share capital: Authorised	2,000,000
Issued (£1 shares)	1,500,000
Revaluation reserve	500,000
Retained profit	206,600
	2,206,600

W1 1,300,000 − 512,000 × 25%.
W2 Includes £120,000 for plant delivered on 31 March 19X6.

Solution 9.5

(a)   *Profit and Loss Account, Year ended 31 Dec. 19X9*

	£	£
Gross profit on trading		416,500
Less: Rent and rates	24,000 W1	
Office salaries	142,600	
Advertising costs	21,000	
Transport costs	23,600	
Depreciation	37,500	248,700
Net profit before tax		167,800
Taxation		83,900
Net profit after tax		83,900
Retained profit at beginning of year		178,500
Retained profit at end of year		262,400

Balance Sheet at 31 December 19X9

	£	£
Freehold property at valuation		650,000
Furniture and equipment at cost	375,000	
Less: Accumulated depreciation	97,000 W2	278,000
Balance c/d		928,000
Current Assets		
Stock and work-in-progress	104,200	
Debts and prepayments	111,000 W3	
Deposit	10,000	
Temporary investment	60,000	
Balance at bank	72,000	
Balance c/d	357,200	

	£	£
Balance b/d	357,200	928,000
Current Liabilities		
Creditors and accruals	85,300	
Taxation due 1 Jan. 19Y0	103,600	
1 Jan. 19Y1	83,900	
	272,800	84,400
Working capital		1,012,400
Financed by:		
Ordinary share capital		600,000
Revaluation reserve		150,000
Profit and loss account		262,400
		1,012,400

W1 30,000 − 6,000 (3 months prepaid).
W2 59,500 + 37,500.
W3 105,000 + 6,000.

(b)   A dividend of 10 pence per share on the share capital of £600,000 would involve a payment of £60,000. There is no doubt that the bank balance at 31 December 19X9 appears sufficient to support this payment, and the after tax profits for the year are £83,900. Consideration must however be given to the company's future commitments. During January 19Y0, a tax payment of £103,600 must be made as well as £40,000 for the new equipment when delivery takes place. This would suggest that bank overdraft facilities will be required during January even if no dividend is paid, although the position could be partially alleviated by the sale of the temporary investment. Funds generated from trading operations during 19X9 amounted to £205,300 (profit £167,800 and depreciation £37,500), and this should soon make good any cash shortage if the results are repeated during 19Y0. Nevertheless a dividend payment of £60,000 is probably unwise at this stage.

Solution 10.1

Rock Ltd — Forecast Results for Additional Sales

Proposal	(i)		(ii)		(iii)	
Additional sales (in units)	25,000	50,000	25,000	50,000	25,000	50,000
Process X						
Materials	5,000	10,000				
Wages	7,500	15,000	80p ×	80p ×		
Depreciation	12,000	12,000	25,000	50,000		
Rent	8,000	8,000				
To Process Y	32,500	45,000	20,000	40,000		
Process Y					180p ×	180p ×
					25,000	50,000
Materials	2,500	5,000	2,500	5,000		
Wages	10,000	20,000	10,000	20,000		
Depreciation	12,000	12,000	12,000	12,000		
Rent	8,000	8,000	8,000	8,000		
Cost of Production	65,000	90,000	52,500	85,000	45,000	90,000
General Expenses	2,000	4,000	2,000	4,000	2,000	4,000
Net Profit (Loss)	(17,000)	6,000	(4,500)	11,000	3,000	6,000
Sales	50,000	100,000	50,000	100,000	50,000	100,000

Solution 10.2

(a)	£	£	£	£	£	£
Sales		46,000		92,000		138,000
Variable Cost	25,300		50,600		75,900	
Depreciation	3,600		7,200		10,800	
General Expenses	10,000		14,000		18,000	
Interest*	3,900		9,300		14,700	
		42,800		81,100		119,400
Profit		3,200		10,900		18,600
*Calculation:						
Cost of plant		36,000		72,000		108,000
Available for investment		10,000		10,000		10,000
Balance to be borrowed		26,000		62,000		98,000
Borrowings at 15%		3,900		9,300		14,700

(b) Eagles can either retain ownership of the business or sell it to Troon Ltd and remain as manager. Under either of these options his income varies according to the level of sales, and is calculated as follows:

Sales	£ Existing	£ + 46,000	£ + 92,000	£ + 138,000
Retain ownership:				
Existing profit	20,000	20,000	20,000	20,000
Profits from exports	—	3,200	10,900	18,600
Total Income	20,000	23,200	30,900	38,600
Sell to Troon Ltd:				
Invest proceeds of sale to				
earn annual interest	12,000	12,000	12,000	12,000
Salary as manager	14,000	14,000	14,000	14,000
Bonus for additional sales	—	3,000	6,000	9,000
Total	26,000	29,000	32,000	35,000

It can be seen that Eagles is better off to sell the business and work as manager unless the largest increase in sales under consideration can be achieved. He must consider whether this is likely. Also, the relief of no longer having the responsibility of both owning and managing the business may be attractive together with the possession of personal capital in the form of cash. These considerations may induce him to sell the business even if he considers the higher income from retention can probably be achieved.

Solution 10.3

(a)   *Summary Profit and Loss Account*

	£000
Sales (60,000 × £5)	300
Variable Costs (60,000 × £3*)	180
Total Contribution	120
Fixed Costs**	100
Net Profit	20

* £5 (Selling Price) − £2 (Contribution) = £3 (Variable Cost)
** Balancing figure

(b) $\dfrac{\text{Fixed Costs}}{\text{Contribution}} = \dfrac{£100,000}{£2} = 50,000$ units

  50,000 × £5 = £250,000

(c) $\dfrac{\text{Fixed Costs}}{\text{Contribution}} = \dfrac{(£100,000 + £4,500)}{(£2 - £0.10)} = 55,000$ units

  55,000 × £5 = £275,000

Solution 10.4

	Jan £	Feb £	March £	April £	May £	June £
Receipts:						
Sales	—	—	12,000	12,000	12,000	12,000
Capital	20,000					
Loan	8,000					
	28,000	—	12,000	12,000	12,000	12,000
Payments:						
Fixed Assets	20,000					
Purchases	—	16,000	8,000	8,000	8,000	8,000
Expenses	800	800	800	800	800	800
Drawings	200	200	200	200	200	200
Interest	—	—	—	—	—	400
	21,000	17,000	9,000	9,000	9,000	9,400
Opening balance	—	7,000	(10,000)	(7,000)	(4,000)	(1,000)
+ Receipts	28,000	—	12,000	12,000	12,000	12,000
− Payments	21,000	17,000	9,000	9,000	9,000	9,400
Closing Balance	7,000	(10,000)	(7,000)	(4,000)	(1,000)	1,600

Solution 10.5

Forecast Trading and Profit and Loss Account

	£	£
Sales (W2)		72,000
Less: Cost of Goods Sold (W3)		48,000
Gross Profit		24,000
Expenses (W1)	4,800	
Loan Interest (0.5 × 8,000 × 10%)	400	
Overdraft Interest	300	
Depreciation (0.5 × 20,000 × 20%)	2,000	
		7,500
Net Profit		16,500

Forecast Balance Sheet

	£	£
FIXED ASSETS		
Cost		20,000
Less: Depreciation		2,000
		18,000
CURRENT ASSETS		
Stock (W3)	8,000	
Debtors (May + June sales)	24,000	
Cash (W1)	1,600	
	33,600	
CURRENT LIABILITIES		
Trade Creditors (June purchases)	8,000	
Accrued Interest	300	
	8,300	
WORKING CAPITAL		25,300
		43,300
Less: Loan		8,000
		35,300
CAPITAL		
Capital Introduced		20,000
Profit		16,500
		36,500
Less: Drawings (W1)		1,200
Closing Capital		35,300

Workings
W1 Forecast cash account produced by adding across the individual columns in the solution to Question 10.4.

Cash Account

	£		£
Capital	20,000	Plant	20,000
Loan	8,000	Creditors	48,000
Debtors	48,000	Expenses	4,800
		Drawings	1,200
		Loan Interest	400
		Balance c/d	1,600
	76,000		76,000

W2   Sales can be calculated in two alternative ways:

(a)   Sales = Cash from debtors + closing debtors*
        = £48,000 (W1) + £24,000 (May + June sales) = £72,000

OR

(b)   £12,000 (monthly sales) × 6 (number of months) = £72,000

W3   Cost of Goods Sold
Purchases can be calculated in two alternative ways:

(a)   Purchases = Payments to creditors + closing creditors*

                = £48,000 (W1) + £8,000 (June purchases) = £56,000

OR

(b)   £16,000 (January purchases) + (5 × £8,000) = £56,000

        Cost of Goods Sold = Purchases − Closing Stock*
        = £56,000 − £8,000** = £48,000

* As this is the first period of trading, there are no opening debtors, creditors or stocks.

		£
**	Purchases	56,000
	Less: Cost of Goods Sold:	
	$\dfrac{100}{150}$ × £72,000 (sales)	48,000
	Closing Stock	8,000

Solution 11.1

(a)

	Plan 1	Plan 2
	£	£
Sales	84,000	112,500
Expenses	76,440	103,500
Net profit	7,560	9,000

(b)   The net profit percentages are:

19X5	19X6 Plan 1	19X6 Plan 2
$\dfrac{5,600 \times 100}{56,000}$	$\dfrac{7,560 \times 100}{84,000}$	$\dfrac{9,000 \times 100}{112,500}$
= 10%	= 9%	= 8%

Both plans give a higher net profit than 19X5 together with a lower net profit ratio. Plan 2 gives the higher net profit, but has a lower net profit ratio. However, as Plan 2 involves a much greater capital investment than Plan 1, its results must be judged on the basis of relative return on capital employed, which is discussed in section 11.3 of Chapter 11.

Solution 11.2

(a) Gross profit margin
$$\frac{54,000}{180,000} \times 100 \ = 30\%$$

Net profit as a % of sales
$$\frac{15,000}{180,000} \times 100 \ = 8.3\%$$

Return on capital employed
$$\frac{15,000}{150,000} \times 100 \ = 10\%$$

(b) An increase in the ROCE to 12.5% would require additional profit of £150,000 × 2.5% = £3,750. The gross profit margin is 30% and an additional turnover of £3,750 × (100 ÷ 30) = £12,500 would produce the required increase in net profit.

Solution 11.3

(a) Workings:

Balance Sheet, 31 December

	19X2		19X3	
	£000	£000	£000	£000
Fixed assets		500		550
Current assets: Stock	150		200	
Trade debtors	125		150	
Cash at bank	25		—	
	300		350	
Less: Current Liabilities: Trade creditors	80		100	
Proposed dividend . .	20		60	
Overdraft	—		20	
	100		180	
Working capital		200		170
Shareholders' equity (capital employed)		700		720

Profit and Loss Account

Sales		2,000		3,000
Less: Cost of sales	1,000		1,450	
Overhead costs	800	1,800	1,300	2,750
		200		250

		19X1		19X2
Return on capital employed	$\dfrac{200}{700} \times 100 = 28.6\%$		$\dfrac{250}{720} \times 100 = 34.7\%$	
Working capital		200		170
Working capital ratio	$\dfrac{300}{100} :1 = 3:1$		$\dfrac{350}{180} :1 = 1.9:1$	
Liquidity ratio	$\dfrac{125 + 25}{100} :1 = 1.5:1$		$\dfrac{150}{180} :1 = 0.8:1$	

(b)   Lock Ltd earned a high rate of return on the shareholders' investment during 19X1, which has been improved on during 19X2. The balance sheet, at 31 December 19X1, shows a strong financial position with the working capital and liquidity ratios each at a high level for a wholesale trading company. There has been a significant decline in the solvency position during the year. The ratios suggest that the company will find it difficult to meet its debts as they fall due for payment. The proposal to pay a final dividend three times last year's level may need to be reconsidered.

Solution 11.4

(a)

	Town £000	Country £000
Profit before interest	600	900
Interest	75	600
	525	300
Return on owners' capital employed	15%	15%

(b)

	Town		Country	
	+50% £000	−50% £000	+50% £000	−50% £000
Profit before interest	900	300	1,350	450
Less: Interest	75	75	600	600
	825	225	750	(150)
Return on owners' capital employed	23.6%	6.4%	37.5%	ZERO OR −7.5%

(c) Both companies produced a return of 15% for their owners in 19X1. The rate of return made by both companies fluctuates widely as a result of changes in the amount of profit, but Country shows a much greater possible fluctuation in return for the same proportional change in profit. This is because Country is highly geared, as is shown by the debt equity ratios:

	Town £000	Country £000
Debt	500	4,000
Equity	3,500	2,000
Debt/equity ratio	14.3%	200%

A large amount of Country's earnings have to be used to meet interest payments, even when profits are low, but a rise in profits produces relatively larger rewards for its owners.

Solution 11.5

(a)   *Trading and Profit and Loss Accounts for 19X5*

	Metalmax £000	Metalmax £000	Precision Products £000	Precision Products £000
Sales		800		950
Less: Variable cost of sales	640		760	
Depreciation	54		54	
Cost of sales		694		814
Gross profit		106		136
Less: Administration expenses	30		30	
Selling expenses	45	75	60	90
Net profit		31		46

Balance Sheets at 31 December 19X5

	Metalmax		Precision Products	
	£000	£000	£000	£000
Plant and machinery at cost		360		360
Less: Depreciation		164		164
		196		196
Current Assets:				
Stocks and work-in-progress	120		200	
Other current assets	120		200	
	240		400	
Less: Current Liabilities				
Trade creditors	120		320	
Working capital		120		80
		316		276
Share capital		200		200
Reserves..........................		116		76
		316		276

(b) *Accounting ratios*	Metalmax	Precision Products
Gross profit margin	13.3%	14.3%
Net profit percentage	3.9%	4.8%
Return on total capital employed	7.1%	7.7%
Return on owners' equity	9.8%	16.7%
Working capital ratio	2:1	1.25:1
Liquidity ratio	1:1	0.6:1

Metalmax is the more solvent whereas Precision Products is the more profitable.

Variable cost of sales is 80% in the case of both companies. Precision Products produces the higher gross profit margin because, on the basis of an identical investment in fixed assets, it produces a significantly higher level of sales. The selling expenses of Precision Products are much higher, perhaps due to the fact that they advertise their products more heavily and distribute them more widely. However, the company retains its advantage and achieves the higher net profit margin. The rates of return on both versions of capital employed are higher at Precision Products. The difference is substantial in the case of return on owners' equity. This is because a large proportion of Precision Products' current assets are funded out of the 'free' finance provided by trade creditors. The consequence of this, however, is that Precision Products' solvency position, at the end of 19X5, is extremely weak. Metalmax, with a working capital ratio and liquidity ratio in line with conventional 'norms', is in a sound financial condition.

Solution 12.1

(a)

	19X2	19X3
Current assets	17,000	23,000
Current liabilities	6,000	10,700
Working capital	11,000	12,300
Working capital ratio	2.8:1	2.2:1

(b) *Work Sheet*

Balance Sheets 31 December

			Differences	
	19X2	19X3	Sources	Applications
	£	£	£	£
Fixed assets at cost	25,000	30,000		5,000
Less: Accumulated depreciation .	5,000	6,500	1,500	
	20,000	23,500		
Stock	11,000	17,000		6,000
Debtors	5,000	6,000		1,000
Cash at bank	1,000	—	1,000	
	37,000	46,500		
Share capital	20,000	20,000		
Reserves	10,000	15,000	5,000	
Debentures	1,000	800		200
Trade creditors	6,000	7,500	1,500	
Overdraft	—	3,200	3,200	
	37,000	46,500	12,200	12,200

Statement of Funds for 19X3

	£	£
SOURCES		
Profit		5,000
Add: Depreciation		1,500
Funds generated from operations		6,500
APPLICATIONS		
Purchase of plant	5,000	
Repayment of debentures	200	5,200
INCREASE IN WORKING CAPITAL		1,300

CHANGES IN WORKING CAPITAL ITEMS
Decreases in working capital

Trade creditors	(1,500)	
Bank (£3,200 + £1,000)	(4,200)	
Increases in working capital		
Stock	6,000	
Debtors	1,000	1,300

(c) The main feature is the heavy build up of stock. This has been financed partly by creditors but mainly by the bank with the result that the cash balance, at the beginning of the year, has been replaced by a large overdraft.

Solution 12.2

Work Sheet	19X1		19X2		Differences Sources	Differences Applications
	£	£	£	£	£	£
Fixed Assets:						
Plant at cost	52,000		70,000			18,000
Less: Depreciation	16,500	35,500	22,700	47,300	6,200	
Transport at cost	10,000		10,000			
Less: Depreciation	3,600	6,400	4,800	5,200	1,200	
		41,900		52,500		
Current Assets:						
Stocks	10,200		12,600			2,400
Debtors	8,300		13,700			5,400
Bank	4,900		—		4,900	
	23,400		26,300			
Less: Current Liabilities						
Trade creditors	5,100		5,800		700	
Bank overdraft	—		1,300		1,300	
	5,100		7,100			
Working capital		18,300		19,200		
		60,200		71,700		
Financed by:						
Share capital		50,000		54,000	4,000	
Profit and loss account . .		10,200		17,700	7,500	
		60,200		71,700	25,800	25,800

Statement of Funds for 19X2

	£	£
SOURCES OF FUNDS		
Profit		7,500
Add: Depreciation		7,400
Funds generated from operations		14,900
Funds from other sources:		
Share capital		4,000
		18,900
APPLICATIONS OF FUNDS		
Purchase of plant		18,000
INCREASE IN WORKING CAPITAL		900
CHANGES IN WORKING CAPITAL ITEMS		
Decrease in working capital		
Bank	(6,200)	
Trade creditors	(700)	
Increase in working capital		
Stocks	2,400	
Debtors	5,400	900

Solution 12.3

Work Sheet   *Balance Sheet 31 March*

	19X3 £	19X4 £	Differences Sources £	Applications £
Share capital	500,000	500,000		
Retained profit	395,800	527,100	131,300	
10% Debentures	200,000	300,000	100,000	
Creditors	179,800	207,500	27,700	
Proposed dividend	50,000	60,000	10,000	
Bank overdraft	—	36,900	36,900	
	1,325,600	1,631,500		
Plant at cost	658,300	796,900		138,600
Less: Depreciation	263,500	371,600	108,100	
	394,800	425,300		
Freehold property	300,000	350,000		50,000
Stock	327,100	608,300		281,200
Debtors	265,700	247,900	17,800	
Cash at bank	38,000	—	38,000	
	1,325,600	1,631,500	469,800	469,800

Statement of Source and Application of Funds

SOURCES OF FUNDS	£	£
Net profit		191,300(1)
Add: Depreciation	295,600(1)	
Loss on sale of plant and equipment	33,000(2)	328,600
Funds generated from operations		519,900
Funds from other sources		
Debentures issued	100,000	
Sale of plant and equipment	169,500	269,500
		789,400
APPLICATIONS OF FUNDS		
Freehold property	50,000	
Plant and equipment	528,600(1)	
Dividend proposed	60,000	638,600
INCREASE IN WORKING CAPITAL		150,800
CHANGES IN WORKING CAPITAL ITEMS		
Decrease in working capital		
Creditors	(27,700)	
Dividend	(10,000)	
Bank	(74,900)	
Debtors	(17,800)	
Increase in working capital		
Stock	281,200	150,800

Workings:

(1)	Plant	Depreciation	Profit
Net increase (work sheet)	138,600	108,100	131,300
Add: Sale of plant	390,000	187,500*	
Proposed dividend			60,000
Gross changes	528,600	295,600	191,300

* Accumulated depreciation £187,500 = Cost, £390,000 − Book value, £202,500.

(2) Loss on sale, £33,000 = £202,500 (book value of plant sold) − £169,500 (sale proceeds).

Solution 12.4   (Work sheet omitted)

(a)   *Statement of Funds for 19X4*

SOURCES OF FUNDS	£	£
Profit (£5,500 + £44,000)		49,500
Add: Depreciation		27,200
Funds generated from operations		76,700
APPLICATIONS OF FUNDS		
Purchase of fixed assets	30,000	
Dividends	44,000	
Debentures repaid	80,000	154,000
DECREASE IN WORKING CAPITAL		(77,300)

CHANGES IN WORKING CAPITAL ITEMS		
Decrease in working capital		
Decrease in trade debtors	(2,700)	
Decrease in bank	(61,500)	
Increase in creditors	(14,200)	
Increase in working capital		
Increase in stock	1,100	(77,300)

(b)   The company plans to pay out nearly all of its profits in the form of dividends, while the funds retained in the business by way of the depreciation charge have been used to purchase fixed assets. There are no other long-term sources of finance and the debentures have been repaid by running down working capital. The result is a large bank overdraft and, probably, severe liquidity problems.

Solution 12.5

(a)   *Statement of Funds for 19X8*

	£000	£000
SOURCES OF FUNDS		
Net profit from ordinary activities		720
Add: Depreciation		350
Funds generated from operations		1,070
Funds from other sources		
Share issue (500 + 200)	700	
Long-term loan	300	
Sale of investment	130	1,130
		2,200
APPLICATION OF FUNDS		
Purchase of plant	410	
Dividends paid	400	810
INCREASE IN WORKING CAPITAL		1,390
CHANGES IN WORKING CAPITAL ITEMS		
Decrease in working capital		
Increase in creditors	(200)	
Increase in working capital		
Increase in stocks	1,220	
Increase in debtors	40	
Increase in short-term loans and deposits at bank	330	1,390

(b)

Accounting ratios	19X7	19X8
Working capital	2:1	3.1:1
Liquidity	1:1	1.2:1

The financial position at the end of 19X7 appears satisfactory when judged on the basis of relevant accounting ratios. The liquidity ratio is 1:1 and the working capital ratio is 2:1, both of which are about right for an engineering firm. At the end of 19X1, the working capital appears to be too high and the company is verging on excess liquidity.

The statement of funds shows that the company both raised and generated long-term funds significantly in excess of present business requirements. Funds generated from operations more than cover the dividend and plant acquisition, yet the company has issued shares, raised a loan and benefitted from the sale of investments. A great deal of the surplus finance is tied up in stocks; a non-income producing asset. The company's system of stock control should be examined to check whether it is being operated efficiently.

The effect of financial developments during 19X8 is a very strong financial position at the end of the year, but there is some doubt whether available resources are being effectively employed. Perhaps additional resources have been raised to finance *future* expansion, but there is no indication that this is the case.

Index